W9-BYN-127

THE RED ROOSTER COOKBOOK

The Story of Food and Hustle in Harlem

MARCUS SAMUELSSON

PHOTOGRAPHS BY BOBBY FISHER

Foreword by Hilton Als

Text with April Reynolds | Recipes and Text with Roy Finamore

Illustrations by Rebekah Maysles and Leon Johnson

A RUX MARTIN BOOK

Houghton Mifflin Harcourt

Boston · New York · 2016

www.hmhco.com

Library of Congress Cataloging-in-Publication Data

Names: Samuelsson, Marcus, author. | Fisher, Bobby (Photographer),
photographer (expression) | Maysles, Rebekah, illustrator. | Johnson,
Leon, date, illustrator.
Title: Red Rooster Cookbook : the story of food and hustle in Harlem / Marcus
Samuelsson ; photographs by Bobby Fisher ; text with April Reynolds ;
recipes and text with Roy Finamore ; illustrations by Rebekah Maysles
and Leon Johnson.
Description: Boston : Houghton Mifflin Harcourt, [2016] | "A Rux Martin Book."
Identifiers: LCCN 2016037226 (print) | LCCN 2016039020 (ebook) |
ISBN 9780544639775 (paper over board) | ISBN 9780544639812 (ebook)
Subjects: LCSH: International cooking. | Cooking — New York (State) — New York.
| Food — New York (State) — New York. | Red Rooster (Restaurant) | Harlem
(New York, N.Y.) | LCGFT: Cookbooks.
Classification: LCC TX725.A1 S344 2016 (print) | LCC TX725.A1 (ebook) | DDC
641.59747 — dc23
LC record available at https://lccn.loc.gov/2016037226

Book design by Toni Tajima

Printed in the United States of America
DOW 10 9 8 7 6 5 4 3
4500642359

TO THE PEOPLE OF HARLEM, ESPECIALLY THE GENERATION BEFORE MINE WHO CARED, RESTORED, AND FOUGHT FOR UPTOWN, TO MAKE SURE HARLEM WOULD BE A SPECIAL NEIGHBORHOOD IN THE GREATEST CITY—A PLACE I AM LUCKY TO CALL HOME.

Contents

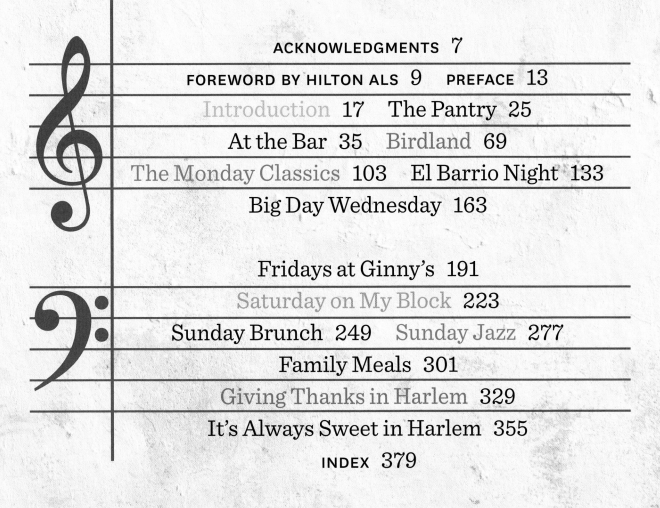

ACKNOWLEDGMENTS 7

FOREWORD BY HILTON ALS 9   PREFACE 13

Introduction 17   The Pantry 25

At the Bar 35   Birdland 69

The Monday Classics 103   El Barrio Night 133

Big Day Wednesday 163

Fridays at Ginny's 191

Saturday on My Block 223

Sunday Brunch 249   Sunday Jazz 277

Family Meals 301

Giving Thanks in Harlem 329

It's Always Sweet in Harlem 355

INDEX 379

Acknowledgments

THE FIRST THANKS ARE TO MY WIFE, MAYA, for allowing us to cook up a mess in the house. Without all your support in the Rooster journey, none of the eating, drinking, cooking, mixing, and celebrating would be possible.

And to the Samuelsson tribe, here and abroad, for your love, guidance, and support in all things I do.

Thank you to Rux Martin and everyone at HMH who have believed in this book since before the days of *Off Duty*.

Thank you to April Reynolds for your time, energy, and words. You brought this story to life and your dedication shines through.

Thank you to Bobby Fisher, for bringing my neighborhood alive on the page. Your bold vision, patience, and keen eye have taken this book to the next level.

Thank you to Roy Finamore, for being our recipe master—making sure every single bite of this book is tasty, every time.

Thank you to Ashley Bode, for your tireless work and dedication.

Thank you to Kim Witherspoon, Leslie Stoker, Victoria Granof, Olivia Anderson, and Nick Krasznai, for making this book beautiful and delicious from cover to cover.

Thank you to my Marcus Samuelsson Group family, for carrying the torch and enjoying the ride. And to Derek Evans, Howard Greenstone, Jeanette Cebollero, Jori Carrington, Jeannette Park, Meaghan Dillon, Erica Morris, Stacy Rudin, Jenn Burka, Angela Bankhead, and Jono Gasparro. To Derek Fleming, Nils Norén, Tracey Kemble, Mahir Hossein, Christina Wang, Jane Ren, Marisa Blanc, Raul Adorno, and Eden Fesehaye, for getting this family started.

Thank you to my Rooster crew, past, present and future, for making this place feel like home. And to my chefs, Patricia Yeo, Adrienne Cheatham, Charlene Johnson, Kingsley John, and Cyed Adraincem, for making delicious food every day that fuels the fire of the Roo, and Lissette Tabales, for your expert mixology and keeping everyone in the bar happy.

Thank you to Andrew, Richard, and the Chapman family, for helping me create something so much more than a restaurant.

Thank you to Dapper Dan, Lana Turner, Bevy Smith, Mayor Dinkins, Marjorie Eliot, Tru Osborne, Rakiem Walker, Kim Hastreiter, Nate Lucas, Billy Mitchell, Thelma Golden, Melba Wilson, and my Harlem neighbors, for lending us your stories and telling us how it really is.

Thank you to Elizabeth Johnson, Sidra Smith, Christina Scott, Cody and Tash, The Rakiem Walker Project, Louis Johnson, Christian Lopez, Daniel Jeffries, AnhDao Nguyen, Fatima Glover, Ulrika Bengston, Angela DiSimone, David Melendez, Ezelia Johnson, and all the others for being the stars in our photos.

Thank you to Gillian Walker and the Maysles family, for letting us stir up trouble in your kitchen and to Rebekah Maysles, for not just her beautiful illustrations but also her stories and friendship.

To the Harlem cooks that came before, Sylvia Woods, Pig Foot Mary, Charles Gabriel, and Crab Man Mike, for showing us all how hospitality should be.

Thank you to The Gordon Parks Foundation, for loaning their iconic images and bearing witness.

Foreword

Hilton Als, writer and critic for The New Yorker, *reminisces about his childhood visits to Harlem and how art, music, and food lured him back to this legendary neighborhood.*

FIRST WHAT WE WOULD DO was collect glass Coke bottles—this was in the late nineteen-sixties. You could get refund money for that, a few pennies for each bottle, but that added up. I would put my little brother in the red wagon we both owned—a gift from our father, who didn't live with us—and then I'd load the wagon up with Coke bottles, the baby and glass bottles clanging delightedly on their way to the store. Then, once the cart was clear, I'd pool my money with my tough first cousin, Donna—she was five years older than me and when big boys bothered me, she beat them up—and then, when we had enough dimes and nickels and pennies rolled up, we'd sneak away from Brooklyn, where we lived, and take the A train all the way to Manhattan and the Apollo, to see James Brown. We weren't allowed to go so far on the train on our own, but we lied, somehow, and once divested of the burden of the truth, there Donna and I would be, sporting our "naturals," Donna, the teenager, grown-like and smoking a cigarette, standing with me in the balcony—who could keep still?—enthralled by rhythms and the feelings rhythms generate, all produced by a genius who spared no physical or psychic expense to express his art, and how our collective heart fit into it. This celebration of bodies and sound—we were one with the Apollo audience; we were the body James wanted to wrest love from—was my first visit to Harlem, and after that Harlem was always one body to me, a beautiful black mass with many questions, including what was its relationship to the rest of the city, the nation as a whole, all those places outside Harlem that, in the nineteen-seventies, didn't give a shit about the neighborhood's fabled past and raggedy present, while Harlem, one black body, fought for, and sometimes won, a kind of self-conferred dignity. While James sang, "Say it loud, I'm black and I'm proud!," and we did because that's the way we felt in our naturals and dashikis, it was something we had to fight for, too, and I remember after seeing James Brown at the Apollo, that I would then go uptown with my older sister, Bonnie, to demonstrate at what was called the "site"—this was in the nineteen-seventies—an area of Harlem we were trying to save, we didn't want the government to build on it, and we would sleep on the ground with so many other people, all in front of where the State Office Building now stands, President Clinton has his office there now, and what I remember most about that experience is how our collective black body tried to stop that which could not be stopped but we tried anyway.

And that was the point: To try. Together. To me, as a child, then, Harlem was a village that represented one black body—black America—who grew through craftiness and invention and intuition, a world where who I was was not separate from who everyone else was, a world where other worlds pertaining to black culture, politics, and so on, nestled deep in the landscape filled with black-owned businesses, the clamor of public debate, and marquees announcing black movies promoting black fantasies. As a student at Columbia University, I rarely went to Harlem; I wanted to be a different self by then. This is the work of youth, to imagine you are not yourself or a self with a past. I did not want to be part of a collective anything; the fantasy was that I was I, and I belonged to me. But things change, and the world teaches you that if you don't belong to any other body than your own, the stars are cold. This changed when I started going to the Studio Museum in Harlem again. When Thelma Golden became the museum's director in 2005, I was reintroduced to the world I had left behind—and that was on the brink of becoming even more itself than when I became one of the region's prodigal sons. Marcus's welcome table was, of course, the place to herald one's return. I first went to the Red Rooster in the spring of 2010, before it opened officially. Marcus and Thelma were hosting a dinner for the artist Mark Bradford. One saw, on the walls, art by Lorna Simpson and Ming Smith—iconic images that described, in photos, painting, and so on, the black body that I once knew but now knew in a different way, in part because Marcus celebrated it in a different way. Without jettisoning blackness, he was introducing blackness to what he knew of the world through his travels in Ethiopia, in Sweden, in London, and Paris.

Harlem was a village that represented one black body—black America—who grew through craftiness and invention and intuition.

Through his food, his milieu, that long-ago evening filled with artists and talk about art, Marcus was celebrating all that which he was doing at the Red Rooster, and all I felt at the Apollo and have always longed for, even when I didn't know it: the joy and ardor it takes to hope, and to effect change.

Preface

RIGHT NOW IN HARLEM, times are changing. An entire neighborhood awakes and wonders about the new thing coming, about the legends closing, about the who and what, despite it all, still remains. Right now in Harlem, 125th Street stretches from river to river. On the west side, Lincoln Fried Chicken is still serving down-home meals behind bullet-proof glass. Right now you can walk a little further east and see a botanical store crammed with religious relics—St. Agnes of Assisi and St. Dominic in glass; St. Sabinus and St. Thomas in clay. The Chinese god of fortune, Caishen, is covered in gold leaf and tucked in the corner of the window display; a blue figurine of Vishnu stands alongside him. Behind the religious souvenirs are a stunning array of plastic flowers. Right now in Harlem, a *florista* is selling items meant to last.

Right now men are gathered, waiting for service at Levels, getting a shape-up, trading stories, telling neighborhood gossip. A six-year-old boy is getting a haircut. His father is just an arm's reach away. Hold still and be brave, Little Man. Right now all along 125th Street, places that have not made it leave markings of their passing. M&G's Soul Food is long gone, but the Capsule clothing shop that's there now doesn't have the heart to take down the sign. If you're lost, *M&G,* printed in money green, and *Soul Food,* written in red and surrounded by a smiling yellow, can orient you. *This is Harlem,* it says, and *I am here.* Just beyond, Showmans' black awning gives the sidewalk shade. This jazz haunt has made music its religion since 1942. That and LaGree Baptist Church anchors the block.

Red Lobster and Chase Banks and the Gap can turn you around in Harlem, but the Apollo and Hotel Theresa point out where you are.

Right now, Harlem is delicious. On the corner of 125th and Frederick Douglass Avenue, I turn my head south and see Little Senegal steeped in barter and food. Then I look north. Charles' Country Pan Fried Chicken is beyond my sight, but I know it's there. Smothered pork chops, hoppin' John, and fried chicken so good it makes you believe in prayer. Charles and his soul food is not alone. Whether hidden or right on an avenue, Harlem is cooking. An entire neighborhood is draped in spice and smells: cumin, garlic, brown sugar. And if that's not enough, take a peek and pause at the folks selling a heart's desire: wooden bracelets, gold-plated necklaces, sun dresses, bed sheets, Jamaican beef patties. You are in Harlem. Right now, Muscle Dan is doing chin-ups on the lamp post; people on tour buses take out their iPhones and snap the sight. Dan's not there for them, he's there for us. He is a lesson for the neighborhood: Look at me, you can get in shape anywhere.

Right now, my Rooster marks the halfway point of 125th Street. I want to stop; I want to talk to our maitre d', Zee Johnson, and our chef, Kingsley John, but more than that I want to walk river to river. I want to see how one street can change and change again. How one street can map success. *Look at me,* it says, *you are standing on a marvel; you are surrounded by the extraordinary.* Harlem is a slow seduction. What is ugly keeps bumping into the beautiful. Right now everything in Harlem turns heads. Chaos is happening underneath the Metro-North bridge. Three ambulances are waiting for folks to get high and drop. Right now, the K2 epidemic is happening; it smells and acts like crack. Walk a block on 125th and wade through 1986. But right now in Harlem, we are beating that back. There is a woman clucking and cooing over a basket perched on the back of the bike. Nothing but a child would receive that kind of care and endless worry. I take a peek through her arms: It's a dog, cleaner than this woman will ever be. What's its name, I ask her. I haven't done that yet, she tells me.

Harlem is a slow seduction. What is ugly keeps bumping into the beautiful.

Right now, at Lexington Avenue, at the mouth of the 4, 5, 6 subway stop, a drug dealer is yelling a job, "15 dollars for 15 minutes. Wanna make 15 dollars in 15 minutes?" Some kid stalls on the stairs. He's twelve, maybe fourteen. I wonder if he is making the same calculation I am. There are 1,440 minutes in a day. 10,080 in a week. 43,200 in a month. He could make rent with all that money; pay back every debt his mother owed, Con Edison and telephone bills handled. A young woman with a Pathmark grocery bag on one hip and a toddler on the other is watching the kid weigh his options. Her gold hoop earrings glint in the sun. "Don't you need to catch the train?"

"Yeah." They walk down the steps. Right now, such small good news doesn't get in the papers, but those of us who live here need to know it all the same. We know alongside the small news, there is great news. Check this. There are Toni Morrisons and Miles Davises; there are Ellas and Mayas and Michael Jacksons in every building on every corner. All of us sing and cook and write our grievances and our triumphs. Nina and Baldwin inspire, but so do little brother and sister around the way. It all goes into my soup. I walk across 125th, looking at what still stands and who walks, through a triple lens: Ethiopian, Swedish, American. I can see Harlem and America and Gothenburg, a fishing village. I'm standing on a Harlem sidewalk, but I can see and feel and taste a dusty road in Addis.

Right now in Harlem, for every bank and chicken wing franchise joint, there is a small business owner who has spent a decade trying to figure out how to cater to a neighborhood he has fallen in love with. For every man or woman who has succumbed to that spell, I want to tell them: Go for it, do it. I want to pass the word like gospel. Let me tell you something: Right now in Harlem authorship is on the move. This is ours, we tell each other. We have made it, chopped it, cooked it, played it. This is our story. Gordon Parks, photographer, musician, writer, film director paved a way for us. *Bear witness,* he told us. That was his gift to the neighborhood. Whatever goes down, whatever turns up—make food and music and dance and story out of it. Right now and since forever, the world keeps telling us there's only room for one: Serena and that's it. Toni and that's it. I wonder if they can hear Harlem across the divide. *Come one, come all.* That's how we wrestle with urban renewal, black removal. The church ladies know this, and so do the hustlers. Right now in Harlem, we don't shy away from the ugly; we don't bow our heads to what's beautiful. We just keep asking, how does all this new shit fit with the old? Right now in Harlem there's room; there's hope; there's inspiration; there's good food. I may not be able to explain the magic, but it is there. To be in Harlem and make it takes luck, but nobody told me different.

One thing is certain, wherever you are, you should come to Harlem—right now.

INTRODUCTION

1.

I HELD THE DOOR OPEN FOR HIM. That was my first mistake. "Give me your fucking money, Man." It was the point of his knife in my back making me rise up on tiptoe, not the menace in his voice. For a second, I thought it was one of my friends playing a joke, but his ripe smell—piss, smoke, funk—told me this wasn't a game. I stood in my building's foyer, my bag of laundry at my side. "I'm serious, Man. Gimme the money."

"Okay. Okay," I said, as I slid my hand into my back pocket for my wallet. I'd never been held up before, but living in New York City, imagining just what would you do if some guy pulled a gun on you, was more than an idle thought. *If it ever happened to me, I'd just hand it over*, I remember thinking, when my friends were trading heroic scenarios. But I never imagined the sweat. Not my attacker's, mine. It was fall in the evening, the air held a bite, but sweat pooled under my arms, down my chest.

"Come on, hurry it up," he hissed, pushing my shoulder, spinning me around. He was a white guy, my height. His red Gap shirt was torn in three places; his jeans were filthy. He had a kitchen knife in his hand. A ten-inch blade. I was being robbed with a chef's knife. I handed over the eighty bucks I had just gotten from the ATM. "The wallet! The wallet, too."

"Okay, okay." I tugged my wallet out of my back pocket and handed it over. He inched away from me, then turned to walk quickly out the building. His knife looked like the kind my grandmother used to cut potatoes and chicken back in Sweden. It was my weapon of choice when I cooked at Aquavit. He didn't know it, but this guy had just mugged me with my family and livelihood. By the time he had gotten to the curb, I realized what he had done and what I was letting him get away with. I took off after him.

It took me a minute to realize I was negotiating with my mugger.

"Wait! Wait!"

"What the fuck, Man. Back off."

"You've got my papers. Give me back my papers." I was working as a chef, but I had come to America with a tourist visa, not a working visa. I had heard stories about people who had been caught without their visas and as punishment weren't allowed to reenter the States for five years. Five years away from America. Five years shut out of New York. No way. I'm not sure what I looked like as I walked closer to him, but whatever my expression, the guy took several steps back.

"What're you talking about? Stop moving."

"Yeah, I will. Just give me my papers!" I followed him as he crossed the street.

"Look. Just stay where you are, okay?" We were separated by the length of a Toyota Camry. He pulled my wallet out of his front pocket and slapped it on the hood of the car. "Okay. So what does it look like? This one?"

He held up my Swedish ID card. "No, but I need that. Let me have that back." It took me a minute to realize I was negotiating with my mugger. My Swedish driver's license wouldn't spend and neither would my Con Edison bill. The more determined I became to get back all those squares of paper that verified my status as an immigrant, as a man, the more scared my robber became. My life sat in a heap on the hood. The robber was shaking.

"You're crazy, Man. Crazy!" Then he took off.

I went to the police station. While sitting on the bench, I thought about the guy who held me up. He had looked like a school teacher who had been out of work for a couple of years. He wore glasses and the left lens was shattered. One of his arms was laced with scars. That guy was broke and scared and desperate. And what had he seen in me? Was there something about my Adidas hat and jeans that screamed loads of money? I left the station after twenty minutes without reporting the incident. Why bother? I clearly wasn't in Sweden anymore. There were bigger problems happening in this station than mine. I had almost forgotten why I had been so absent-minded, why I held open the door for my mugger to walk through in the first place.

That day, I moved to Harlem.

2.

I was doing a promotion for Aquavit at the Observatory Hotel in Sydney, Australia, when the World Trade Center was struck. My good friend and chef de cuisine, Nils Norén, woke me up with the news, and together we watched footage of the attack on BBC. The video ran on a loop, and because the reporter failed to mention the cross streets, I imagined all of Manhattan under rubble and ash. The chef of Windows on the World, Michael Lomonaco, was kind enough to let me cook there a week before. The breakfast crew had helped me set up. They were great guys. Even before I returned to a stunned city, I knew the world had changed. On my hotel bed, with my head in my hands, hard questions hounded and haunted me: *What am I doing? What is this all for? Should I still cook?*

3

"I'm out."

"Excuse me?" I was talking with Mark, good friend of mine, and a fellow chef over a beer after work.

He waved his hand over his chef whites, "This. I'm getting out of this." Mark had this idea of opening a place with beer and organic apples. He wanted to set up TVs to show soccer matches. And he'd do it all in Brooklyn.

"Brooklyn?"

"Yeah. Brooklyn. I'm going to call it The Diner." I felt as if Mark was speaking Welsh. What the hell? We were chefs, and not to sound conceited, we were chefs who operated at a certain tier. Our lives were about chasing James Beard awards and visiting places in France. We created highly technical dishes, ones that took tweezers and squeeze bottles to plate. And foam. Yes. I did foams. So did Mark. "Joey's getting out, too."

"Really?"

"Yeah, he wants to open this place downtown. Extra Virgin. No muss, no fuss."

"I mean . . . I think." I laughed and took a swallow of beer.

"I'm going to go for it. I think I'm ready to cook and be happy," he paused. "At the same time."

Harlem is the Apollo and the young woman who stands inside thinking, *I'm going to get this*. Harlem is poverty. Harlem is wealth. Harlem is America.

I took the train back to home to Harlem and replayed the conversation over in my head. To cook and be happy. I was happy with cooking, wasn't I? I started to think about all the culinary techniques I had learned, skills that I performed with precision every day. My dishes had a point of view—edgy Swedish cuisine with a lot of Asian notes underneath. I noticed peaking food trends and then riffed on them. So was I happy with cooking? No. I was in love with it. I approached my profession with this overwhelming desire, tinged with vanity. My life was foie gras and microgreens. But what if it didn't have to be like that?

My mother had frequently asked me over the course of my career: "Why do you always have to travel so far to cook in your restaurant? You should cook in your neighborhood. Not just fine folk would like to eat your food." Remembering my mother's gentle admonishment, along with Mark's departure, made me think about next steps. Where was I happiest? Harlem. It was the only place I had ever lived where I felt both invisible and noticed. I could be Chef and just a black guy. When I was twelve years old, my adoptive father introduced me to my heroes: James Baldwin, Maya Angelou, James Brown, Nina Simone. "Look up to them, Marcus. Follow their footsteps. Or try to. *Förstår du?*" I wasn't sure if I really did understand, but I nodded solemnly anyway. These men and women had outsized lives and achievements. They were that good; what they could create was that rare. To read Ellison, to listen to Ella was like watching magic unfold. My twelve-year-old self listened to my father and thought the people who he told me to look up to were *magisk neger*. Magical Negroes. I didn't know it at the time, but most of my heroes had found a home in or been inspired by Harlem.

It's one of the many reasons that I go to sleep and wake up with thoughts of authorship. Who writes our stories? Who chronicles our tales of cooking it, playing it, writing it? Baldwin, Gordon, the Apollo, Jacob Lawrence, Paul Mooney, James Brown, Malcolm— that's my neighborhood. Why *wouldn't* I want to cook for the people who lived there?

Opening Rooster has meant I get to cook and be happy. At the same time. We make dishes inspired by the South and the Great Migration. I offer the food I grew up with, big dishes that made you suck your fingers. Good lumpy gravy with odd-shaped *kroppkaka,* Swedish potato dumpling. But my food also comes out of church cooking, home cooking, diners, and the Southern tradition of meat and three. It's black culture, but it's for everyone. It's the bird and the pig. It's bourbon. I don't think I changed so much from living and working in Harlem, as I found a certain kind of orientation. The meet-and-greet that happens in Harlem is real and important. Honey and sugar aren't ingredients, they're words of endearment used to say hello. Up here, we like it when you eat with your whole body, elbows and all. Women restaurateurs like Leah Chase, B. Smith, Edna Lewis, Alberta Wright, Melba Wilson, and Sylvia Woods set the tone. And I think I was smart enough to follow their example.

Muscoota, **that's what Native Americans called this section of Harlem. Run your eye across the page quickly enough, and the name looks like the word** *music.*

But what I love best is how Harlem and the Rooster allow me to play, to learn, to dream. *Muscoota,* that's what Native Americans called this section of Harlem. Run your eye across the page quickly enough, and the name looks like the word *music.* Which fits. Music, food, dance, song. In Harlem you can do all of that inside four walls. There's room for me here. My pickled herring runs alongside the mac and cheese and my neighbors love it. To be given the space to do my own thing is a gift.

Five years later and Rooster is a happy place. In all the restaurants I worked at before, I never considered being truly happy. Or being satisfied with the work I had done, instead thinking about everything I hadn't gotten to. This doesn't mean I'm skipping in place, but most days I revel in the joys. Instead of bowing to pressure, I'm prone to riding that tension and letting it take me to someplace new. I think of all those who have authored Harlem. I wonder if my personal scrawl is worthy to be read alongside theirs. I thank all the troubles I've been though. They got me here. They got me to Harlem.

4.

What Harlem is, is constantly changing. It is a place that comes at you like a duet or a trio. Some avenues reveal a quartet of interest, while on side streets, a soloist steps out and breaks into song.

Harlem is Langston. Harlem is allure. Harlem is jazz. Harlem is my wife, standing on an avenue sidewalk with chickpea flour perched on her head. "Come on, Marcus, let's hurry." We walk as if we are hungry and destined. Harlem is love. And strife. And sorrow. Harlem is art. Harlem is the Apollo and the young woman who stands inside thinking, *I'm going to get this*. Harlem is poverty. Harlem is wealth. Harlem is America.

Harlem is my home.

THE PANTRY

FOUR AVENUES CONVERGE to inform the pantry at the Red Rooster.

First is the food of the Great Migration, dishes brought north by Southern blacks and subtly changed in their new environment.

Second is the global emigration—the Italians, Jews, Chinese, Puerto Ricans, Mexicans, Caribs, West Africans who form the ever-changing landscape of Harlem.

Third is my own background: my roots in Sweden, my training as a chef in Europe, my work as a chef on cruise ships, my discovery of the cuisine of Ethiopia, where I was born.

Last is the moment we are cooking in today. This is where we find our link to other restaurants.

It is an eclectic mix, and it gives rise to an eccentric pantry. You'll find many of the ingredients in supermarkets or ethnic markets, and all of them are available online.

Vinegars

I'm a pickle guy, so naturally I love vinegar, but I also love the acidic brightness it adds to stews, soups, and greens. I use them all: apple cider, balsamic, black, sherry, red wine, white wine, and distilled white vinegar. You should be able to find all of them in your grocery store, or visit kalustyans.com. Check Chinese markets for black vinegar—the perfect dumpling dip.

MAKING WINE VINEGAR

Combine mother, wine, and oxygen, and you'll get vinegar. The *mother* of vinegar is the substance that helps turn alcohol into acetic acid. Bragg sells organic, unfiltered apple cider vinegar "with the 'Mother.'" This makes things easy. Strain the cider vinegar, shaking the bottle if you need to so the mother slips out. Put the mother into a clean wine bottle and pour in leftover wine. Leave the bottle open for a day or two, then cork it and leave it alone for a week or so. Uncork it and give it a sniff. You'll be able to tell if it's ready. Then taste it.

You can replenish the bottle with more wine as long as the mother hasn't dried out. Follow the same process: open for a day, then a week for aging.

Wines

I'm going to say what every chef will say: Use good wine when you cook. It doesn't have to be the most expensive bottle, but it does have to be something you enjoy drinking. And if you don't want to open a bottle of white wine, substitute dry vermouth. It's crisp and floral, and because it's fortified it keeps in the refrigerator much longer than an opened bottle of wine will.

Mirin. A low-alcohol rice wine, essential in Japanese cooking. Check your grocery store, Asian markets, or online (kalustyans.com and amazon.com).

Shaoxing wine. This Chinese rice wine is used both in cooking and as a beverage. Look for it in wine shops or substitute dry sherry.

Mustards

Dijon mustard. White wine releases the flavor of mustard in this classic condiment.

Extra strong Dijon mustard. Prepared mustard loses its pungency over time. If you like to feel mustard in your nose, buy the jars labeled "extra strong" or "extra forte."

Chinese mustard. You'll find jars of Chinese mustard in the Asian section of most grocery stores, but if you want truly searing mustard, make it yourself: Mix 1/4 cup Chinese mustard powder (though Colman's will certainly work) and 1/2 teaspoon freshly ground (make it fine) white pepper with 1/4 cup water. Let it sit for 10 to 15 minutes before using. This loses potency fast, so use it right away.

Sweet mustard. The sweet mustard called for in my recipes is the Scandinavian one. You can find it (look for Lars Own brand) in some specialty stores, markets like Whole Foods, and online from amazon.com.

Flours, Grains, and Rice

You should be able to find most of the flours in grocery stores or specialty markets. If not, you can get them online from bobsredmill.com.

All-purpose flour. Use unbleached in all these recipes.

Rice flour. Gluten-free and easy to digest.

Potato flour. Another gluten-free option. It's a great thickener.

Chickpea flour. Gluten-free and loaded with protein. This is the essential ingredient for shiro (see *The* Breakfast, page 266). It's also called garbanzo bean flour and gram flour.

Semolina flour. Most often used to make pasta.

Teff flour. Ground from a small East African cereal grass. It's the main ingredient of injera, Ethiopian flat bread.

Cornstarch. A great thickener. Combine it with all-purpose flour to make a shattering crust for fried foods.

Corn flour. A finer grind than cornmeal. Great for delicate breading.

Cornmeal. Use stone-ground cornmeal in these recipes. Yellow or white? It's up to you. Many farmers are grinding their own meal, so look for it at your farmers' market.

Grits. Get the best grits you can and store them in the freezer. Ansonmills.com and hoppinjohns.com are both great online sources.

Jasmine rice. This is my white rice of choice. You'll find it everywhere.

Rice powder. I use this as a coating in Double-Dragon Rice (page 116) to give it extra crunch. You can find it in Chinese markets, where it costs pennies, or make your own: Toast jasmine rice in a cast-iron skillet—add a piece of ginger or a stalk of lemongrass if you want—over very low heat until golden brown. Stir often; it will take about 45 minutes. Discard the ginger or lemongrass. Cool completely, then grind to a powder in a spice grinder.

Herbs, Spices, and Spice Mixes

Curry leaves. The Indian cooking authority Julie Sahni says these leaves, which are members of the citrus family, have "a bitterish taste and a sweetish, pungent aroma almost like lemongrass." You'll find them in Indian markets (and online at amazon.com). They freeze well, and there's no need to thaw them before using. Avoid dried curry leaves; they have no flavor at all.

I spread fresh rosemary out on paper towels and zap it in the microwave in 30-second bursts to dry it. And when I've grown a pot of oregano, I pull up the plant, shake off all the dirt, and hang it upside down out of the light. When it's dry, I squeeze it over a piece of waxed paper to release all the leaves and store them in a jar.

Ajwain. Common in Indian cooking, this tiny pod has a complex, bitter flavor and smells like thyme. You can find it in Indian markets (or online from kalustyans.com, penzeys.com, and thespicehouse.com).

Aleppo pepper. Thank you, Paula Wolfert, for introducing us to this fruity and moderately hot pepper named after the Syrian city on the famed Silk Road. Look for it in markets with a big spice section (or online from penzeys.com and thespicehouse.com).

Ancho chile powder. Mild and smoky. You should be able to find ancho chile powder in most grocery stores.

Chipotle chile powder. This chile powder packs some heat. Like ancho chile powder, it's in most grocery stores.

Berbere. A complex spice mix from Ethiopia. You'll likely need to shop online for berbere (kalustyans.com and penzeys.com). But you can also make your own (see below).

BERBERE

▶ Put 2 teaspoons coriander seeds, 1 teaspoon fenugreek seeds, ½ teaspoon black peppercorns, 3 or 4 allspice berries, 6 cardamom pods, and 4 whole cloves into a small skillet. Toast over medium heat, swirling the skillet, until fragrant, about 4 minutes. Pour the seeds into a spice grinder and cool. Add ½ cup dried onion flakes and 5 stemmed and seeded chiles de arbol. Grind to a fine powder.

▶ Put the spice powder into a bowl and whisk in 3 tablespoons pimentón, 2 teaspoons kosher salt, ½ teaspoon grated nutmeg, ½ teaspoon powdered ginger, and ½ teaspoon ground cinnamon.

▶ This makes about ¾ cup. Store in a sealed jar, out of the light, for up to 6 months.

Garam masala. There are many different recipes for this Indian spice mix. Look for it in markets with a big spice section, online (kalustyans.com and penzeys.com), or try making your own from the many recipes online.

FRESH GINGER

- Look for fresh ginger with a smooth peel. Wrinkled peel is a sign of older, dry, and very fibrous ginger.
- Use a spoon to peel it. And if the recipe calls for grated ginger, use a rasp grater.
- Here's a little trick for chopping ginger. Cut the ginger into thin coins. Then smash them with the flat of a chef's knife the way you would smash garlic. Chop or mince. Smashing not only does most of the work for you, it starts to release the juices, so you get a tastier dish.

Horseradish. I prefer the nose-clearing bite of horseradish grated fresh to the bottled kind. Peel what you need and use a rasp grater.

Lavender, culinary. Floral, delicious with poultry. If you grow your own, you can use the fresh buds. If you buy it and it isn't labeled culinary, it has probably been sprayed. Available in some specialty stores or online from thespicehouse.com and amazon.com.

LEMONGRASS

- There's a lot of flavor in this herb, but you need to be brutal to get to it.
- Trim off the woody root and discard the very tough outer layers. Slice the lemongrass lengthwise and set, cut side down, on your cutting board. Grab your biggest chef's knife by the handle, blade pointing up, and smash down on the lemongrass with the end of the handle, working your way up from the root end to break the lemongrass into long fibers. It's now ready to mince.
- You can also grate lemongrass on a rasp grater. The result will be finer, but it takes more time.

Pickling spice. You'll find it in the spice section in your grocery store.

Ras el hanout. The Moroccan equivalent of garam masala, the name can be loosely translated as "top of the shop," meaning the best of a spice merchant's goods. Look for it in markets with a big spice section, online (kalustyans.com and penzeys.com), or try making your own from the many recipes online.

Shichimi togarashi. Japanese seven-spice, a mix of sansho (a Japanese pepper), ground red chile, dried tangerine rind or orange zest, ground or flaked nori, white and black poppy seeds, sesame seeds, and dried garlic. Look for it in markets with a big spice section and online (kalustyans.com and amazon.com)

Wasabi powder. Much of the wasabi powder on grocery shelves is actually horseradish flavored with mustard flour and colored with spinach. Look for brands like Eden Foods that contain at least some wasabi. Sushi Sonic sells 100 percent wasabi; you can find it at amazon.com.

Pink curing salt (curing salt #1, Instacure #1, or Prague Powder #1). This preservative is added to meats that are cured to prevent the growth of bacteria. It is a mixture of sodium nitrite and table salt dyed pink.

Williams-Sonoma carries it (in stores and online); you can also find it at spicejungle.com.

Tomato powder. This powder, made of ground dehydrated tomatoes, has an intense flavor. Use it whenever you need a little tomato taste and don't want to open a can. You can find it in specialty stores or online (spicejungle.com and amazon.com). Store in the refrigerator so it doesn't clump.

Filé powder. Also called gumbo filé, this earthy and spicy herb is the ground leaf of the sassafras tree. If you can't find it in your grocery store, look online at amazon.com. Buy the pure stuff.

Pastes and Sauces

Aji amarillo. This hot and fruity pepper is a keynote ingredient in Peruvian cuisine. You can find the paste online at tienda.com and amazon.com.

Chipotles in adobo. These are dried, smoked ripe jalapeños cooked and packed in a slightly sweet red sauce. The chipotles themselves have fairly intense heat; the sauce on its own is a great ingredient when you want to add a hint of smoky heat. You'll find it in the Latin section of most grocery stores.

Fish sauce. A Southeast Asian sauce made of anchovies fermented with salt and water. It adds a distinct flavor and aroma. You can find it in large grocery stores, Asian markets, or online from kalustyans.com.

Indian curry paste. A great cheat ingredient. You'll find many different kinds of curry paste (hot, mild, vindaloo) at Indian markets (or online from kalustyans.com).

Ketjap manis. Think of this as Indonesia's soy sauce, sweetened with palm sugar. You will find it at some specialty shops and online (kalustyans.com and amazon.com).

Korean hot pepper paste (gochujang). Moderately hot, with a hint of sweetness. Buy it at Korean markets—Haechandle is the number one brand—or online at amazon.com.

Mala sauce. Look for this numbingly hot Sichuan sauce for noodles in Chinatown markets. Or substitute Chinese chili oil.

Miso. I love the salty funk that this fermented soybean paste adds to food. Look for it in most grocery stores and Asian markets. The recipes in this book call for white miso.

Beat a couple of tablespoons of miso into a stick of softened butter and use it on salmon, on chicken, on chops or steaks, on vegetables.

Plum sauce. I add this sweet and sour Chinese condiment to braising liquids. Use it as a dip for anything fried. You'll find it in the Asian section of your grocery store and at Asian markets.

Sambal oelek (chili garlic sauce). This ground chili paste from Southeast Asia adds great heat. Try to find Huy Fong brand in Asian markets (or online from amazon.com).

Sriracha. Has this Thai hot sauce become the new ketchup? Look for it in the Asian section at your grocery store or at Asian markets.

Tomato paste. Why open a can when you just need a tablespoon or two? The double-concentrated tomato paste in tubes is terrific.

Yuzu kosho. This Japanese paste is made of ground yuzu (a very aromatic citrus fruit), chiles, and salt. You can find it in Japanese markets (or online from amazon.com).

XO sauce. A spicy Chinese condiment made with dried scallops, dried shrimp, ham, garlic, and oil. You'll find it in Asian markets (or online at amazon.com).

Specialty Oils

Mustard oil. As you would expect from an oil made from mustard seeds, this is pungent. Look for it in specialty stores (or online from kalustyans.com and amazon.com).

Pumpkin seed oil. I discovered this finishing oil years ago in Austria. Use it to make a salad dressing, put a few drops into soups—you can even drizzle a little over vanilla ice cream. Your best bet is buying it online. Look for Austrian or Styrian oils on amazon.com.

Cheeses

Burrata. The name may mean "buttered," but this fresh mozzarella is filled with cream. Serve it at room temperature.

Mascarpone. One of the main ingredients in tiramisu, this soft Italian cheese is great when you want to add richness to a sauce.

Queso fresco. Mexican "fresh cheese" is mild, with a little salty kick, and crumbly. You can substitute a mild feta.

Flavors from the Sea

Dried shrimp. Tiny, pungent dried shrimp are an important umami flavoring in many Asian cuisines. You'll find small packages of them in Asian markets or online (amazon.com).

SHRIMP POWDER

You can find shrimp powder in West African markets, or you can make your own by grinding tiny dried shrimp in the spice grinder. Clean the grinder after by grinding a few tablespoons of raw rice and a teaspoon of baking soda.

Nori and dried kelp. Find them in many grocery stores and health food markets and use them to add ocean brightness. Toast nori by waving it back and forth a few times over an open flame, them crumble it into a salad.

The Melting Pot

Banana leaves. Whether you use them to wrap tamales or to steam fish, banana leaves impart a delicate flavor. You'll find them frozen at Mexican markets. You can also get them online from mexgrocer.com.

Black beluga lentils. These may be the tiniest of the lentil family, and they glisten like caviar when they're cooked—hence the name. You'll find them in some good markets, specialty stores, or online (kalustyans.com and amazon.com).

Brioche buns. More and more bakeries are shaping tender, buttery brioche into hamburger buns large and small. But you can also find them in grocery stores that have great bread departments (there are some fine commercial bakeries making them).

Canned chestnuts. You could spend an afternoon roasting chestnuts, shelling them, and then blanching and peeling them. Or you can buy them packed in water in a can, ready to eat. What's your pleasure? Check your specialty store or amazon.com.

Coconut milk. The recipes in the book use unsweetened coconut milk. It's easy enough to find in grocery stores. Asian coconut milk seems to be thicker than the Latin brands.

WHIP IT

Coconut milk makes super delicious whipped cream. And it's vegan!

▶ Put a can of Asian coconut milk in the refrigerator overnight. The fat will rise and firm up. Open the can and scoop the fat out and into a bowl. Leave all the coconut water behind.

▶ Whip with a whisk or an electric mixer until you have stiff peaks. Flavor it as you will. A little vanilla extract? Some sugar? A pinch of ground cardamom? It's up to you.

Kimchi. These fermented vegetables—countless varieties of them, though Napa cabbage is the most common—are a staple on every Korean table. Some are mild, but most have a good dose of Korean hot pepper paste and hot pepper flakes and can be fiery. Check farmers' markets and Korean markets for kimchi that's homemade, but you'll also find it in the refrigerated sections of big grocery stores (near the tofu).

Korean rice cakes (*dduk,* also spelled *tteokguk* and *thuck*). Do what you can to find this great product; it's a revelation. Rice cake is sticky rice that is steamed, pounded, and then shaped into a cylinder. It's a blank canvas that sops up whatever flavor you pair it with, and it's seriously chewy. You'll find sliced rice cakes in the refrigerator and frozen sections of Korean markets. H&Y Marketplace sells rice cakes online (hy1004.com), but they don't ship everywhere. Sometimes you can find vendors on amazon.com. If you can't find sliced rice cakes, buy the whole ones and slice them yourself, on the diagonal and about $1/4$ inch thick.

Pickled ginger. It's not just a condiment for sushi. I love the gingery brightness and bite it adds to greens. You'll find it in Asian markets and many grocery stores. Very young ginger will turn pale pink when it's pickled; the brighter pink stuff is dyed.

MAPLE SYRUP

Real maple syrup is graded on a combination of flavor and color, and it's always been confusing. Is grade A "better" than grade B? It's not. The light-colored syrups (the old grade A), are produced early in the sugaring season; the darker ones (grade B) come later. A new system of grading is coming into place. Vermont has started, and the other syrup-producing states will soon be following.

Here's what to look for:

▶ Golden Color, Delicate Taste

▶ Amber Color, Rich Taste

▶ Dark Color, Robust Taste

Good Things to Have on Hand

These aren't ingredients in any of the recipes. They're just yummy.

Canned sardines. They could be the perfect snack. But they're great in a potato salad, too.

Chicharrón. Fried pork belly or pork rinds. Sit in front of the television and eat them out of hand like popcorn, or crumble them into a salad for crunch.

Fish roe spread. It comes in a tube and it's Scandinavia's instant canapé. If you've got an Ikea near you, you're in luck. Squirt some onto a Ritz cracker. But you could also spread a thin layer onto black bread and top with thin slices of cucumber and some chopped dill.

Lemon pickle. At its simplest, it's lemon, red chile powder, turmeric, and salt—though there are many variations, and it's India's antidote for indigestion. Eat it with rice. Or naan. Or with curry. Or fried chicken.

Pickled okra. This is one of the treasures of the South. Sure, you can just eat it as a pickle, but it makes a killer dirty martini.

BOOKS TO THINK ON AND COOK FROM

- ► *The Dooky Chase Cookbook*, by Leah Chase. Recipes from the New Orleans restaurant and Leah's stories of her Creole heritage.
- ► *The Taste of Country Cooking*, by Edna Lewis. Recipes and reminiscences from a born cook.
- ► *The Welcome Table: African-American Heritage Cooking*, by Jessica B. Harris. Food from church suppers, family reunions, and Sunday school picnics, all spiced with history.
- ► *Southern Food: At Home, on the Road, in History*, by John Egerton. The name says it all.
- ► *Hoppin' John's Lowcountry Cooking: Recipes and Ruminations from Charleston and the Carolina Coastal Plain*, by John Martin Taylor. *The* book about the food of the Carolina lowcountry, tracing its history to Africa.
- ► *The Ideal Bartender*, by Tom Bullock. An early classic by an African-American bartender.
- ► *Building Houses out of Chicken Legs: Black Women, Food, and Power*, by Psyche A. Williams-Forson. Forson examines how black women used chicken as a tool of self-determination and self-reliance.
- ► *The Lee Bros. Southern Cookbook: Stories and Recipes for Southerners and Would-Be Southerners*, by Matt Lee and Ted Lee. The word from the new generation.
- ► *Southern Homecoming Traditions: Recipes and Remembrances*, by Carolyn Quick Tillery. A cookbook and celebration of the five historic black colleges and one university that comprise Atlanta University Center.
- ► *Soul Food: Recipes and Reflections from African-American Churches*, by Joyce White. An Alabama native finds her roots in the churches of Harlem and Brooklyn's Bed-Stuy.
- ► *The Hot Bread Kitchen Cookbook: Artisanal Baking from Around the World*, by Jessamyn Waldman Rodriguez and Julia Turshen. The recipes come from around the world because the women who bake them at this Harlem bakery come from around the world.
- ► *The Jemima Code: Two Centuries of African American Cookbooks*, by Toni Tipton-Martin. This book digs deep to unearth histories of unknown black cooks and their books.

AT THE BAR

COPS LIFT A GLASS and toast grifters they haven't caught yet. Men dressed in summer wool gabardine and women in silk sip and nibble as they watch the exchange. Two men hold hands and neck when they think no one is watching, and older people look on and cluck about the outrageousness of young love. Musicians and hustlers grip the curve of the bar counter for dear life, since both need a kind of reprieve they can only find inside these four walls. Everybody is listening to the saxophonist play "Yesterdays." The song both swings and hurts at the same time.

Always, there is a bite of this, a taste of that, and oysters for everyone. Women ask for peach wine and get it. Brothers call out, "Give me that hooch," and the bartender knows exactly what they mean. All kinds of elbows touch: mailmen's and maids', church goers' and choir girls', politicians' and their potential constituents'. Both black and white patrons taste their drinks, and every now and then, they eat Southern food at the bar and savor, since everybody knows the real world waits right outside the door. Just for a moment, the best drinks in Harlem smooth over differences between race and status. And well, if they don't do that, they give folks enough room to learn something they didn't know about themselves: With the right sort of music, all manner of people can groove to the same beat.

Just for a moment, the best drinks in Harlem smooth over differences between race and status.

No, I'm not talking about my restaurant. I'm talking about the original Red Rooster on 138th Street and Adam Clayton Powell Boulevard. Opened on October 12, 1933, the original Red Rooster joined over five hundred speakeasies, juke joints, and bars already opened for business in Harlem in the nineteen-thirties. The time was ripe for such a venture. In the Great Migration, approximately six million Southern black folk from Louisiana, Georgia, Arkansas, and Tennessee heard the clarion call—get here!—and traveled north to a promised land to make it. Some left family, swearing they would send for them "when they got settled," and so many more gathered everything of value in cardboard suitcases or pillow slips to escape intolerable living conditions and maybe even make it big. According to Leah Dickerman, curator of *Jacob Lawrence: The Migration Series,* a song gunned their journey:

> *Lord, I work all week in the blazing sun*
> *Can't buy shoes Lord, when my payday comes.*
> *I ain't treated better than a mountain goat*
> *Boss takes my crop and poll tax takes my vote.*
> *I'm leaving here cause I just can't stay,*
> *I'm going where I can get more decent pay.*

Many found that decent pay in Chicago, Philadelphia, and St. Louis, but close to a million black Southerners set up shop in New York's Tenderloin and later in Harlem. Along with things they wouldn't dare leave behind, they also carried with them an abundance of hope, the foods they ate back home, and a taste for moonshine and peach wine. Al Douglas, a New York hotelier, and George Woods, the owner of the original Red Rooster, when thinking about a joint venture, wanted to cater to this burgeoning clientele. Their first advertisement in 1933 modestly asked for Harlemites to stop by the Red Rooster and partake in the "sensational, colossal, terrific, gigantic, stupendous, and magnificent" show they were staging. Most of Harlem showed up. So did the rest of New York.

Through the thirties, forties, fifties, and even the sixties, out-of-towners, the downtown set, and folks living in Harlem frequented the Rooster. It was the place to be. It housed good music and better food and the best cocktails. On Wednesdays, it offered the ultimate culinary high and low: chitterlings and champagne. And unlike Connie's Inn, a nightclub with black entertainers which catered only to white people, it welcomed all. Blacks, whites, gays, straights, musicians, artists. Even politicians. So when I found myself dreaming of opening a restaurant in Harlem, I didn't think about the Cotton Club or the Savoy, or even Minton's Playhouse. What captivated me was the story of the original Red Rooster. A place in the North where you could eat a good Southern meal. A place where Frank Sinatra and Adam Clayton Powell Jr. stopped by to quench their thirst. A place where Ethel Waters, aka Sweet Mama Stringbean, stopped in to belt it out. A place where everybody was welcome.

Harlem desperately needed a watering hole.

For an ambitious young man (and that would be me), the Red Rooster and all of its stories were something to aspire to. It gave me a reference. The more I studied and biked past its shuttered doors, the clearer picture I had of what I could bring to this neighborhood that was now my home. The unique community of Woods's Rooster gave me a peek into Harlem's cultural DNA: its style, its artistry, its music. The original Red Rooster wasn't the Cotton Club, an exclusive place where black and white were separated at the door; it

was a watering hole. A place where both folks in the neighborhood and white moneyed clientele were served full-strength drinks and a good meal. By the time I decided to take the plunge and open a restaurant uptown, I was acutely aware of three things—the first Red Rooster had closed in 1984; just a handful of Harlem speakeasies/bars remained; and Harlem desperately needed a watering hole.

I wanted a place where we didn't roll down the gates at night when we closed. I wouldn't have done that on Fifth Avenue, so why would I do it in Harlem?

So when I began thinking about *our* Rooster, I immediately thought about the bar. I needed drinks that catered to the neighborhood, but also to Swedes who knew their vodka and to a downtown set who knew great French wines. As I walked from my place on 118th to our then newly leased space on 125th and Lenox, my neighbors approached me with questions and advice. "You moving up here?"

"Yeah."

"Food gonna be tight, right?"

"Absolutely."

"Yo, Chef, them drinks gone be tasty?"

"Definitely."

"Chef, them drinks gotta be on point. Hear me?" I did. Black people know a good cocktail. Ours is a cocktail culture. We like our drinks sweet. And we know our hooch. Again and again, my neighbors let me know that they expected a full dining experience *at the bar*. Traditionally, bars in black neighborhoods were places where you eat *and* drink. A watering hole is where you catch up with friends. Where you spread the news: both good and bad. Where you listen to great live music. Where you eat food that makes you want to call your momma. But they were also establishments where you could get a free drink when you were short on money and you returned the favor by dropping off a roast turkey at Thanksgiving. In my line of business, you called those places "a bar, bar." My challenge was to make all of that happen at my Red Rooster.

Screw being hip, I wanted the bar to be the shape of hips.

It took us a month. I was terrified it wouldn't work, but my friend Andrew Chapman and his family were really the driving force. They believed in me and Harlem in ways I couldn't imagine, providing support, guidance, and freedom to chase my dream. As native New Yorkers, the Chapmans understood what makes Harlem so special and, like me, believed it was time to remind the rest of the city. And though I was afraid, I knew what I wanted. I wanted Lenox Avenue to have a life after seven o'clock. I wanted a bar that didn't operate as if it were backup—a place where you waited until your table was ready. I wanted a place where we didn't roll down the gates at night when we closed. I wouldn't have done that on Fifth Avenue, so why would I do it in Harlem? I wanted a restaurant that housed fine, fun dining and welcomed everybody—Latinos, Italians, Haitians, Africans, Jewish people. I wanted a bar anchored by the beats. The music had to move from gospel to jazz to hip-hop seamlessly. I wanted customers to look out at the show happening on a windy Lenox Avenue and fall in love the way I did. The M7 and M102 stop right outside our Rooster. All walks of life ride those buses. On 125th there's a kind of chaos on the corner that creeps midblock. Brothers are tending to business; sisters are loud-talking anyone who looks at them funny. African ladies hawk their skills. "You? You. I braid your hair. Come here. Meet my sister." My future patrons were in that crowd. And hopefully they wanted to share drinks with folks from downtown or tourists from around the world. I wanted a bar that invited people to ask, "See that? You peep this?" It was those kind of questions that followed me when I first visited Harlem. So no gates. And the bar counter itself needed to be voluptuous. Screw being hip, I wanted the bar to be the shape of hips. God knows all of Harlem needed something to hold on to.

Once we had sketched the shape of the bar, the rest of the details naturally grew up around it. Designing the Red Rooster reminded me of the lining of a suit or of a woman's lingerie. It didn't matter if the world didn't see it. I did. I knew it was there. And I wasn't about to step out in holey drawers. Whether it was the floor, or the Harlem artists on the shelf, or the brownstone mirror hung on the wall, all those details would give me confidence. For those who would pause and take it all in, maybe it could instigate a conversation. It should definitely be something they remembered after they left. Luckily, I met a young black artist from the neighborhood and began explaining my plans for Red Rooster. "I want our bar to be voluptuous. Sexy, you know? Like Angie—"

"Or Jill Scott?"

I let go of the breath I had been holding.

The next step was the cocktails. I had Tom Bullock on my mind. He was the first black bartender to publish a cocktail handbook. His drinks were so legendary that when Teddy Roosevelt declared he didn't have a drinking problem, that in fact he only had a sip or two of a mint julep at the St. Louis Country Club, the *St. Louis Post-Dispatch's* editorial board found the claim incredible. "Who was ever known to drink just a part of one of Tom's juleps?"

I didn't think I could fill those shoes, but I did want to give a nod to Mr. Bullock and the first black bartenders. In order to do that, our cocktails needed to introduce the neighborhood, they needed to taste like life in Harlem and, well, that's some complicated hooch.

In the end, we created the Savoy, the Brownstoner, Rum Rum Punch, and the Bloody Rooster, names that give voice to Harlem neighborhoods and that start conversation.

A while back, a friend of mine asked me if I got what I wanted. Did I get my imagined main bar that sits on a wind-swept Lenox? Am I satisfied that Rooster doesn't gate its window? Have I created a space that welcomes everybody from everywhere? Maybe. Sometimes. Yeah, sure. Bevy Smith comes for brunch, then moves to the bar and orders a Savoy and oysters. She pulls out her work and gets it done. She stays for dinner. I watch this accomplished woman move around the Rooster and think, *Okay, maybe I created a bar, bar.* I watch her smile as she listens to Rakiem, our saxophonist, wailing his heart out. The neighborhood keeps me honest. If Red Rooster's bar tried to do otherwise, folks on the street would look at me funny and give me an earful. "You have food, right? We got seats? Alright, then. Let's eat."

People who sometimes avoid looking at each other on the street gather around our bar and talk.

Every once and a while, I think I've done it. I've made space at our bar for all kinds of celebration—Cinco de Mayo, Black History Month, St. Patrick's Day, the Jacob Lawrence exhibit at MoMA. All kinds of elbows touch. People who sometimes avoid looking at each other on the street gather around our bar and talk. Nothing fascinates me like watching brunch and church ladies wearing hats that look like pastry who can't hide their grins behind the cocktails they're drinking. Or Fridays at eight, when every race and every hue is headed downstairs toward Ginny's to drink up. In the wee hours, here comes last call and most want to order a final cocktail to go with the tacos they get from the Nook.

The sun is setting and Gerald Tucker isn't at the bar. Dressed in a three-piece suit, he traveled uptown every day from the Lower East Side to sit here. He was beloved. The plaque we placed in his honor, "The Mayor of Red Rooster presided here," hasn't yet soothed the sting of his absence.

When I think about my friend's question, "Did you get what you wanted?" I want to lift a glass and toast it all. I want to celebrate in every language and culture I know.

Skål...

Cheers...

To every brother who pours a sip on the curb in memory of...

Drink up.

THE BAR PLAYLIST

"LITTLE RED ROOSTER"   Big Mama Thornton

"LIQUID LOVE"   Chris Turner

"I'LL NEVER FALL IN LOVE AGAIN"   Dionne Warwick

"CRAZY LOVE"   Akie Bermiss

"COME TO MY DOOR"   José James

"LITTLE RED ROOSTER"   The Rolling Stones

"AS"   Stevie Wonder

"HARLEM RIVER DRIVE"   Bobbi Humphrey

YES, CHEF

MAKES 1 COCKTAIL

We named this cocktail after my memoir. It's got a lot of flavor, and just a little hint of spice.

Honey syrup is simply equal parts honey and water brought to a boil and cooled. It will keep in a jar in the refrigerator for months.

---

2 sprigs mint

¾ ounce honey syrup
(see headnote)

¾ ounce Homemade
Ginger Beer

¾ ounce pineapple juice

½ ounce fresh lime juice

1½ ounces vodka

1 mint leaf

1 Rub the mint sprigs between your palms and drop them into an old-fashioned glass.

2 Add the honey syrup, ginger beer, pineapple juice, lime juice, and vodka to a cocktail shaker. Fill with ice and shake.

3 Pour the drink into the old-fashioned glass and garnish with the mint leaf.

HOMEMADE GINGER BEER

► Pour 2 quarts water into a large saucepan. Add 2 cups peeled and ground ginger (use the food processor), 4 cups light brown sugar, the juice of 2 limes, and 5 Thai bird chiles. Bring to a boil, then strain through a sieve lined with several layers of cheesecloth.

► Pour into bottles and refrigerate. This makes 2 quarts and will keep for about 1 week.

ere's our take on the Manhattan. It's a little sweeter, but it's still boozy. It's a very popular cocktail at our bar—particularly with women.

BROWN-STONER

MAKES 1 COCKTAIL

1 Pour the Cherry Heering, St-Germain, and bourbon into a mixing glass. Fill with ice and stir well.

2 Strain into a cocktail glass and garnish with the orange wedge.

¾ ounce Cherry Heering

¾ ounce St-Germain liqueur

2 ounces Nutmeg Bourbon (see below)

1 orange wedge

Shaking and stirring drinks does more than just combine ingredients. It starts to melt the ice and that water is an important ingredient.

Hold the mixing glass as you stir and the glass will tell you when the cocktail is ready. It will be very cold.

INFUSED BOURBONS

It's all about the flavor.

▶ **Nutmeg Bourbon.** Pour 1 liter bourbon (we use Bulleit) into a pitcher, add 5 whole nutmegs, and cover. Infuse for 48 to 72 hours—taste it to see how deep you want the flavor. Strain and pour back into the bottle.

▶ **Fig and Pear Bourbon.** Pour 1 liter bourbon into a large pitcher, add 10 ripe figs and 6 sliced Asian pears. Cover and infuse for 48 to 72 hours—taste it to see how deep you want the flavor. Strain and pour back into the bottle.

DARK AND STORMIER

MAKES 1 COCKTAIL

½ ounce fresh lime juice

¾ ounce simple syrup

1½ ounces Goslings Black Seal rum

1½ ounces Homemade Ginger Beer (page 46)

Lemon wheel

The flavors—rum and ginger—are there, but our homemade ginger beer gives this cocktail an extra bite.

1 Put the lime juice, simple syrup, rum, and ginger beer in a shaker. Fill with ice and shake for at least 15 seconds.

2 Strain into a collins glass filled with ice and garnish with the lemon wheel.

American Prohibition, which lasted from 1920 to 1933, led to the creation of speakeasies, where patrons could indulge in alcohol, bar snacks, and, more than occasionally, drugs like marijuana and cocaine. But Prohibition also spurred on legal nightlife, and it was the time of legendary Harlem clubs like the Savoy Ballroom and the Log Cabin, where Billie Holiday sang. At the original Red Rooster, some of the greats of the twentieth century came to sip drinks and listen to jazz. We've tried to honor that tradition with cocktails that are layered and complex but don't have too many steps.

THE SAVOY

MAKES 1 COCKTAIL

This is our tribute to the Savoy Ballroom, "the home of happy feet" on Lenox Avenue between 140th and 141st Streets, where blacks and whites danced together. We served this sprightly drink the night the Rooster first opened its doors.

---

3 seedless green grapes

4 seedless red grapes

½ ounce fresh lemon juice

¾ ounce agave syrup

1¼ ounces vodka

1 Put 2 green grapes and 2 red grapes into an old-fashioned glass and muddle. Pour in the lemon juice, agave, and vodka and fill the glass with ice. Transfer to a cocktail shaker and shake well.

2 Pour back into the glass. Spear the remaining grapes onto a small bamboo skewer and lay across the top of the drink.

Lissette Tabales has been behind the bar at the Rooster since we opened, and this is her favorite cocktail. Herby, puckery Campari and bourbon make a perfect cocktail. "It's a drink for the Campari lover," she says.

BOURBON NEGRONI

MAKES 1 COCKTAIL

1 Pour the vermouth, Campari, and bourbon into a cocktail shaker. Fill with ice and shake well.

2 Strain into a cocktail glass and garnish with the orange wedge.

½ ounce sweet vermouth (we use Antica Formula)

¾ ounce Campari

2 ounces Fig and Pear Bourbon (see page 47)

1 orange wedge

Dark rum, white rum, pineapple and lime juices, and coconut water make this cocktail an island carnival!

RUM RUM PUNCH

MAKES 1 COCKTAIL

1 Pour the coconut water, pineapple juice, lime juice, and both rums into a cocktail shaker. Fill with ice and shake well.

2 Strain into an ice-filled collins glass.

2 ounces coconut water

2 ounces pineapple juice

½ ounce fresh lime juice

2 ounces white rum

2 ounces Goslings Black Seal rum

Most Bloody Marys have a lot of mix and a little vodka. Ours packs a punch.

BLOODY ROOSTER

MAKES 1 COCKTAIL

1 Pour the Bloody Mix and vodka into a collins glass and stir. Fill the glass with ice and stir again.

2 Spear the lemon wedge and okra on a bamboo skewer and garnish the cocktail.

1½ ounces Bloody Mix

1½ ounces vodka

1 lemon wedge

1 pickled okra

BLOODY MIX

Mix a big can (48 ounces) of tomato juice with 1 cup prepared horseradish, ½ cup fresh orange juice, ½ cup fresh lime juice, ½ cup Cholula hot sauce, ¼ cup Worcestershire sauce, and ¼ cup green olive brine. Cover and refrigerate. You'll have a bit more than 2 quarts, and it will keep for a day or so (the flavors of fresh citrus juices fade).

PIG EARS *with* HOT MUSTARD

SERVES 6

Pig Foot Mary must not have had a fryer, otherwise she'd have been selling pig ears from her baby carriage at 135th and Lenox in the 1910s and '20s instead of the boiled pigs' feet that made her fortune.

Pig ears are an old taste that's new again. They're just about shatteringly crisp. Look for pig ears in ethnic grocery stores and butchers or ask a pig farmer at the farmers' market.

FOR THE HOT MUSTARD

3 tablespoons extra strong Dijon mustard

1 tablespoon Chinese mustard

1 tablespoon olive oil

1 teaspoon soy sauce

1 teaspoon rice vinegar

Juice of 1 lime

½ teaspoon wasabi powder

FOR THE EARS

2 pounds pig ears

6 cups water

1 cup apple cider vinegar

1 bay leaf

½ cup cornstarch

½ cup all-purpose flour

2 teaspoons smoked paprika

1 teaspoon coarse kosher salt, plus more for seasoning

½ teaspoon cayenne

Peanut oil for frying

Smoked paprika

FOR THE HOT MUSTARD

1 Whisk all the ingredients together. Scrape into a serving bowl, cover, and refrigerate until you're ready to serve. (Makes about ½ cup.)

FOR THE EARS

2 Slice off and discard the thick ridged sections on the cut sides of the ears. Cut the ears into ¼-inch strips.

3 Put the water, vinegar, and bay leaf into a large saucepan and bring to a boil. Add the ears and bring to a simmer. Cover, turn the heat down to low, and simmer until very tender (you'll be able to cut them with a fork), about 2 hours. Drain the ears and spread them out on a baking sheet lined with several layers of paper towels. Leave them to dry and cool. Discard the bay leaf.

4 Put the cornstarch, flour, salt, smoked paprika, and cayenne into a large bowl and whisk to combine.

5 Fill a large saucepan one-third full with peanut oil. Set over medium-high heat and heat the oil to 360°F.

6 Working in batches, toss the ears in the seasoned flour. Put them in a sieve and shake off excess flour. Fry until crisp and browned, 4 to 5 minutes. Keep an eye on the heat and adjust it to keep the oil between 350° and 375°F. Drain on a rack set over a rimmed baking sheet. Be careful while you fry; the ears will spit.

7 Season with salt and paprika while they're hot. Serve with the hot mustard.

The streets of Harlem are filled with food. Find a construction site, and you can be sure the tamale lady will be there come lunchtime. And you're never surprised when you're sitting in the barber chair and an aunty comes in selling her sweet potato cake.

CAULIFLOWER FRITES *with* GREEN MAYONNAISE

SERVES 4 TO 6

Picture this. You're sitting at the bar. You've got a cold beer, a plate of beer-battered cauliflower florets, and a small bowl of gently spicy mayo perfumed with herbs. You dip, you eat, you get a little greasy around the lips—in the best possible way. You use your napkin and drink your beer. Life is good.

FOR THE BEER BATTER

½ cup lager beer

¼ cup water

Juice of 2 limes

1 tablespoon soy sauce

2 drops Tabasco sauce

1 cup all-purpose flour

1 tablespoon cornstarch

1 teaspoon coarse kosher salt

½ teaspoon baking powder

½ teaspoon ras el hanout
(see page 28)

¼ teaspoon freshly ground
black pepper

FOR THE FRITES

1 cauliflower, cut into
small florets

1 tablespoon ras el hanout

1 teaspoon smoked paprika

Peanut oil for frying

Coarse kosher salt

FOR SERVING

Green Mayonnaise
(recipe follows)

FOR THE BEER BATTER

1 Whisk the beer, water, lime juice, soy sauce, and Tabasco together.

2 Whisk the flour, cornstarch, salt, baking powder, ras el hanout, and pepper together in a bowl. Pour in the wet ingredients and whisk until perfectly smooth. Let stand for 30 minutes.

FOR THE FRITES

3 Meanwhile, bring a large pot of salted water to a boil. Add the cauliflower, bring back to a boil, and blanch until the cauliflower is just tender, about 5 minutes. Lift the cauliflower out with a spider or slotted spoon (so you don't break the tender florets) and drain on a baking sheet lined with paper towels.

4 Mix the ras el hanout and smoked paprika together.

5 When you're ready to fry, fill a large saucepan one-third full with peanut oil. Set over medium-high heat and heat to 360°F.

6 Working in batches, dip the tops of the cauliflower florets into the spices and then drop them into the batter, coating them completely. Let the excess drip off and fry until golden brown, about 2 minutes. Drain on a rack set over a baking sheet and sprinkle with salt while they're hot. Use a spider to remove any bits of batter in the oil between batches. Keep an eye on the heat and adjust to keep the oil between 350° and 375°F.

7 Pile the cauliflower onto a platter and put out next to the bowl of mayonnaise so your guests can pick and dip.

GREEN MAYONNAISE

► Heat 2 tablespoons olive oil in a skillet over medium heat. Add 2 peeled garlic cloves and 2 stemmed jalapeños and cook, turning the garlic and jalapeños, until the garlic is golden (about 3 minutes) and the jalapeños are blistered all over (about 5 minutes). Put the garlic into a food processor when it's done. Cut the jalapeños in half lengthwise and return to the skillet, cut side down. Cook for 1 minute, then add 1 packed cup baby spinach and cook, tossing with tongs, until the spinach wilts, about 90 seconds. Scrape everything into a food processor. Pulse until chopped coarse. Scrape down the sides.

► Add 2 large egg yolks, 2 tablespoons rice vinegar, 2 teaspoons Dijon mustard, 2 tablespoons chopped fresh cilantro, and 2 table-spoons chopped fresh mint. Process until you have a smooth puree. Scrape down the sides again. With the processor running, pour in 6 tablespoons olive oil in a steady stream to make an emulsified mayonnaise. Add the juice of 1 lime and process until combined. Taste and season with salt and pepper. Scrape the mayo into a serving bowl. Cover and refrigerate until you need it. This makes about 1½ cups and will keep for 5 days.

FISH CROQUETTES

MAKES 30 CROQUETTES

Like the best bar food, these two-bite morsels are perfect for sharing. The surprise is the mix of seafood and chorizo. And the very crisp breading, which is actually instant potatoes!

1 (12-ounce) russet potato, peeled and cut into big chunks

Coarse kosher salt

¼ pound sea scallops, chopped

6 ounces snapper fillet, chopped (you could substitute scrod or sole)

4 ounces Portuguese chouriço or Spanish chorizo, minced

2 garlic cloves, minced

2 teaspoons chopped fresh dill

2 teaspoons minced fresh chives

1 tablespoon mayonnaise

1 teaspoon Dijon mustard

1 teaspoon fish sauce

6 ounces crab meat, picked over

Peanut oil for frying

¼ cup cornstarch

2 large eggs

2 cups instant potato flakes

Green Mayonnaise (page 57)

1 Put the potato into a small saucepan and cover with cold water by at least 1 inch. Add a big pinch of salt and bring to a boil over high heat. Turn the heat down to medium-high and boil until the potato is tender, 15 to 17 minutes. Drain. Put the potato into a mixing bowl, mash it with a fork, and cool to room temperature.

2 Put the scallops and snapper into a food processor and process to a smooth paste. Scrape into the bowl with the potato. Add the diced sausage, garlic, dill, chives, mayo, mustard, and fish sauce and mix well. Fold in the crab meat. Shape into 30 walnut-sized balls.

3 Fill a large saucepan one-third full with peanut oil. Set over medium-high heat and heat to 360°F.

4 Put the cornstarch in a shallow bowl. Beat the eggs in a second bowl. Put the instant potatoes in a third bowl.

5 Roll the croquettes in the cornstarch, dip in the eggs and let the excess drip off, then dredge in the instant potatoes. Put them on a rack as they're coated.

6 Working in small batches, fry the croquettes until they're golden brown, 5 to 6 minutes. Keep an eye on the heat and adjust it to keep the oil between 350° and 375°F. Drain the croquettes on a rack set over a rimmed baking sheet.

7 Pile them onto a platter and serve with a bowl of green mayonnaise.

People do come and eat full meals at the Rooster bar, but I make sure we always have something bite-sized and full of flavor for people who want to nosh a little before dinner. Bar food shouldn't ruin your appetite; it should make you hungry for more.

BEEF KITFO
with AWASE

SERVES 4 TO 6

Kitfo is the ultimate celebration dish in Ethiopia. The spiced raw beef was an important part of my wedding feast, but it is also served after a long vegetable fast. It can be refined, as it is here, but at its simplest, kitfo is simply chunks of raw beef dipped in the spicy dip called awase. We serve several versions of kitfo at Rooster. This one reminds me a little of the English bookmaker sandwich—the one made with roast beef, mustard, and horseradish.

You can use the awase as a dip for vegetables, as a sauce for grilled fish, or as a rub for rack of lamb (page 216).

FOR THE KITFO

3 ounces trimmed beef kidney or beef heart, cut in ⅓-inch slices

2 cups water

1 teaspoon distilled white vinegar

Coarse kosher salt

2 tablespoons Spiced Butter (recipe follows)

2 garlic cloves, minced

2 shallots, minced

1 jalapeño chile, minced

1 tablespoon berbere (see page 27)

1 to 2 teaspoons cayenne

1 teaspoon Chinese mustard

1 pound beef tenderloin, diced

FOR THE AWASE
(MAKES ABOUT ½ CUP)

3 tablespoons berbere

1 teaspoon cayenne

1 tablespoon horseradish, preferably freshly grated

2 tablespoons olive oil

1 tablespoon red wine vinegar

Juice of 1 lemon

Whole wheat bread, toasted

FOR THE KITFO

1 Put the beef kidney in a small bowl with the water, distilled vinegar, and a pinch of salt. Cover and refrigerate for 2 hours. Drain and dry it well with paper towels. If you're using beef heart, you only need to salt it and refrigerate for 1 hour.

2 Cook the spiced butter, garlic, shallots, and jalapeño in a skillet over medium heat until the vegetables are softened, about 3 minutes. Scrape into a bowl.

3 Return the skillet to high heat. When it's hot, sear the kidney or heart for 30 seconds on each side. Dice and add to the bowl with the vegetables.

4 Stir in the berbere, cayenne, and mustard. Toss in the tenderloin, mixing well. Taste and season with salt.

FOR THE AWASE

5 Stir all the ingredients together in a small bowl.

6 Put out the bowl of kitfo, the awase, and a stack of toasts. Rip off pieces of toast, pile with kitfo, and dip in the awase.

SPICED BUTTER

We use this butter as a flavor enhancer—you find it in a lot of recipes in the book. It has a hint of funk, like the funk of fermented foods, the new wave of flavor to follow umami.

There are a lot of versions of spiced butter in Ethiopia. My version is true to that made by my wife Maya's tribe, the Gurage.

► Melt 8 sticks (2 pounds) unsalted butter in a saucepan over low heat. Add 2 minced garlic cloves, 2 minced shallots, a 2-inch piece ginger (peeled, sliced, and smashed), 1½ tablespoons coriander seeds, 1 tablespoon cumin seeds, 1½ teaspoons fenugreek, 1½ teaspoons ajwain (see page 27), 1 teaspoon freshly ground black pepper, ½ teaspoon ground cinnamon, and ½ teaspoon ground turmeric. Simmer very gently for 30 minutes to infuse the flavors. Keep an eye on this; you don't want the milk solids to brown.

► Skim off all the foam and any floating seeds and let the butter sit for about 10 minutes for the milk solids to settle on the bottom.

► Carefully pour the spiced butter through a sieve lined with a few layers of cheesecloth into a container, leaving the solids behind. Let it cool, then cover and refrigerate. It will keep for months.

► This makes about 3 cups.

CORN BREAD

MAKES 1 (9-X-5-INCH) LOAF

The his is right up there with the Fried Yardbird as a core recipe at the Rooster. We even have someone dedicated to making all our corn bread. Charles Webb, a former Alvin Ailey dancer, is the keeper of our secrets.

I knew from the beginning how I wanted it to taste, but we continue to tinker and change the recipe. This version is very moist, almost custardy. It will keep for 4 days, but a better plan is to freeze individual slices.

1 cup cake flour

1 cup coarse yellow cornmeal

¾ cup sugar

2¼ teaspoons baking powder

1½ teaspoons Aleppo pepper (see page 27)

1½ teaspoons coarse kosher salt

1¾ cups sour cream

1½ cups buttermilk

2 large eggs

1 large egg yolk

2 tablespoons unsalted butter, melted and cooled

⅔ cup corn kernels (fresh or thawed frozen)

1 Preheat the oven to 325°F. Spray a 9-x-5-inch loaf pan with pan spray.

2 Whisk the flour, cornmeal, sugar, baking powder, Aleppo pepper, and salt together in a bowl.

3 Whisk the sour cream, buttermilk, eggs, yolk, and melted butter together in another bowl until smooth.

4 Pour the wet ingredients into the dry and stir until combined. Fold in the corn.

5 Scrape the batter into the loaf pan and smooth out the top. Bake until the bread is browned and pulling away from the sides of the pan and a skewer poked into the center comes out clean, about 60 minutes.

6 Cool on a rack for 20 minutes. Run a knife around the sides of the pan to loosen the sides and turn out the loaf. You can cut it now— the slices will be messy— or cool completely.

There are plenty of things to spread on corn bread—like either the Bird Funk or Chicken Liver Butter (both on page 82)—but I do love the way sage honey butter melts into the bread when it's warm: Beat 2 tablespoons honey and 12 ripped fresh sage leaves into 8 tablespoons (1 stick) softened unsalted butter. Check it for salt. Cover and refrigerate the honey butter for at least an hour to give the sage a chance to work its flavor into the butter, but take it out of the refrigerator at least 15 minutes before serving.

CORN BREAD CRUMB VINAIGRETTE

Like every restaurant, we need to be frugal. Crumbs from leftover corn bread, along with some chile and shallot, make for a very tasty vinaigrette. Use it on sturdy greens like romaine or escarole.

► Heat ¾ cup olive oil in a skillet over medium-high heat. Add 2 minced garlic cloves, 2 minced shallots, 1 minced poblano chile, and 3 tablespoons corn bread crumbs. Sauté, stirring or tossing, until the shallot and poblano have softened and the crumbs are browned, about 5 minutes. Whisk in 3 tablespoons rice vinegar and the juice of a lemon. Season with 1 tablespoon toasted sesame seeds, a few drops of Worcestershire sauce, 1 teaspoon Aleppo pepper (see page 27), and salt and pepper. Scrape the vinaigrette into a bowl and keep it covered on the counter for an hour or two or use it immediately. Right before you use it, stir in 1 tablespoon minced fresh chives.

► Makes about 1½ cups.

THE QUINTESSENTIAL HARLEM GIRL

The fabulous Bevy Smith currently rules the roost on Bravo's Fashion Queens. *She is also the creator of Dinner with Bevy, a roving dinner party where she brings together all manner of people. Here's what she had to say about life, love, and community in Harlem.*

I am a quintessential Harlem girl, and we have gifts that I refuse to squander. Great art has been made in the name of this place, and I want to follow suit. I was born on Fifth Avenue, yes, in a hospital, Baby, but I've always said that that avenue set me up for greatness. My dad taught us how to read very early. He is a man of letters without a formal education. Everywhere I go in the world, my father has an anecdote about it. Sydney, Milan, Paris. He's from the South, South Carolina. We used to spend summers down there. My mom is from North Carolina, she's a spitfire and amazing. So we have all this South in Harlem, and they raised a Harlem girl.

There's this housing development called the Dunbar and when I was a kid, there was a roll call of all the famous people that came out of there and by the time I was a kid in the eighties, that roll call hadn't changed. But I started to understand that there's greatness around me. And because I was aware of the history and the legacy, it never dawned on me that I should leave Harlem. Which is what most people did in my generation. See I never got priced out, 'cause I never left.

I've been in my apartment since I was twenty-nine. They will carry me out of this juke joint in a box. The only reason I never left is because I knew it was important for young black kids, young brown kids, to see somebody in the neighborhood who had made it. Someone they could see in a magazine, a person who looked like them. There's lots of kids in my building who are like, "Hey, I know you," 'cause they would see me in *Vibe.* They would see my luggage and they would be like, "Where you going?" And I would tell them, "I'm off to Europe." That's something to look up to. And then I would tell them, "I'm just like you." And that's not just a race conversation. We are changing, we have million-dollar brownstones, but we also have to stay true; we have to fold those rich folks into us. And you know they want it, Lovely. Why else would they move here?

See, Marcus didn't want to swoop in; he wasn't like, "Let me slap an awning up here." He was actually about learning about Harlem. Getting us, 'cause he knew how cool we could be. He ain't staring at us, he's in it. A lot of people came here and wanted to run from the old Harlem. Marcus was one of the ones who came here and understood the texture and the grit, and then he put that in the cooking, he put that in the restaurant. That's so rare for those who are not born and raised here. And without that, without digging the old Harlem, you might as well fucking go downtown, you know? He gets our mélange.

The only thing I'm worried about is that the African-American heart and soul stays in Harlem. That's what's important to me. And I'm not into leaving anybody in the diaspora out of the conversation, Baby. The stuff that I do in the community, working with the Girl Scouts, talking with the girls there, that all matters. What I did was tell all my black friends, hey, take all that money you spend downtown and come spend it up here. You should move up here. I give walking tours. And when they get up here and everybody is like, "ohhh . . . ahhh," 'cause it's so friendly and so cool, folks get real hyped. See they didn't know it was *that* cool up here. They were like, "Oh my god, I don't have that on West 79th Street."

I started Dinner with Bevy when I ran out of money and I was making the journey from Bevy Smith, advertising executive, to Bevy Smith, TV personality. It's really about the communal act of dining, making connections. That's my passion.

I'm also going to bridge the gaps. Art, architecture, fashion, food, design, film. I want it to be said that I was a complement to this community. I was an asset. Because, Baby, I am Bevy Smith. And I am in Harlem. And I'm at the Red Rooster, Darling.

BIRDLAND

I WAS BORN INTO a tribe of chicken. The Amhara tribe traditionally makes *doro wat*, a treasured Ethiopian dish with poultry, onions, and berbere that is often eaten during celebrations. But I grew up on salmon and mackerel. When I worked at Aquavit, eight dishes featured salmon. My chicken was salmon. The way most people look at a bird and can think of twelve ways to cook it, that's how I understood Sweden's national fish. I never expected that I would come full circle. But I knew that if I wanted to make my mark in Harlem, I had to learn to think about chicken in the same way.

While pork can often divide along religious lines, chicken, that most holy bird, unites. Chinese, Puerto Rican, Irish, Mexican, Senegalese, Jewish—all have treasured poultry recipes. Almost every home cook on the planet has a favorite chicken recipe in their back pocket, and two stashed in a top drawer. Moving uptown to Harlem meant I had to combine fine dining with fun dining. My menu had to reveal my love of comfort food—Swedish and Ethiopian—and now that Harlem was my home, my kind of soul food. Pork may be more important in Southern cooking, but the bird is iconic. Mothers and favorite uncles throw in secret spices when no one is looking, and when you ask what's on that bird, their smiles are as wide as they are mysterious. So when I decided to open the

Red Rooster, I knew I had to create a chicken dish that lived up to the name. I had to nail fried chicken.

I could taste my fear. It tasted like chicken.

I was scared to death. So many nationalities have perfected fried chicken—the Koreans twice fry it and bathe it in a spicy gochujang sauce, the Italians dredge their cutlets in bread crumbs and Parmesan cheese. I wanted my fried chicken to have global flavors, but still be recognized as that quintessential American dish. More, I wanted people to taste Harlem when they ate my version. I wanted my fried chicken to be in the same orbit as that of Charles Gabriel's Country Pan Fried Chicken. And that meant, whatever I dreamt up, its foundation had to be traditional Southern cuisine transformed by city living. For two years I thought about how to put my culinary stamp on America's favorite dish. So I mined my own childhood memories. We had roast chicken almost every Saturday. I still remember our bird, stuffed with carrots and onions, surrounded by potatoes—the entire aromatic concoction spiced with caraway and fennel. And then Sunday. The carcass and leftovers were the main ingredients for soup and dumplings.

I started to obsess. And when I obsess I do three things: I research, I run or bike, and I talk to everyone. I dove into the archival stacks at the Schomburg Center for Research in Black Culture; I visited M&G Diner, Sylvias, Pan Pan, I even went to Kennedy Fried Chicken over and over again, tasting and thinking, thinking and tasting. To everyone I had more than a five-minute conversation with during those two years—look, I'm sorry. People who casually asked me about the weather or the time of day or just stopped me to say hello found themselves knee-deep in a conversation about chicken. What's your favorite place in the neighborhood? How did your mother cook it? How do you cook it?

What I learned during those two years was eye-opening. If you are having conversations with people about fried chicken, watch out. Their stories are steeped in lore and myth. Regular people fry their bird with a rabbit foot in their pockets, with their uncle's secret cooking hat perched on their heads. Not only do they have special pans—cast-iron skillets top the list—but they have *the* special pot. You know, the one their great, great, great grandmother forged from volcanic rock. It wasn't just the recipes that dazzled—though I'm sure folks left out an ingredient or two—it was the love and reverence with which they spoke about a legendary bird. Some told me stories about the special fried-chicken picnic and all the jokes they shared that made the chicken taste so good. For others, figuring out their grandmother's chicken was a journey of tears. Happy or sad, triumphant or chagrined, those stories struck me with their common emotion of initial frustration. So what *is* the perfect temperature? *Do* you marinate? *Which* part of the bird goes in first? The answers I received from home cooks, neighbors, and professional chefs were all over the map. Oh, yes, I was told. Hell, no, I was admonished. And your special super-secret spices? The look I got when I asked that question: I realized I might as well have asked people to show me their dirty underwear. Folks didn't want to talk about the particulars, they wanted to discuss that first taste that revolutionized their palate, the trembling they felt when they finally got their hands on the secret recipe.

The home cooks and the chefs had similar experiences. Somebody's Little Sister from around the way sounded just like Ben Barrow, the owner of Pan Pan who patiently walked me through cooking fried chicken. While listening to advice and stories, I was

also experimenting with flavors. Marinate in buttermilk? That's good, even great, but it's a well-known technique. How do you get that crispy skin? How do you turn a chicken into the juiciest bird you've ever tasted? How do get that sound—you know that *crunch*—that made people make that other sound—*yum*. The more I sped around the neighborhood on my black bike, the more I researched, the more I spoke to anyone who had even looked at a chicken, the more I wanted to curl into a fetal ball. There was no way I could scale this mountain. A low point came when one of the ladies from the neighborhood marched up to me and spoke her mind, "What do you know about chicken?" I could taste my fear. It tasted just like chicken.

I finally hit a turning point when I was talking to my friend John. As we shared cocktails, I gave him the ins and outs of my chicken saga. He was a good listener. He nodded when he should have, and when I paused in the middle of telling my story, he gave me encouraging grunts to continue. Finally, I was done.

"Marcus?"

"Yeah?"

"Just fry the damn bird!"

Maybe having John Legend yelling at you about fried chicken makes you pay attention. Maybe I had reached a breaking point with my two-year obsession about frying the perfect bird. Or maybe I was just ready to hear that shout. Whatever the case, John's exasperation made my mouth water. Sometimes, I think his yell gave me permission to return to what I knew and loved best. I started to think about the bird. All of it. I had killed myself for Georges Blanc, transforming chicken into a high art. Could I mine those flavors? And when I was growing up, Helga, my grandmother, left nothing to waste. She used every little bit of the chicken when she made two meals from that one Saturday bird. I wanted to do the same. What could I do with the wings? Or the skin? The liver. The gizzards. With the carcass, I could make stock.

I found myself running over two years of conversations, and this time, I really listened. Black people have always made something delicious from almost nothing at all. Dishes that blew your hair back were created with a bit of this, a scrap of that. I also heard the advice of my mentors. The great New Orleans chef Leah Chase's words of wisdom helped me understand not only chicken but running a restaurant in a black neighborhood. "Don't forget to always aim up. Maybe your audience doesn't know what they want, so give them your everything. That'll help them decide. And keep cooking. You hear me?" She was fierce. "You need to find that love in the food. And pass it on!" Her advice gave me confidence. Now, I'm not going to lie. It didn't get any easier. I didn't suddenly hear a choir of angels who sung me the secret recipe of the perfect fried chicken. I still was in the kitchen for months testing and retesting recipes. But now the confidence that had eluded me for almost two years came home.

Suddenly, I felt a kind of clarity about the whole dish. I was shooting for an instant classic. That's where I wanted to land. Our fried chicken, the Yardbird, needed to have both the deliciousness and the cultural familiarity of Sylvia's chicken. It needed to have that crispness of Jonathan Waxman's bird. You can't just talk about that. You have to do it. Over and over and over. You have to earn it. And I could do this. I could take the Swedish frugality I grew up with and combine it with the creativity poor Southern folk had to have in order to eat. The landscape was different; the paths were the same. All I had to do was remember, "Just fry the damn bird."

For the buttermilk, I traded coconut milk perfumed with lemon. I thought we should steam it. Instead of working with chicken breast, I fell in love with dark meat—short thighs, drumsticks, wings. Bone in. That's where you find the flavor. But perfecting our fried chicken was just the beginning.

"Just fry the damn bird," gave me license to play. Michael Garrett, my sous chef at the time, and I turned chicken skin into cracklings and folded it into our deviled eggs. Our chicken and waffles came with a side of Chicken Liver Butter. We made Wild Wild Wings and our signature Bird Funk. At brunch we serve chicken liver omelets. Occasionally, we offer a dish called Just Fry the Damn Bird. Brioche and chicken liver, chicken gravy, every piece of the bird cooked in schmaltz. What I could do with chicken became the anchor of Red Rooster. The bird is our heartbeat, and it grounds our menu. We make use of every part of it. A ladle of chicken stock goes into just about everything.

The bird is our heartbeat, and it grounds our menu. We make use of every part.

When I want to riff on my grandmother's meatballs, I go to chicken. Best of all, our recipe for the Yardbird (which is the best-selling item on our menu) has evolved. We've tinkered with the temperature, added a couple of spices, taken a couple away. All the tweaking and tasting makes for a better dish.

Every once in a while something jumps off and makes me think I'm getting it right. At dinner, two Mercedes-Maybachs pull up to the curb right outside Rooster. A prominent New York family steps out of one car; a famous American rapper, along with his entourage, steps out of the other. Both parties have a driver. And by coincidence, they have been seated in booths right next to each other. After a while, the patriarch of the New York family signals his server. "Could you please tell the group next to us to quiet down? Please?" We can do that, sure.

Half an hour later, the rapper lifts an arm and crooks a finger to signal his server. "Yo, could you tells those guys next to us to speak up? They're making us feel self-conscious." Both parties ordered the Yardbird.

So I keep an eye on what Zagat and the *New York Times* are saying, but I cater to Harlem.

BIRDLAND PLAYLIST

"CHASIN' THE BIRD" Charlie Parker

"BLACKBIRD" The Beatles

"BACK HOME AGAIN IN ARIZONA" New Orleans Swamp Donkeys

"SO HIGH" (CLOUD 9 REMIX) John Legend
featuring Lauryn Hill

"CISSY STRUT" The Meters

"I CAN'T BE SATISFIED" Muddy Waters

"WHEN MY TRAIN PULLS IN"
(ACOUSTIC) Gary Clark Jr.

BIRD BROTH

MAKES ABOUT 4 CUPS

Broth is an essential in any good kitchen. For our bird broth, we looked to the ramen culture of Japan. It looks innocent, just like any other broth. But then you taste it, and there's this explosion of flavor on your tongue, and you say, "Damn! What is that!"

Eat it hot. Eat it cold. It's always right. And yes, like Grandma's, it's what you want when you have a cold.

Save up the bones and backs and necks and wing tips when you're butchering chickens—even the carcasses when you roast—and freeze them until you have enough for this broth.

---

2 tablespoons grapeseed oil

2 pounds chicken parts (see headnote)

2 red onions, sliced thin

2 garlic cloves, smashed

1 jalapeño chile, stemmed and halved lengthwise

1 carrot, sliced

2 sprigs thyme

1 cup dry white wine

4 cups water

1 tablespoon white miso

1 teaspoon shrimp powder (see page 30)

1 (3-inch) piece kelp

1 teaspoon sherry vinegar or black vinegar

Coarse kosher salt and freshly ground black pepper

1 Heat the oil in a large saucepan over medium-high heat. Add the chicken, onions, garlic, jalapeño, carrot, and thyme and cook, stirring once in a while, until the chicken and onions start to brown, about 7 minutes.

2 Add the wine and stir and scrape to deglaze the pan. Add the water, miso, and shrimp powder. Bring to a simmer, then turn the heat down to low and simmer for 20 minutes. Add the kelp and simmer for another 20 minutes.

3 Strain the broth and discard the solids. Season with the sherry vinegar and salt and pepper to taste.

But then you taste it, and there's this explosion of flavor on your tongue, and you say, "Damn! What is that!"

RAMEN

This broth is a great starting point if you want to improvise ramen.

► Start by adding 2 boneless, skinless chicken thighs to the broth when you add the kelp so you'll have meat to shred and add to the ramen.

► Sauté some greens. It could be chopped broccolini. Or maybe shredded collards or mustard greens or even Swiss chard. Dice some extra-firm tofu if you'd like.

► Boil fresh ramen noodles (look for them in the refrigerator cases in Asian markets) for no more than 30 seconds; you want them to still have that distinctive bite. Put the noodles in a soup bowl, pour in the boiling broth, and garnish with the shredded chicken, the greens, and tofu. Top with a poached egg—or a pickled egg (page 245) cut into quarters.

► Advanced ramen makers might experiment with adding a handful of peeled medium shrimp or Pickled Fresno Chiles (see Pickles at the Rooster, page 244) before you pour in the broth.

WILD WILD WINGS

SERVES 4 TO 6

Where there's a bird, there are wings, and they were meant to be eaten. You can't eat chicken wings pretty. You get sauce all over your fingers and lips, and you're a kid again. Your face betrays you. It says, "I ate wings!"

Deep-fried chicken wings dressed with vinegary hot sauce (Frank's) and butter may have started the craze for Buffalo wings, but there are countless versions now. Ours uses Cholula hot sauce and a good hit of ginger, so the heat is sweet.

→ **Start the day before.**

FOR THE WINGS

4 cups water

¼ cup sugar

¼ cup coarse kosher salt

3 pounds chicken wings, separated into flats and drumettes

FOR THE WING SAUCE

1 tablespoon unsalted butter

1 tablespoon minced garlic

1 tablespoon minced peeled ginger

1 cup hot sauce (we use Cholula)

1 tablespoon sugar

FOR FRYING

1 cup all-purpose flour

1 cup cornstarch

¼ cup cornmeal

3 tablespoons chipotle chile powder

Peanut oil for frying

FOR THE WINGS

1 Bring 2 cups of the water, the sugar, and salt to a boil. Remove from the heat, add the remaining 2 cups water and cool the brine completely.

2 Put the wings in a bowl and pour in the brine, making sure all the wings are submerged. Cover with plastic wrap and refrigerate overnight.

FOR THE WING SAUCE

3 Melt the butter in a small saucepan over medium heat. Add the garlic and ginger and cook, stirring constantly, until the garlic and ginger are golden brown, about 5 minutes. Add the hot sauce and sugar and bring to a simmer. Turn the heat down to low and simmer for 5 minutes to develop the flavors. You can leave the sauce on the back of the stove until you need it.

FOR FRYING

4 When you're ready to fry, drain the wings and pat them dry with paper towels.

5 Put the flour, cornstarch, cornmeal, and chipotle chile powder in a large bowl and whisk to combine.

6 Dredge the wings in the seasoned flour, making sure each piece is well coated. Leave them on a rack while you heat the oil.

7 Fill a large saucepan one-third full with peanut oil. Set over medium-high heat and heat to 360°F.

8 Working in batches, fry the wings until they're fully cooked and golden brown, 8 to 9 minutes. Keep an eye on the heat and adjust it to keep the oil between 350° and 375°F. Drain the wings on a rack set over a rimmed baking sheet.

9 When you've fried all the wings, put them into a large bowl, pour in the wing sauce, and toss to coat all the wings with sauce. Pile the wings onto a platter and serve.

Make a quick dip for the wings by stirring ½ cup crumbled blue cheese into ¾ cup plain yogurt. And put out a plate of chilled radishes.

It matters when you get the sauce on the wings. Hot wings and warm sauce will make a marriage.

BIRD FUNK *and* CHICKEN LIVER BUTTER

MAKES ABOUT 2¹/₂ CUPS BIRD FUNK AND 2¹/₂ CUPS CHICKEN LIVER BUTTER

Chicken skin. Chicken livers. Odd bits turned into something yummy. It's poverty food—and sublime.

Bird funk has the bite of Nina Simone. It's sultry, and it has deep flavor with an edge—the gift of miso and dried shrimp. Like Nina's music, it can be addictive, particularly when you spread it on sweet corn bread.

Then there's liver butter, with the electric smoothness of Luther Vandross that makes even Dionne Warwick smile. Oh, it's so smooth, so silky. Spread it on a whole wheat cracker or a waffle. Pipe it into a donut (page 186). Smile.

→ **Make sure your pan is good and hot when you sauté the livers. And don't crowd the pan.**

FOR THE BIRD FUNK

2 cups chopped chicken skin

1 cup ground chicken thighs

1 cup small dried shrimp, pulsed in a food processor until chopped fine

4 garlic cloves, minced

1 lemongrass stalk, trimmed, smashed, and minced (see page 28)

1 (2-inch) piece ginger, peeled and minced

¹/₂ cup rice vinegar

2 tablespoons soy sauce

2 tablespoons white miso

2 tablespoons oyster sauce

FOR THE CHICKEN LIVER BUTTER

4 sticks (1 pound) unsalted butter, softened

¹/₂ pound chicken livers, halved, trimmed, and patted dry

1 teaspoon coarse kosher salt

¹/₄ teaspoon ground allspice

1 whole clove

Leaves from 1 sprig thyme

1 tablespoon bourbon

2 tablespoons maple syrup

2 tablespoons brandy

TO SERVE

Corn Bread (page 63)

Softened butter

FOR THE BIRD FUNK

1 Line a rimmed baking sheet with plastic wrap. Spread out the chicken skin and freeze for 30 minutes. Put through a meat grinder or pulse in batches in a food processor to mince the skin. Scrape the skin out into a saucepan. Add the remaining ingredients and turn the heat to low. Cook, stirring occasionally, until the fat renders and the funk begins to brown, about 45 minutes. Keep cooking, stirring frequently and scraping the bottom of the pan, until the funk is a deep, rich brown, about another hour and 15 minutes.

continued on page 84→

2 The funk will keep, tightly covered, in the refrigerator for about 1 week.

FOR THE CHICKEN LIVER BUTTER

3 Melt 4 tablespoons of the butter in a large skillet over medium-high heat. When the butter stops sputtering, add the livers, salt, allspice, clove, and thyme and sauté until the livers are cooked and browned but still light pink inside, about 3 minutes. Turn off the heat, add the bourbon, and stir, scraping up any browned bits. The butter, bourbon, and liver juices will become almost syrupy. Scrape everything into a food processor and cool to room temperature.

4 Add the maple syrup and brandy to the livers. Turn on the processor and add the remaining 3½ sticks butter bit by bit, scraping down the sides as needed. Process until the butter is completely incorporated and the liver butter is smooth.

5 If you want a more refined spread, pass it through a fine strainer. Otherwise, just transfer it to a container with a tight cover and refrigerate. It will keep for about 1 week.

TO SERVE

6 Take the liver butter and the funk out of the refrigerator about 30 minutes before serving.

7 Cut ½-inch-thick slices of corn bread, spread very lightly with butter, and toast on a griddle or in a cast-iron skillet.

8 Slather each slice with about 2 tablespoons of the liver butter and top with the funk.

CHICKEN SHAKE

▶ Whisk ¼ cup berbere (page 27), ¼ cup hot smoked paprika, 2 tablespoons ground cumin, 2 tablespoons freshly ground white pepper, 2 tablespoons celery salt, 1½ teaspoons granulated garlic, and 1½ teaspoons coarse kosher salt together. Store in a jar, out of the light. It makes about 1 cup and will keep for 6 months.

The New Orleans chef Leah Chase said it to Julia Child, and there's nothing more true. "I don't care where you're from or who you are. There's nothing like a good piece of fried chicken."

I went for dark meat only for our fried chicken. It's juicier, and it's got the crunch that I love hearing.

→ **Start the day before.**

FRIED YARDBIRD

SERVES 4

1 Put 2 cups of the water and the salt in a saucepan over high heat and bring to a simmer, stirring to dissolve the salt. Pour into a large container, add the remaining 6 cups water, and cool to room temperature. Add the chicken, cover, and refrigerate for 1½ hours. Drain.

2 Whisk the buttermilk, coconut milk, garlic, and chicken shake together in a 9-x-13-inch baking dish. Submerge the chicken in the marinade, cover, and refrigerate overnight.

3 Fill a large saucepan one-third full with peanut oil. Set over medium-high heat and heat to 360°F.

4 Coat the chicken while the oil heats. Put the flour, semolina, cornstarch, and white pepper into a bowl and whisk to combine. Let any excess marinade drip off the chicken, then roll in the flour coating, packing it on. Place on a rack set over a rimmed baking sheet. If the coating looks damp, roll it in the flour again.

5 Working in batches, fry the chicken until it is a rich brown and has an internal temperature of 165°F, about 10 minutes per batch. Keep an eye on the heat and adjust it to keep the oil between 350° and 375°F. Drain on a rack set over a rimmed baking sheet.

6 Season the Yardbird with a sprinkle of chicken shake.

8 cups water

1 cup coarse kosher salt

4 chicken thighs

4 chicken drumsticks

2 cups buttermilk

¾ cup coconut milk

2 garlic cloves, minced

1 tablespoon Chicken Shake (opposite), plus additional for serving

Peanut oil for frying

2 cups all-purpose flour

¼ cup semolina flour

2 tablespoons cornstarch

1 tablespoon freshly ground white pepper

FRIED BIRD ROYALE

"Just fry the damn bird!"

Even after I perfected the fried Yardbird, those words kept resonating. And then it hit me. I had to fry the *whole* damn bird. Not just parts. I wanted a glorious whole chicken, all of it moist and completely coated in shattering breading. It's the best of both worlds because you get the bits—like the pope's nose and the tiny tender shreds buried in the backbone—you'd pick at in the kitchen when you roast a chicken.

► It's a feast fit for royalty, so it comes with all the fixings. Brown butter biscuits, waffles, chicken liver butter, collards, mace gravy. Plus some hot sauce and more chicken shake.

► If you've got a turkey fryer and a sense of adventure, you can make this at home. Get a 3½-pound chicken and take out the stockpot so the bird will stay submerged in the brine and marinade. Follow the Fried Yardbird recipe on page 85, but double the ingredients for the brine and double the ingredients for the marinade.

► When you're ready, coat the chicken with the flour coating and heat 2 gallons peanut oil in an outdoor turkey fryer to 360°F. Fry the whole bird until the thickest part of the thigh reaches 165°F on an instant-read thermometer, 15 to 20 minutes. Drain it on a rack set over a rimmed baking sheet for 10 minutes before serving.

Put it out whole, and be proud.

MACE GRAVY

Gravy was subsistence food for poor folks in the South. If you had some bacon grease or a little back fat to render, some flour, and water, you could make something flavorful to spoon over biscuits. Maybe you had a sausage; you'd fry that up and make gravy for the family. If you were flush, you'd make gravy with milk, and you'd put it on vegetables, or on chicken-fried steak. It went by lots of names: gravy, white gravy, cream gravy, sawmill gravy. White folks in Kentucky made it; black people in Alabama made it.

We honor this legacy with our mace gravy.

► Dice 6 slices bacon and cook them in a large saucepan over medium-low heat with 3 tablespoons butter until the bacon is limp and the fat is rendering, about 5 minutes. Add ½ cup minced shallots and a tablespoon ground mace and cook until the shallots have softened, 2 to 3 minutes. Sprinkle in 2 tablespoons all-purpose flour to make a roux and cook, stirring constantly, until the roux is golden brown, 6 to 7 minutes. Stir in 3 tablespoons bourbon, then add 3 cups chicken broth and whisk to dissolve the roux. When the gravy starts to simmer, whisk in another 3 cups broth and add a bay leaf. Cook at an active simmer, whisking occasionally, until reduced by half. Whisk in 2 tablespoons apple cider vinegar, then 3 cups heavy cream and a sage leaf. Cook at an active simmer until the gravy is thick. Remove the bay leaf and sage leaf and season with salt and pepper.

BB ROO CHICKEN SANDWICH *on a* POTATO ROLL

SERVES 4

I took off my chef hat when I thought about putting breaded fried chicken on a soft potato roll, but it's because this lunch favorite is just plain delicious. I love the barbecue feel you get from the Red Stripe sauce, and the slaw and scallion sauce add even more layers of flavor.

→ **Put out plenty of napkins.**

FOR THE RED STRIPE Q SAUCE

2 cups ketchup

1 cup chopped onion

½ cup sliced whole scallions

½ cup diced mango

1 (1-inch) piece ginger, peeled and minced

¼ packed cup light brown sugar

2 tablespoons apple cider vinegar

1 tablespoon soy sauce

1 tablespoon tomato paste

2 teaspoons ground allspice

1 cup beer (we use Red Stripe)

1 whole habanero or Scotch bonnet chile

FOR THE CUCUMBER-APPLE SLAW

¼ cup Greek yogurt

¼ cup sour cream

2 tablespoons olive oil

Juice of half a lemon

1 cucumber, roughly peeled and seeded

2 green apples, cored and peeled

2 whole scallions, chopped

Coarse kosher salt

FOR THE SCALLION SAUCE

3 whole scallions

1 cup sour cream

Juice of 1 lemon

1½ teaspoons chipotle chile powder

Coarse kosher salt

FOR THE CHICKEN

4 boneless, skinless chicken thighs

2 boneless, skinless chicken breasts, cut into 4 equal portions

Coarse kosher salt

Peanut oil for frying

2 cups Greek yogurt

2 large eggs

2 tablespoons Aleppo pepper (see page 27)

2 cups all-purpose flour

2 tablespoons cornstarch

TO SERVE

4 large potato rolls or other soft hamburger buns

Softened unsalted butter

FOR THE RED STRIPE Q SAUCE

1 Put all the ingredients— *except* the beer and chile— into a saucepan over medium-high heat. Bring to a simmer, then turn the heat down to low and simmer until the onion and mango are soft, about 20 minutes. Add the beer and chile (make a slit in it) and simmer until the sauce is thick and glossy, another 20 minutes. Strain the sauce and discard the solids.

2 You can serve the sauce now or refrigerate and reheat it later. It will keep for about 1 week.

FOR THE CUCUMBER-APPLE SLAW

3 Whisk the yogurt, sour cream, olive oil, and lemon juice together in a bowl.

4 Use the big holes on a box grater to grate the cucumber and apples onto a clean kitchen towel. Gather up the ends and squeeze out as much liquid as possible. Add the cucumber, apple, and scallions to the dressing, season with salt, and toss well.

5 Cover and refrigerate until cold. This is best the day it's made.

FOR THE SCALLION SAUCE

6 Heat a grill pan over high heat. Turn the heat down to medium and grill the scallions until softened and charred in spots, 3 to 4 minutes. Cool to room temperature.

7 Chop the scallions and mix with the remaining ingredients. Cover and refrigerate until you're ready to serve. This will keep about 3 days.

FOR THE CHICHEN

8 Pound the thighs and breast just enough to give them even thickness. Season with salt.

9 Fill a large saucepan one-third full with peanut oil. Set over medium-high heat and heat to 360°F.

10 Whisk the yogurt, eggs, and 1 tablespoon of the Aleppo pepper together in a deep dish. Whisk the flour, cornstarch, and remaining 1 tablespoon Aleppo pepper together in another deep dish.

11 Dip the chicken into the wet ingredients. Let the excess drip off, then coat liberally with the dry ingredients, packing them on. Place on a rack.

12 Working in batches, fry the chicken until a rich golden brown with an internal temperature of 165°F, about 7 minutes. Keep an eye on the heat and adjust it to keep the oil between 350° and 375°F. Drain on a rack set over a rimmed baking sheet.

TO SERVE

13 Reheat the sauce.

14 Heat a griddle or grill pan over medium-high heat.

15 Split the buns, butter them lightly, and toast them on the griddle.

16 Spread some scallion sauce on the bottom of the buns. Put a thigh and breast on each bun, spooning a generous amount of sauce over each. Add some slaw, put the top on, and serve.

LEMON CHICKEN *with* GREEN HARISSA *and* ROAST EGGPLANT PUREE

SERVES 4

I was looking for something that felt light, almost the opposite of Yardbird. This chicken is tender, moist, and very lemony. The eggplant is a luxurious foil. And then there's the magic harissa. It's bright and fresh; the Anaheim chiles give it a gentle heat, unlike the fire of the Tunisian stuff.

→ **Start this the day before.**

FOR THE GREEN HARISSA (MAKES ABOUT 1 CUP)

8 tablespoons olive oil

4 garlic cloves, chopped

2 shallots, chopped

2 Thai bird chiles, minced

3 Anaheim chiles, seeds and ribs removed, chopped medium

1 teaspoon chopped fresh thyme leaves

Coarse kosher salt

½ teaspoon coriander seeds

½ teaspoon caraway seeds

½ teaspoon cumin seeds

Juice of 1 lime

FOR THE CHICKEN

1 (3½-pound) chicken

Coarse kosher salt and freshly ground black pepper

1 cup fresh lemon juice

2 tablespoons olive oil

3 garlic cloves, minced

1 teaspoon chopped fresh rosemary needles

FOR THE EGGPLANT

2 medium Japanese (long/lighter purple) eggplants (about 1¼ pounds)

4 garlic cloves, unpeeled

1 jalapeño chile

2 packed cups baby spinach

Coarse kosher salt and freshly ground black pepper

FOR THE GREEN HARISSA

1 Heat 2 tablespoons of the oil in a large skillet over medium heat. Add the garlic, shallots, chiles, thyme, and a pinch of salt and cook until the shallots are translucent, about 5 minutes. Clear a space in the center of the skillet and add all the seeds. Toast them for 1 minute, then stir everything together and cook for 1 minute so the flavors can mature.

2 Scrape everything into a food processor and cool slightly. Add the lime juice and remaining 6 tablespoons olive oil and process to make a fairly smooth puree. Taste and season with salt. You can make the harissa 1 day

ahead. Store it covered in the refrigerator.

FOR THE CHICKEN

3 Cut the backbone out of the chicken (freeze it for another use) and cut the chicken in half through the breast bone. Season the chicken on both sides with salt and pepper and put it on a rack set over a rimmed baking sheet. Refrigerate uncovered for 24 hours (or at least 8 hours).

4 Put the lemon juice, oil, garlic, and rosemary in a 1-gallon zip-top bag. Add the chicken to the bag and seal it, squeezing out all the air. Marinate on the counter for 1 hour, turning the bag over after 30 minutes.

5 About 20 minutes before you are ready to roast, preheat the oven to 325°F.

6 Put the chicken, skin side up, in a roasting pan. Pour in the marinade and roast for 20 minutes. Turn the oven temperature up to 375°F.

FOR THE EGGPLANT

7 Cut the eggplants in half lengthwise and score the flesh deeply in a crosshatch pattern. Rub each half with 1 teaspoon of the harissa and set them, cut side up, in a rimmed baking sheet. Add the garlic cloves and the jalapeño. Slide the baking sheet into the oven.

8 Roast the chicken until it registers 165°F in the thickest part of the thigh, 25 to 30 minutes longer, and roast the eggplant until it is soft and browned, about 20 minutes.

9 When they're cool enough to handle, scrape the eggplant flesh out of the skins with a spoon and put it in a food processor. Peel the garlic, stem and slice the jalapeño, and add to the processor. Puree.

10 Bring ¼ cup of the chicken pan juices to a boil in a skillet over high heat. Add the spinach and cook, stirring, until it wilts, about 1 minute. Turn off the heat and fold in the eggplant puree. Taste and season with salt and pepper.

11 Divide the eggplant among four dinner plates. Top each with a quarter of the chicken and a spoonful of harissa.

CHICKEN-FAT CHALLAH *with* CRACKLINGS *and* ONION

MAKES 1 LOAF

There was a time when Harlem was a Jewish neighborhood. Nobody really talks about it anymore, but the evidence is there. In the *New York Times* David W. Dunlap told us to look at the Star of David medallions atop the Baptist Temple Church. Or the cornerstone of the Mount Neboh Baptist Church that says it was built in 5668. Or the marble pediment leading to the baptismal pool at the Mount Olivet Baptist Church, on which is inscribed the Old Testament verse: "Jehovah is in his holy temple; be silent, before him, all the earth.'"

The Jews would call it schmaltz and gribenes, but we call it fat—or grease—and cracklings. Makes no nevermind. It makes a loaf of bread that can go onto the most elegant table imaginable.

FOR THE CHICKEN FAT AND CRACKLINGS

3 pounds chicken thighs

3 tablespoons grapeseed oil

1 medium onion, chopped

Coarse kosher salt

1¼ cups water

FOR THE CHALLAH

⅓ cup honey

1 packet (2¼ teaspoons) active dry yeast

2 large eggs, beaten

2½ teaspoons coarse kosher salt

5 cups all-purpose flour

FOR THE EGG WASH

1 large egg

3 tablespoons water

1 tablespoon sugar

1 teaspoon caraway seeds

1 teaspoon coarse or flaky sea salt

FOR THE CHICKEN FAT AND CRACKLINGS

1 Pull the skin off the chicken and trim all the visible fat. Reserve the chicken for another use. Cut the skin into ½-inch dice (the small pieces are important for rendering the fat and ending up with small cracklings). There's no need to dice the fat.

2 Heat the grapeseed oil in a skillet over medium heat. Add the chicken skin and fat and stir to coat. Cook until the fat is rendering and the skin has curled and is just starting to brown, 5 to 6 minutes. Add the onion and a pinch of salt and cook, stirring, until the cracklings and onion are a rich brown, 14 to 15 minutes. Strain the fat into a bowl. Measure out ½ cup and save the rest to add to the egg wash. Scrape the pan and reserve the cracklings separately.

3 Return the skillet to the heat and pour in the water. Bring just to a simmer, scraping the bottom of the

skillet to dissolve all the brown bits. Pour into a mixing bowl and cool to room temperature.

FOR THE CHALLAH

4 Whisk the honey and yeast into the water from the skillet and let sit until it's creamy, about 10 minutes. Whisk in the ½ cup chicken fat, then the eggs, then the salt. Stir in the flour, 1 cup at a time, to make a soft dough. Turn the dough out onto a lightly floured surface. Flatten it out, put half the cracklings in the center, then pull the edges of the dough over the cracklings and knead for 2 minutes. Flatten the dough out again, add the rest of the cracklings, pull the edges over and knead until the dough is smooth and elastic and the cracklings are distributed throughout, about 10 minutes.

5 Put the dough into a lightly oiled bowl, cover with plastic, and leave it to rise in a warm spot until doubled, 1 to 1½ hours.

6 Turn the dough out onto your work surface and flatten it into a rectangle. Cut it into 4 equal pieces. Roll and stretch each piece into a 20-inch rope. Pinch the ends so they're half the width of the rest of the rope.

7 To braid the challah, twist one end of the ropes together. Lift the far right rope over the one next to it. Then pick up the rope that's second from left and lift it over the two ropes to its right. Now lift the far left rope over the one next to it and lift the rope that's second from right over the two ropes to its left. Repeat the braiding, first from the right and then from the left until you reach the ends of the ropes. Pinch and twist the ends together. Transfer the loaf to a rimmed baking sheet and fold the twisted ends

under the loaf. Cover loosely with plastic. Leave it to rise in a warm spot until doubled, about 1 hour.

8 Thirty minutes before the challah completes its rise, preheat the oven to 375°F.

FOR THE EGG WASH

9 Beat the egg, water, sugar, and leftover chicken fat together in a small bowl.

10 Brush the challah with the egg wash and bake until lightly browned, 15 minutes. Brush it again with the egg wash and sprinkle with the caraway seeds and sea salt. Bake until the loaf is a deep rich brown, 15 to 20 minutes.

11 Cool on a rack for at least 30 minutes before serving. Use a serrated knife to slice it.

Toast it and spread it with Chicken Liver Butter (page 82) or drizzle with Spiced Maple Syrup (page 212).

Use leftovers to make the savory Andouille Bread Pudding (page 260) or a strata.

CHICKEN MAN

Soul-food chef and fried-chicken maestro Charles Gabriel, owner of the famous Charles' Country Pan Fried Chicken, is loath to part with all his culinary secrets, but his words of wisdom are a guide to understanding yourself as a cook. And to the big question: So what's the secret to killer fried chicken? According to Charles, the answer is literally at the tip of your tongue.

I just grew up cooking like this. We had our own pigs. We lived so far away from stuff, couldn't do nothing but cook for yourself. We had to walk seven miles to school, just to get to the highway, to get to the bus, to get to school. We had to get up at four o'clock in the morning to get to the bus stop. It be dark in the morning when you get up, and dark in the evening when you get home.

The thing is you got to like cooking, you got to like it. 'Cause you don't like it, it's not gonna work for you, no matter what you do. I buy my chicken every day. I have to catch the market, 'cause I go to three different markets, 'cause of the prices. Sometimes they got a sale, sometimes they don't. This one might be a good price for the chicken, this one might be a good price for the collard greens. They know me, so when I call they tell me head of time, oh, this what we got going today. Then they get it ready for me.

It's chicken, so you have to make it the way you like. Doesn't matter what kind of chicken you buy. I buy the whole bird and cut it up myself, but you don't have to do that. You can buy the pieces, too. You don't want no big chicken, neither, so get them regular sized. I get nine pieces out of one chicken. Now, *you* ain't gone get nothing but eight. But I get nine. And that's a secret how I do that. I ain't telling

you that. Hahaha. Then you season it; you taste it. I can't tell you what you like. If you can eat it, well, someone else can have it, too. But if you can't eat it, you in a world of trouble. Anything that I make—if I don't like it, I can't sell it.

As far as seasoning, salt and pepper and whatever you like. Look in your cabinet. What's in there? Little bit of this; little bit of that. Salt and pepper is the basic. And sometimes you ain't gotta have all them seasonings. You just gotta have the salt and the pepper. Then you got to let it set. You can't just put that salt and pepper on and go. That's what a lotta people do. They put on that salt, then put that chicken in right away. That's not seasoning. If you gone eat that chicken tomorrow, you gone season it today. You gone wrap that chicken up and put it in the fridge. Tomorrow you gone eat.

And whatever you gone season it with, put it all together. Don't put that seasoning on one at a time. Mix it all up together and then put it on that chicken at the same time. Mix it, then sprinkle it on there. That way the seasoning even. And use that same stuff for your egg wash. So you season your flour, your egg wash, and your chicken. And the egg wash is milk and eggs, that's it. See I might use six eggs to a half gallon milk. Something like that. It's watery. That's why that skin get so crispy. And you just need all-purpose flour and you put your own seasoning in there.

So you put the breast and everything in the pan. Everything. You put it in all at the same time and it all comes out at the same time. So what I do is put the big pieces around the pan and the little pieces in the middle of the pan. And you should do that at home. So the middle doesn't get as hot as the outside, and that's why you do it that way. Once they inside, they don't burn.

Don't cook too fast, it need to be sizzling just a little bit. If it's spitting at ya, you gotta cut it down. See you do it too fast and it'll brown on ya and you think it's done, but it's not done. See you got to drop it in there and cook it slowly then let it come up by itself. Cook it at medium. And that there's a good chicken.

It's chicken, so you have to make it the way you like. Doesn't matter what kind of chicken you buy.

THE MONDAY CLASSICS

FOR A CITY THAT NEVER SLEEPS, New York is notoriously quiet on Mondays. Broadway goes dark and mum; museums shut down and hide their artistry, and before making rent became such a struggle, restaurants closed their doors, in effect telling diners, "Try a home-cooked meal." When I first arrived in New York in the nineties, I marveled at Monday's silence. Chefs, artists, musicians, dancers, we take Monday off. We need it. Since I was sixteen years old, I've worked in a professional kitchen, slogging away in great kitchens across Europe, honing my craft, playing with ingredients, and learning from the masters. In practical terms, that meant I always worked hardest when folks wanted to celebrate and get down: Friday and Saturday nights, that graduation celebration, Mother's Day, the leisurely Sunday brunch. I love doing it. I love the sheer exhaustion that can sometimes come with it. When Monday morning finally rolls around, I collapse into bed. But by the afternoon, I'm ready for something to jump off. I want to listen to some music, hang out at a jazz bar, maybe eat something surprising or start a conversation with someone I find fascinating. The problem is most things are closed. What are people like me doing on sleepy Mondays? Where are they?

I've always understood this opportunity as a particular kind of challenge. I am African, and now an American, and Harlem represents both worlds. I was born into the Amhara tribe in

Ethiopia—a people proud of its regal history. But being newly adopted into America also means being proud of a different kind of past while possessing an irrepressible optimism. We are a country that represents what is possible. I felt as if moving to Harlem and opening Red Rooster was forcing me to answer certain questions. How do you thread all this together: immigration and migration, taste and sound, music and dance, majesty and vanity, bourbon and wine? How can I become a twenty-first century African-American in Harlem?

I decided to look to my elders for guidance. None of the iconic institutions in Harlem is *just* a place. The Lenox Lounge wasn't *just* a club; the original Rooster wasn't *just* a bar; the Apollo isn't *just* a music hall; Sylvia's isn't *just* a restaurant. The reason these establishments are so revered and respected is because they're committed to serving the community *and* introducing Harlem's special brand of a good time to the outside world. The Apollo showcases R&B royalty *and* the young woman around the corner whose voice can bring an audience to tears. Sylvia's is home to wonderful soul food *and* a meeting place for the politically minded. More importantly, Lenox, Apollo, and Sylvia's map a way back to black culture. They provided venues for the greats: Miles, Fela, Herbie Hancock, artists adored by both locals and visitors.

I wanted our Red Rooster to be a part of that tradition, while being open to an alternative, one that was rooted in funk and storytelling. Done right, Red Rooster would give us an opportunity to own our culinary narrative. Zee, a hostess for Rooster, was deeply interested in black art. Soon she became a cocurator of the ever-evolving collection of black art on the shelves that run the length of the bar: headshots of Billy Dee Williams, vinyls of Ella Fitzgerald and Nina Simone. I also added to the shelf photos of culinary artists who inspired me: Jonathan Waxman, Edna Lewis, Daniel Boulud, and Leah Chase.

We had the space; we had the art. What we needed now was the music. My partner Andrew and I both agreed: In order to follow in the footsteps of the greats of Harlem, we needed to bring the best of what is on Harlem streets inside. The Chinese, Mexicans, Puerto Ricans, Jews, Italians, Haitians, Senegalese—they are just some of the people who have created a home in Harlem. How could Red Rooster highlight those communities? And what should that representation taste like? How should that bourbon be sipped? We wanted to become a classic. We wanted to hold our own, on the same side of the street as the iconic Sylvia's, down the way from Lenox Lounge, and around the corner from the Apollo; we needed to be more than *just* a restaurant.

In order to follow in the footsteps of the greats of Harlem, we needed to bring the best of what is on Harlem streets inside.

This was an opportunity to build a bridge—one that stretches from Harlem to downtown, from Sweden to cosmopolitan cities in Africa.

One of the supporting beams was music.

Great food, cocktails, sweet old music. That would be our foundation. Gospel, jazz, salsa, soul, reggae—the music and the artists who played it—would organize the nights and days of the Red Rooster. Andrew and I started talking about what music belonged on which day. My good friend Derek Fleming was charged with being on the hunt for Harlem talent. What we wanted to achieve was layered. There were so many small communities within Harlem that we wanted to pay tribute to with both our menu and our music. I worked with my culinary team to create a menu that tapped out several cultural beats, but what about the music? Something about a restaurant band didn't appeal. We decided not to do an open mike because we wanted to promise excellence every night. But even as we went back and forth about our music and menu, my mind was on the quiet Monday. And on the people who had that day off. All I needed to do was send out the right invitation. But how? I got lucky and met Rakiem Walker.

He was a guy from the neighborhood who was born with a saxophone in his mouth. By the time I had met him, he was playing his music in Central Park. I had seen him often as I walked from my apartment to the Rooster, and we had said hello the way Harlem neighbors say hello. "Hey, Brother, how you doing?"

"Yo, Man, I'm good. I'm good." I didn't know it at the time, but Rakiem mainly exchanged pleasantries with me because he was sure he knew me, but he just couldn't figure out from where. Finally, he had chalked me up as a neighbor whose daily walking commute had recently changed and now our paths crossed. "How's it going, Man?"

"Don't pay to complain."

Mother's Day, 2011, Dr. Calvin Butts, head pastor of the Abyssinian, almost a hundred congregants, my friend Derek, and I were all jamming to Rakiem and the band he was playing with. When there was a break, Rakiem and Derek saw each other and started a conversation. Rakiem told me later, that's what musicians do. You have to stay hungry. You case a room and hope you'll have a conversation that may turn into a gig. What Rakiem played after the break made Derek and me offer him a regular gig on Monday.

"Nobody's around on Monday."

"Not right now. But we got you, right?"

Rakiem smiled. That doesn't mean we opened Monday night and were slammed by people clamoring to get inside. Actually it was better. The growth was steady. Couples from up the block came in to

hear up close the music they heard drifting outside. I invited folks from downtown who had always found me no matter where I was. Best of all, they all came back. Rakiem and I would go out at two, three o'clock in the morning and, over drinks at the Shrine or Paris Blues, would talk about what kind of food and music we should have for our good-time Mondays. During those conversations, Rakiem and I became close, like brothers. It helped that he lives three blocks away from me and he's a musician in love with his craft and always striving toward distinction. We wanted folks to leave and wake up the next day with a happy headache and a secret grin that made their coworkers ask, "What are you smiling about?" Most of all, we agreed that Mondays should be an invitation for folks like us—writers, painters, dancers, folks in the hood, all those downtown people who know a good time when they see it, hip-hop kids from Brooklyn, Swedish tourists. This should all be about finding our tribe, I told him.

"Yo, Man, that's a funky tribe."

"Well, Rooster should be all about the funk, right?"

And if Rooster is about funk, then Monday night is our beating heart. Rakiem owned it. The Rakiem Walker Project started out as a seven-person band that grew into ten. Guitar, drums, two people on keys, bass, trumpet, three vocalists, and Rakiem, killing it on the sax. Every Monday the bar fills with a distinctive brand of hip-hop, soul, and R&B. But the arrangement is all jazz. There's no list of songs that Rakiem decides to play any given night. He and his musicians just jam from seven o'clock until whenever. The move from classic R&B, to new soul, to jazz standards is flawless. Underscoring it all is this feeling of church. The music invites an audience's call and response. But when the trumpet cuts into Mary J. Blige's "What's the 411?" and the hook is sung in three-part harmony, the audience knows Rakiem is treading on different ground. The whole vibe has a juke-joint feel where the unexpected happens.

One night Rakiem and his band had the whole place rocking. Zee came over. She was frowning. "You know Rakiem moved Billy Dee." She had to shout to be heard, and she was eying Rakiem as if he had rummaged through her panty drawer without permission.

"Okay."

"And he moved the Langston Hughes, too. I don't even know where he put it."

Alright, I was about to tell her, I'll talk to him about it. Then Rakiem stepped up with his three singers, and together they sang a four-part harmony. One by one, his singers dropped back and suddenly he was playing solo. He blew a key and held it. High. Higher. When I looked at Zee again, she had a smile on her face as Rakiem played and held this impossible note. "You know what? Don't worry about it, Marcus. I'll find the stuff."

Along with the music, I hope we have created a menu that offers a funky riff on the classics. As a nod to the fish fry, our catfish is dredged in flour and grits. Slivered almonds, apples, capers, and raisins, along with a dollop of butter, make the sauce. The mac and greens became an instant classic. Collard greens, little florets of cauliflower, and three cheeses. The best reward is when I hear our devoted customers read their favorites from our menu out loud. "Yardbird. Helga's Meatballs." It sounds like a song.

When I recently reminded Rakiem that we've been at this for almost six years, we both threw our heads back and laughed. It felt like no time at all. Monday has become a great night when the young meet their elders, the artist lifts a glass to the tourist, and Harlemites and downtowners all groove to the same beat. Everybody wants in on the show, because you never know who might turn up. Is Wynton coming? Maybe. You think Mary J. Blige might walk through the door? Who knows. Black men in bow ties and two-piece suits set the tone and the mood. Don't hunt me, their loafers announce; I'm here for a good time and nothing else, screams a well-tucked handkerchief. Mike and Eddie live down the street and have been coming on Mondays since the beginning. Grand Puba and Nas come by on Mondays to eat and nod to the music. Sometimes we have crazy takeover sessions. Ne-Yo fixes his hat and sings. Pedro Almodóvar brings his whole crew and treats them to our cocktails. What can happen behind the mike and in front of it is equally entertaining.

One night I watched two Swedish ladies dancing their butts off. They called out to Rakiem, who was on the other side of the room, "*Spela* ABBA!" Play ABBA! The brother standing next to them thought they were toasting him, so he joined in. "*Spela* ABBA!" I broke down laughing. I was so happy to be here with my crew, with the wonderful people who make sure to come by every week—with my tribe.

MONDAY CLASSICS PLAYLIST

"AH YEAH" Robert Glasper Experiment featuring Musiq Soulchild & Chrisette Michele

"I BLAME YOU" Ledisi

"INSIDE" Kem

"GEORGY PORGY" Eric Benét featuring Faith Evans

"JUST IN CASE" Jaheim

"LOUNGIN" LL Cool J

"ONE" Mary J. Blige featuring U2

"SOMETIMES" Bilal

"SPOTLIGHT" Jennifer Hudson

"JUMP AND SHOUT" Lakecia Benjamin featuring ChinahBlac

"LA NAVE DEL OLVIDO" Buika

"UNCONDITIONAL" Rakiem Walker Project

"TIME" Rakiem Walker Project

"THE ARCHITECT" Rakiem Walker Project

"CHECK IT OUT" Grand Puba featuring Mary J. Blige

JERK BACON *and* BAKED BEANS

SERVES 6

Bacon and beans sound homey and rustic, don't they? They are, but this simple homemade jerk bacon served with baked beans is far from conventional. I know there are a lot of ingredients, but most of them are pantry items, and you're building up a lot of flavor. Marinating, baking, and chilling the pork belly takes time, but it's not active time, and the result is bacon that's better than anything you'll find at the butcher's. Think about doubling the recipe, because the bacon freezes beautifully (see opposite).

→ **Soak the beans the night before.**

FOR THE JERK SAUCE (MAKES ABOUT 1 CUP)

½ packed cup dark brown sugar

½ cup olive oil

¼ cup soy sauce

2 tablespoons molasses

1 tablespoon water

4 garlic cloves, chopped

2 tablespoons hot red pepper flakes

1 teaspoon fresh thyme

1 teaspoon ground allspice

1 teaspoon ground cinnamon

1 teaspoon freshly grated nutmeg

1 tablespoon coarse kosher salt

FOR THE JERK BACON

1 tablespoon dark brown sugar

1½ teaspoons smoked paprika

1½ teaspoons berbere (see page 27)

1½ teaspoons coarse kosher salt

1 teaspoon freshly ground black pepper

2 pounds pork belly, skin removed

1 pineapple, peeled, quartered, and cored

2 jalapeño chiles

FOR THE BEANS

5 slices store-bought bacon

½ cup diced onion

4 garlic cloves—2 minced and 2 whole, peeled

½ cup diced plum tomato

¼ cup diced celery

3 sprigs thyme

3 tablespoons tomato paste

3 tablespoons dark brown sugar

1 tablespoon Dijon mustard

1 pound navy beans, soaked overnight and drained

6 cups chicken broth

1 habanero chile

Coarse kosher salt

1 ripe tomato, halved through the equator

1 jalapeño chile, halved lengthwise

FOR THE JERK SAUCE

1 Put all the ingredients into a blender and puree until smooth. You can store the sauce in a jar in the refrigerator for 4 or 5 days.

FOR THE JERK BACON

2 Mix the brown sugar, paprika, berbere, salt, and pepper together in a small bowl. Rub the spice mix into both sides of the pork belly. Set the belly on a baking sheet and refrigerate, uncovered, for 2 hours.

3 Preheat the oven to 350°F.

4 Put the pineapple and jalapeños on a small baking sheet lined with parchment.

5 Slide both baking sheets into the oven and bake for 20 minutes. Turn the heat down to 225°F. Slow-roast until the pineapple is tender (about 1 hour longer) and the pork belly is fork-tender (about 2 hours longer).

6 Cover the pork belly with a sheet of parchment and another baking sheet. Weight with a cast-iron skillet for 1 hour (compacting the meat makes it easier to slice). Wrap in plastic and refrigerate until you're ready to serve. The pineapple and jalapeños can stay on the counter.

FOR THE BEANS

7 While the pork belly is roasting, chop 3 of the bacon slices and put them in a large saucepan. Turn the heat to medium and cook until the fat has rendered, about 5 minutes. Add the onion, minced garlic, plum tomato, celery, and thyme and cook, giving it an occasional stir, until the onion is softened and translucent, about 10 minutes. Add the tomato paste, brown sugar, and mustard and cook, stirring, until the tomato paste turns brick red, about 2 minutes. Add the beans and broth and bring to a simmer. Cut the habanero almost in half—leave it attached at the stem—and add it to the pot. Turn the heat down to medium-low and simmer until the beans are tender, 1 to 2 hours, depending on your beans. Keep an eye on the pot and add water if necessary to keep them juicy. Taste and season with salt.

8 Turn the oven heat up to 375°F.

9 Pour the beans into a wide casserole. Top with the remaining 2 slices of bacon, the 2 whole garlic cloves, the tomato halves, cut side up, and the halved jalapeño, cut side down. Bake until the bacon is cooked and slightly browned (it won't be crisp), about 45 minutes.

10 Mash the garlic onto the side of the casserole. Take out the bacon, tomato, and jalapeño, chop them all, and scrape them back into the casserole. Stir, making sure you get the garlic off the sides and into the beans.

TO FINISH

11 Cut the pork belly into 1/3-inch-thick slices. Put it into a couple of skillets, turn the heat to medium, and cook, turning several times, until the jerk bacon is richly browned, about 15 minutes.

12 Layer the jerk bacon on a platter, spooning on some jerk sauce and using the back of the spoon to spread the sauce over each piece of bacon before adding another layer. Slice the pineapple and jalapeños and add them to the platter.

13 Set out the bacon with the pot of beans and dig in.

Last season's dried beans will take longer to cook than ones that are only a few months old. Be patient, and add water if you need to, to keep them juicy.

FREEZING BACON

► Cut the jerk bacon into 1/3-inch-thick slices and spread them out on baking sheets. Freeze for a couple of hours, then gather the slices up and put them in a zip-top plastic bag.

► No need to defrost them before browning them.

Go to most restaurants and the fish on the menu will be salmon. Not at Rooster. Our customers love catfish.

I grew up with something we called catfish, but it was completely different from the catfish I found here. In Sweden, catfish tastes of the sea, so I was surprised by the mild flavor of the American freshwater varieties. It has a real meatiness that holds up to nuts. So here we've got a quick fry, topped with a shower of pecans, apples, raisins, and capers. Love that play of salty and sweet.

CATFISH *and* PECANS

SERVES 4

1 Whisk the flour, cornmeal, cornstarch, and paprika together in a shallow bowl.

2 Heat 1 tablespoon of the grapeseed oil in a large cast-iron skillet over medium heat.

3 Dredge 4 of the catfish fillets in the seasoned flour and pat off the excess. Add to the pan and cook until browned, about 3 minutes. Flip the fish over, add 1 tablespoon of the butter and 1 tablespoon of the dill to the skillet, and cook until the catfish is cooked through (it will feel firm when you press down on it with your finger), about another 2 minutes. Spoon the butter and the dill over the fillets. Transfer to a platter and cover with foil to keep warm. Wipe out the skillet and repeat.

4 Add the pecans to the skillet and toast over medium heat. When the pecans are golden, add the apple, raisins, capers, and soy sauce and cook for 2 minutes to barely soften the apple. Spoon over the fish and serve.

½ cup all-purpose flour

1 tablespoon coarse cornmeal

1 tablespoon cornstarch

1½ teaspoons paprika

2 tablespoons grapeseed oil

8 (3- to 4-ounce) catfish fillets

2 tablespoons unsalted butter

2 tablespoons chopped fresh dill

2 cups pecan halves

1 Granny Smith apple, peeled, cored, and chopped

2 tablespoons raisins

2 teaspoons capers

1 tablespoon soy sauce

Love that play of salty and sweet.

DOUBLE-DRAGON RICE *with* GRILLED SHRIMP

SERVES 4

We've been serving this classic from the beginning. The rice is cooked two ways, and there's fire in the rice and fire in the Green Papaya Salad (recipe follows) that I like to serve alongside. I add sweet shrimp to tame the dragons.

Please try to get head-on shrimp so you can squeeze the juices from the shrimp heads over the rice before you suck them. If you can't, just use the biggest shrimp you can find.

→ **Start the rice the day before.**

FOR THE RICE

1 cup jasmine rice

2 cups water

1 tablespoon rice powder (see page 27)

2 teaspoons brown sugar

1 teaspoon coarse kosher salt

1 cup peanut oil

4 slices bacon, diced

2 poblano chiles, diced

2 garlic cloves, minced

1 teaspoon minced peeled ginger

½ teaspoon shrimp powder (see page 30)

Freshly ground black pepper

2 large eggs, beaten

Juice of 2 limes

1 tablespoon chopped kimchi

FOR THE SHRIMP

4 or 8 head-on, shell-on shrimp (see headnote)

Olive oil

Coarse kosher salt and freshly ground black pepper

Smoked paprika

1 lime, quartered vertically

1 tablespoon chopped fresh cilantro

FOR THE RICE

1 Cover the rice with cold water and soak overnight.

2 Drain the rice and put it in a saucepan with the water. Bring to a simmer over medium-high heat. Cover, turn the heat down to low, and cook for 10 minutes. Turn off the heat. Put a kitchen towel over the pot, put the lid on tightly, and steam the rice for 10 minutes. Spread the rice out onto a rimmed baking sheet and cool completely.

3 Rinse the rice, separating all the kernels, and dry thoroughly on kitchen towels.

4 Combine the rice powder, brown sugar, and salt in a medium bowl. Add half the rice and toss.

5 Heat the peanut oil in a large skillet over medium-high heat. When it is almost smoking, add the coated rice and stir-fry until golden brown, about 2 minutes. Drain the rice and spread it out on paper towels.

6 Combine the bacon, chiles, garlic, and ginger in a large skillet over medium heat and

sauté until the bacon browns, about 10 minutes. Add the other half of the rice and the shrimp powder and cook, stirring, until the rice is hot. Taste for salt and pepper, then stir in the fried rice, eggs, lime juice, and kimchi. Take the skillet off the heat while you make the shrimp.

FOR THE SHRIMP

7 Rub the shrimp with olive oil and season with salt, pepper, and smoked paprika.

8 Heat a grill pan over medium-high heat. When it's hot, grill the shrimp and lime for 3 minutes per side. The shrimp should be almost cooked through (residual heat will finish the job), and the lime should be charred.

9 Divide the rice between four plates. Top each serving with shrimp and a shower of cilantro and garnish with the grilled lime.

GREEN PAPAYA SALAD

Green—or unripe—papayas are used as a vegetable throughout Southeast Asia. The texture is similar to a mango, and the fruit has a very subtle flavor. To take the rice and shrimp over the top, make a salad of 1/2 cup chopped kimchi, 1 cup julienned green papaya, 2 cups julienned cucumber (seed before slicing), 1/4 cup grated carrot, a handful of cherry tomatoes, halved, and a tablespoon of minced chile (use your favorite). Season with 2 teaspoons brown sugar, 1/2 teaspoon shrimp powder (see page 30), salt, and pepper and toss with the juice of 2 lemons. Serve icy cold.

MAC AND GREENS

SERVES 10 TO 12

Sometimes you put a dish on the menu to try it out, and it takes over. You find that out when you take it off the menu and there's a chorus of disappointed voices. That dish has become a classic.

I wanted comfort food, but I knew I needed something to cut the richness. Collards give you something to chew on and a different kind of richness. Then I took another left turn and slipped in some cauliflower for another level of texture. Everybody agrees. Mac and Greens is yummy.

→ **Cut the cauliflower into very small florets—the size of a fingernail.**

FOR THE MAC AND GREENS

4 tablespoons (½ stick) unsalted butter

½ cup thinly sliced shallots

2 garlic cloves, minced

2 tablespoons all-purpose flour

4 cups (1 quart) heavy cream

1 cup milk

1½ cups tiny cauliflower florets

½ cup crème fraîche

8 ounces cheddar cheese, shredded

4 ounces Gruyère cheese, shredded

4 ounces Parmesan cheese, grated (½ packed cup)

1 teaspoon mustard powder

¼ teaspoon freshly grated nutmeg

Coarse kosher salt and freshly ground white pepper

1 pound orecchiette or other small, sturdy pasta, cooked until just tender

2 cups Killer Collards (page 123), reheated

FOR THE TOPPING

⅓ cup dry bread crumbs

¼ packed cup fresh parsley leaves

2 packed tablespoons fresh basil leaves

2 ounces Parmesan cheese, grated (¼ packed cup)

¼ teaspoon coarse kosher salt

⅛ teaspoon freshly ground white pepper

FOR THE MAC AND GREENS

1 Set a rack in the center of the oven. Preheat the broiler. Butter a 9-x-13-inch baking dish.

2 Melt the butter in a large pot over medium heat. Add the shallots and cook, stirring often, until turning golden, 9 to 10 minutes. Stir in the garlic and cook until fragrant, about 30 seconds. Add the flour and cook, stirring, for 1 minute. Pour in half the cream and cook, stirring, until the sauce thickens and comes to a simmer. Pour in the remaining cream, the milk, and the cauliflower and cook, stirring, until the sauce boils. Turn off the heat and add the crème fraîche and cheeses. Whisk until the

cheeses melt. Whisk in the mustard, nutmeg, and salt and pepper to taste. Add the pasta and collards and stir well. Pour into the baking dish.

FOR THE TOPPING

3 Put all the ingredients into a food processor and pulse until the herbs are minced. Strew evenly over the mac and greens.

4 Broil until the topping is golden, 3 to 4 minutes. Leave this to rest for 30 minutes before serving.

CHEESE BROTH

In case you haven't heard, the rinds from Parmesan cheese are an umami ingredient, adding amazing depth of flavor to any broth. To beans, too.

This starts as a broth, but orzo and kimchi turn it into a great light lunch.

► Heat ⅓ cup olive oil in a large saucepan over medium heat. Add 2 sliced shallots, 2 ancho chiles (stem, seed, and chop them first), 1 cup diced carrots, and 2 sprigs each thyme and oregano. Cook until the shallots soften, about 5 minutes.

► Add 4 Parmesan rinds, 1 (15.5-ounce) can of white beans (rinsed and drained), 1 tablespoon white miso, 1 cup dry white wine, and 5 cups water. Bring to a simmer, then turn the heat down to low and simmer for 45 minutes. Remove the rinds.

► Turn the heat up to medium-high and add ½ cup orzo, ½ cup chopped kimchi, the juice of 2 limes, and salt and pepper to taste. Bring to an active simmer and cook until the pasta is just tender, about 5 minutes.

Everyone has a mom or aunty who knows "the best" way to make collards, so I knew we'd have controversy when I skipped the ham hock or salt pork and made them lush with a lot of spiced butter. I love it! That kind of argument makes for the liveliest dinner table conversation.

KILLER COLLARDS

SERVES 6 TO 8

1 Melt the spiced butter in a large stockpot over medium-high heat. Add the onion and chiles and sauté until the onion has softened, about 5 minutes. Add the collards and stir in the vinegar, brown sugar, and salt to taste and bring to a simmer. Turn the heat down to low, cover, and simmer until the greens are very tender, about 1½ hours.

2 Serve hot or warm.

1 cup (8 ounces) Spiced Butter (page 62)

1 onion, chopped

2 Thai bird chiles, minced, or ½ teaspoon hot red pepper flakes

2 pounds collard greens, stemmed and chopped

¼ cup apple cider vinegar

2 tablespoons brown sugar

Coarse kosher salt

HAM HOCKS *with* MUSTARD GREENS *and* KRAUT

SERVES 4

Southern cooks will throw a ham hock into a pot of greens or beans to give them a little flavor, but there's never enough to turn it into a main dish. Well, here we've got two pieces of succulent ham hock—the kind of cut that leaves your lips sticky— for each person.

→ **There's lots of pot likker here, so have a loaf of Chicken-Fat Challah (page 97) or good rye bread on the table so those who don't want to drink the likker with a spoon can sop it up. And put out mustard—Dijon mustard, grainy mustard, or Chinese mustard—for those who want it.**

4 slices bacon, chopped

2 onions, chopped

4 garlic cloves, chopped

2 Fresno or jalapeño chiles, stemmed, seeded, and chopped

2 teaspoons mustard seeds

Coarse kosher salt

1 teaspoon ground cumin

2 cups chicken broth

2 cups beer (such as a pale ale)

¼ cup apple cider vinegar

2 bay leaves

8 (4-ounce) pieces smoked ham hock

1 cup water

6 packed cups chopped mustard greens

½ cup green lentils

1 cup bottled sauerkraut

2 Granny Smith apples, peeled, cored, and chopped

2 tablespoons honey

1 Put the bacon in a very large saucepan. Turn the heat to medium and cook, stirring occasionally, until the fat is rendered and the bacon is beginning to brown, 5 to 6 minutes. Add the onions, garlic, chiles, mustard seeds, and a pinch of salt and cook, stirring occasionally, until the onion is softened, about 8 minutes. Add the cumin and cook, stirring, for 1 minute.

2 Pour in the broth, beer, and vinegar. Add the bay leaves and ham hocks, turn the heat up to medium-high, and bring to a simmer. Cover, turn the heat down to low, and simmer for 1 hour.

3 Pour in the water and stir in the mustard greens and lentils. Bring back to a simmer, and simmer, uncovered, for 30 minutes. Stir in the sauerkraut (rinse and drain it, if you want) and apples, bring back to a simmer, and simmer until the lentils and apples are tender, about 20 minutes. Stir in the honey. Remove and discard the bay leaves.

4 Divide the ham hocks between four large soup plates. Ladle in everything else, dividing it equally.

MARROW DUMPLINGS *with* CHARRED BROCCOLINI *and* CHILES

SERVES 4 TO 6

Ask me what marrow tastes like, and I'll tell you it tastes like "More, please!" It's got what I call *lipstick fat,* something that coats your lips just enough when you eat it. Combine marrow with pork and shrimp, and you've got a killer filling for potato dumplings. The broccolini and chiles make it a complete meal.

→ **You'll need to talk to your butcher about getting the pipe-cut marrow bones, which are lengths of bone that have been split lengthwise. Believe me, it's worth the effort. However, if all you can get are shin bones, go for them. You'll need 15 inches of bones. You may need to roast them a little longer to be able to get the marrow out.**

FOR THE FILLING

3 (5-inch) pipe-cut beef marrow bones

½ pound ground pork

1 teaspoon ground cumin

Coarse kosher salt and freshly ground black pepper

½ pound shrimp (any size), peeled and chopped

4 garlic cloves, chopped

FOR THE DUMPLINGS

2½ pounds russet potatoes, scrubbed

1 large egg

1 large egg yolk

¾ cup all-purpose flour, plus more for dusting

1 teaspoon kosher salt

½ teaspoon freshly ground white pepper

FOR THE BROCCOLINI AND CHILES

3 garlic cloves, unpeeled

3 Fresno or jalapeño chiles

¼ cup olive oil, plus more for sautéing the dumplings

2 cups chopped broccolini

1 cup chopped bok choy

Coarse kosher salt and freshly ground black pepper

FOR THE FILLING

1 Preheat the oven to 450°F.

2 Put the bones cut side up on a rimmed baking sheet. Roast for 5 minutes to release the marrow. When the bones are cool enough to handle, scrape the marrow out onto a cutting board with a spoon and chop it.

3 Heat a cast-iron skillet over medium-high heat. Add the marrow, pork, cumin, and salt and pepper to taste. Cook, stirring to break up the pork, until crumbly and browned, 7 to 8 minutes. Stir in the shrimp and garlic

It's got what I call *lipstick fat,* something that coats your lips just enough when you eat it.

and sauté until the shrimp are cooked, 1 to 2 minutes. The marrow will render as you cook. Scrape the filling into a bowl and cool to room temperature. Cover and refrigerate until you need it.

FOR THE DUMPLINGS

4 Preheat the oven to 375°F.

5 Prick the potatoes all over with a fork and bake them directly on an oven rack until tender, 60 to 75 minutes. Cool the potatoes for 5 minutes.

6 Cut the potatoes in half and peel them. Mash them well (a ricer is the best tool) and spread out on a rimmed baking sheet. Cool completely.

7 Beat the egg and yolk together and add to the potatoes with the flour, salt, and pepper. Knead until you have a smooth, soft dough. Be gentle; you don't want to activate the gluten in the flour.

8 Line a rimmed baking sheet with parchment and dust with flour. Take the filling out of the refrigerator and stir it.

9 Turn the dough onto a floured surface and use your hands to roll it into a 12-inch log. Cut it into 12 equal pieces. Flour your hands and roll a piece of dough into a thin round. Flatten it into your palm, pushing down in the center to make a well, and add about 2 teaspoons of the filling. Pinch the dough over the filling, and roll to make a round ball, making sure no filling escapes. Put the dumpling on the baking sheet and repeat. Set aside the leftover filling. Cover the dumplings with a kitchen towel.

10 Line a rimmed baking sheet with a kitchen towel. Bring a large pot of salted water to a boil. Add half the dumplings to the water. When they rise to the top, simmer for 8 minutes—keep an eye on the heat; you want the dumplings to *simmer*, not boil. Use a slotted spoon or skimmer to transfer them to the baking sheet. Cook the remaining dumplings and leave them uncovered while you cook the vegetables.

FOR THE BROCCOLINI AND CHILES

11 Cook the garlic and chiles in a cast-iron skillet over medium heat until the garlic and chiles are charred in spots and the chiles are blistered all over, about 10 minutes. When they're cool enough to handle, peel and mash the garlic and stem, seed, and chop the chiles.

12 Add the oil to the skillet and heat over medium-high heat. Add the broccolini and bok choy and sauté until the broccolini is starting to char, 4 to 5 minutes. Add the leftover filling and cook, stirring, until it's hot, about 2 minutes. Scrape into a bowl, stir in the garlic and chiles, and season with salt and pepper.

13 Wipe out the skillet and return it to medium-high heat. Add a slick of olive oil. Sauté the dumplings, turning them gently, until golden brown, 2 to 3 minutes.

14 Put the dumplings on a platter, top with the vegetables, and serve.

Save those bones. You can freeze them, then roast later and add to the pot when you're making broth.

"BREAKING NIGHT" AT THE ROOSTER

Wise beyond his twenty-six years, Tru Osborne comes to Rooster every Monday as a vocalist of the Rakiem Walker Project. And because he loves the music and vibe, he often shows up Tuesday through Sunday.

The best way to explain how the Monday house band, the Rakiem Walker Project, functions is that it is an artist collective. There are set members, and we allow other musicians to come and partner with us. We never know what you're going to get either. You can come here, see the same band, sing some of the same songs every Monday, but you hear it differently. That is New York culture in a nutshell.

You really join a membership when you're here. You become someone with a family at Rooster and once international family members come, you gain access to networks in countries you've never been to. Many of the people who come in on a Monday night don't have passports themselves, but they have friends that live in Belgium or Ivory Coast.

I met some international soccer players here. One of them had on a shirt that was so hilarious that I said, "Hey Man, I love your shirt." He took it off in the middle of the dining room and handed it to me, saying "It's yours,"

then bought me a beer. I took my blazer off in the middle of a song, and I covered him with my blazer, and he bought me another beer. Right afterward, they spent the entire evening making sure I had the time of my life. I literally broke night with these gentlemen and had the most amazing time.

And just like every night, when the set was over, we all sang, *Thank you for being a friend. Travel down the road and back again. Your heart is true, you're a pal and a confidant.* We sing that *Golden Girls* theme song all the time because it really expresses our feelings about the people we share ourselves with every week.

I actually went to middle school right here. It operated on one floor above this restaurant. The current Red Rooster door was the door of my school. I remember in the fifth grade, I was outside, where Rooster's outdoor seating is now, doing my first street performance with my mentor. This place is my home.

You can come here, see the same band, sing some of the same songs every Monday, but you hear it differently. That is New York culture in a nutshell.

EL BARRIO NIGHT

MY MOUTH WATERS every time our restaurant manager, Raul Adorno, tells me stories about his childhood in El Barrio. I can smell the bowl of sofrito sitting on his grandmother's East Harlem kitchen table. I can almost taste the goodness of the carne guisada—beef stew—and the bistec encebollado, a fragrant beef with onions. Raul chuckles when he tells me about stealing tostones from a warm platter. In his grandfather's brownstone where he and his extended family lived, Raul's most vivid memories are of Christmas and birthdays and always, the food that surrounded the celebrations. Uncle, aunts, and cousins surrounded his grandmother's dining room table laden with traditional Puerto Rican dishes—mofongo, arroz con pollo, bacalaítos fritos, rice with pigeon peas and, as the table's centerpiece, a succulent pernil pork. In a house full of music and family, what Raul remembers most were the silences prompted by food so good there was nothing to say.

So many in Spanish Harlem have stories like Raul's. El Barrio is a neighborhood where little kids block off side streets with garbage cans and play Saturday stickball. Where Puerto Rican flags, draped from fire escapes, announce a pride in an island's culture. In January, Mexicans, Puerto Ricans, and Dominicans stand in the cold and watch their children in the annual Three Kings Parade—little boys in tuxedos and little girls in chiffon and silk walk Third

Avenue surrounded by a zoo of lambs, donkeys, camels, nine-foot papier-mâché puppets, and politicians in turbans. It's also a neighborhood grooving to a Latin soundtrack: Eddie Palmieri and Daddy Yankee take turns with reggaeton, plena, and bomba music for attention. Every time I walk those blocks, I find myself nodding to the beat.

The enclosed cluster of shops running from 111th to 116th became the place where a neighborhood could buy its heart's desire.

And then there is La Marqueta. In 1936, Mayor La Guardia had the city build an enclosed space under the Park Avenue viaduct as a way to bring order to the pushcarts that dominated the neighborhood. Almost from the beginning, La Marqueta was known as the life of East Harlem. The enclosed cluster of shops running from 111th to 116th became the place where a neighborhood could buy its heart's desire: bouquets of cilantro, bunches of plantains, pineapples, fresh fish. Mothers could come and buy school clothes for their children. Fathers smelled the spices wafting from the chorizo and dreamt of their childhood homes. All of my friends who grew up in El Barrio have a story about La Marqueta. About how they were taught to check for the ripeness of a pineapple or how they fell in love with getting lost because that was the only way to discover something new.

Their stories are plump with Spanish Harlem memories. There's that moment when a kid hit a homer, the warm pride of participating in the parade impervious to the cold, or the comfort they felt because all their family lived on the same block, or that wonderful rush that happened when they tasted the first bite of sweet budin on the Christmas table. Those are the stories of El Barrio.

Unspoken, but there all the same, is a story of leaving Spanish Harlem. You can't help but hear it. Those who come to Spanish Harlem sooner or later leave the neighborhood for the Bronx, New Jersey, sometimes as far away as California. The leaving of Spanish Harlem, the flight from East Harlem. That's a tradition, too.

Those who come to Spanish Harlem sooner or later leave the neighborhood for the Bronx, New Jersey, sometimes as far away as California.

The New York and Harlem Railroad, constructed in 1837, turned rural farmland into what we now know as East Harlem. Soon thereafter, Germans, Irish, Scandinavians, and Eastern European Jews hopped the train and settled in. For the next forty years, some sixty-five thousand tenements were built, creating a neighborhood full of the cheapest housing in the city. Italians came in droves—both from the mother country and from the Lower East Side. By the nineteen-thirties, East Harlem housed the largest Italian community in the country. The neighborhood was then known as Italian Harlem. After the Second World War, the demographic of the neighborhood changed again. Puerto Ricans moved in, and the neighborhood was renamed Spanish Harlem. By the nineteen-nineties, their numbers had dwindled and they were replaced by mostly Mexicans and some Chinese.

By the nineteen-thirties, East Harlem housed the largest Italian community in the country. The neighborhood was then known as Italian Harlem.

In so many ways, East Harlem's history is like that of neighborhoods all over the city. Hundreds of thousands of immigrants flocked to a particular area. They set up shop; garbage-strewn tenement lots were cleaned up and turned into gardens—the shape and study of zucchini and tomatoes became the conversation of the day. But in other ways, East Harlem is utterly unique. Robert Moses, arguably the most influential city official who never ran for office, made El Barrio his personal plaything for fifty years. Tenement basements that were used for private worship and backyards dedicated to growing vegetables were knocked down. And in their place, one project house after another was erected. El Barrio became infamous. Those thirty square blocks held the most concentrated public housing in the city. With notable exceptions—Franklin Plaza springs to mind—you had to be dirt poor to get into that kind of public housing and to stay in, you had to stay poor. It's little wonder that the immigrants who lived and ate and worshiped in Spanish Harlem took their hopes elsewhere. Maybe they could make it in the Bronx or Brooklyn or New Jersey.

That's why I can't help but to be drawn to El Barrio's history; in some ways it mirrors my own.

Those who stayed—grandmothers who commissioned wax replicas of lungs and hearts and livers and arms for the annual festival of the Madonna of the Mount Carmel, Puerto Rican vendors who set up shop inside La Marqueta—fought the good fight. When Moses opened Thomas Jefferson Park, complete with a pool and baseball field, he put "Whites Only" on the welcoming door. For a neighborhood that housed every shade of brown, it was an affront. Italians, Jews, and Puerto Ricans fought the whites-only policy and won. But despite that victory, Italians and Jews still pulled up stakes and moved elsewhere. Puerto Ricans a generation later followed suit. It felt like a neighborhood plagued with bad luck. Too many battles needed to be waged. And even when folks won, it felt like a loss. To know El Barrio is to understand that it oftentimes wasn't the final destination, it was a first step. To know Spanish Harlem is to understand America as an immigrant.

Most who moved here and looked at the acreage of tenement apartments or later at the carved skyline of housing projects had a raging hope. They all heard that first beckoning, "Hurry up, man. You should come over here," told to them by family and close friends. That siren song was strong enough to get them to stuff everything of value in a suitcase and head over to a promised land. Italian Harlem, Spanish Harlem, East Harlem has always been teeming with that suggestive phrase, *"Du solltest hierherkommen. Gib zikh a traisel. Vieni qui, veloce! ¡Ven aquí! Ni ying-gai lai le."* I have heard the proposition in both my adoptive language and in my mother's tongue; I know the power of its seduction, *"Kom over hit. We-de, ena gara, me-metat, ale-bachu."*

That's why I can't help but to be drawn to El Barrio's history; in some ways it mirrors my own. I landed on the Lower East Side on a friend's massage bed. But what I have in common with the good people of El Barrio is the excitement of arriving in New York City. We are eager, often afraid, but always ready. Full of hope and ambition and the overwhelming desire to make it. For me, my dreams took me uptown. It took a long time (at least by my clock) to make Harlem my home. And I find myself thinking about why folks come to my neighborhood and why they stay or what makes them go. And then I remember Raul's stories—old men showing a thing or two to the young as they do the merengue; that first sweet savory bite of tostadas. Jews, Italians, Puerto Ricans may flee East Harlem, but they are constantly drawn back to what they left behind: music and food.

The heyday of Italian Harlem may be gone, but Rao's is still there, on Pleasant Avenue, vibrant as ever. And life in Spanish Harlem teems with street vendors who sell antojitos. On Sundays, in the summer, I wander up and down Second, Third, and Lexington Avenues, and pass the men and women who offer food that soothes every little craving—tacos, tamales, gorditas, tostadas, chalupas, tlayudas, tortas. In the mornings, I pick up warm churros sprinkled with cinnamon and sugar. The church bells from St. Cecilia, Holy Rosary, and St. Paul are ringing, calling their congregants to mass. And in the afternoon, people block off the side street and dance merengue and bomba. Men with bongos tucked between their knees keep the beat. I get elote—a boiled or roasted corn on the cob slathered with crema and lime juice then dusted with chile powder. The neighborhood is still peppered with shops selling cuchifritos, their neon signs light up the night, and the heady smell of fried goodness and pineapple juice lures in customers. Amor Cubano and Cafe Ollin still serve the best Puerto Rican dishes in Spanish Harlem.

The longer I live in Harlem, the more I realize you can't just be *of* the community, you have give your heart and your work *to* the community.

La Marqueta has shrunk in size and scope, but Raul and his family still make the yearly pilgrimage to pick up pigeon peas and cilantro. The city has poured money into renovating this space and it shows. New vendors have joined the old guard—La Bodega Gourmet, Velez Groceries—and offer the neighborhood local produce and baked goods.

The longer I live in Harlem, the more I realize you can't just be *of* the community, you have give your heart and your work *to* the community. That feeling came home, Spring 2014, on a perfect March day when tragedy struck Spanish Harlem. I remember walking to the restaurant when the blast happened. I felt its vibration in my knees. But the sight that I keep returning to over

and over again is the shocked profile of every face around me. We all turned our heads toward the sound. "Yo, what was that?"

"I don't know. I don't know." And then we all ran east. It was a weird moment. Spanish Harlem was suddenly quiet—as if every person who lived in the neighborhood turned their music off at the same time. I remember walking past the graffiti and murals that depict life in El Barrio and hoping that whatever caused the sidewalk to move underneath my feet wouldn't move an artist to find a blank wall. El Barrio didn't need another R.I.P mural with a portrait of an eight-year-old kid. But as I ran toward the sound, surrounded by other people in the neighborhood running with me, my stomach started to hurt. Men and women were leaning out of windows, standing in doorways, calling out to all of us on the move, *"¿Se enteró que?"* Did you hear that? *"¿Que esta pasando?"* What's going on? By the time I got to Park Avenue, just a block away from La Marqueta, I saw nothing but rubble. There had been a gas explosion, and two buildings had fallen. I saw New York City police and firemen tackling the blaze. I could now answer the questions that had followed me all the way to Park Avenue, but I didn't want to.

The whole neighborhood still had the music off and spoke in whispers, as if speaking in a normal voice would scare up something we didn't want to hear. When I passed the Edible Schoolyard at P.S./M.S. 7, where we had built an organic garden, I shoved my hands in my pockets and swallowed. I had taught a cooking seminar at this school; maybe some kid who was a part of the class was lost under the rubble, or maybe their mom or dad or aunty or cousin was lost.

Later, Rooster hosted a fund-raiser to aid families who were displaced by the blast. I'll always remember that night, as we all raised a glass and felt the fierce love for this community.

And so, I honor Latin culture at the Red Rooster. Lissette, the boss of the bar, who is half Dominican and half Puerto Rican, knew a neighborhood band, Johnny Mambo and Friends, who could play salsa and merengue like nobody's business. Part of creating Latin Night at the Rooster is rising to a culinary challenge—we wanted a menu that nods to the Spanish community in our neighborhood: sour tomato soup with shrimp ceviche, coconut fluke ceviche, grilled bass with jicama slaw, snapper in banana leaves, and a forever evolving taco menu.

On Tuesdays, folks come and stay for the show we put on. People eat pork tack tack—Rooster-style tacos—and listen. Once Buika, the world-renowned Spanish-African poet, composer, and singer, showed up and took over. Her music sounds like jazz, flamenco, and soul: rumbling. She kicked off her shoes and sang with her head bowed, as if praying.

Men and women make a space on the bar floor and dance the bachata and the mambo and the merengue. The young know the steps, but the old men in panama hats own it, hands down. They take a break and eat tacos filled with pork and mango salsa, food that feels like home and faraway. I hope they can taste El Barrio on Sundays in the summer. I want everyone who visits us on Tuesdays to walk away carrying the story of how music, food, and dance, Latin style, come together at the Red Rooster.

EL BARRIO PLAYLIST

"THE OFFENSE OF THE DRUM"   Arturo O'Farrill

"MI POLLO"   Eddie Palmieri

"MAMBO VIVO"   Elio Villafranca and the Jass Syncopators

"CABRON"   Red Hot Chili Peppers

"LENGUA DE OBBARA"   The Pedrito Martinez Group featuring Wynton Marsalis

"CUMBIA UNIVERSAL"   Gregorio Uribe Big Band featuring Rubén Blades

This cold soup is light, refreshing, and perfect for a hot summer's day. Think gazpacho with an Asian twist.

SOUR TOMATO SOUP *with* SHRIMP CEVICHE

SERVES 4 TO 6

FOR THE SOUP

1 Heat the oil in a large saucepan over medium heat. Add the shallots, garlic, ginger, lemongrass, coriander seeds, cilantro and mint stems, and a good pinch of salt. Cook, stirring once in a while, until the shallots have softened, about 6 minutes. Add the tomatoes, stock, vinegar, pickle juice, lime juice, and honey. Turn the heat up to medium-high and bring to a simmer. Turn the heat down to low and simmer for 20 minutes. Cool to room temperature.

2 Working in batches, puree the soup in a blender. Push the puree through a fine sieve. Discard any of the solids that don't make it through the sieve. Taste the soup for salt, cover, and refrigerate.

continued on page 144 →

FOR THE SOUP

3 tablespoons grapeseed oil

2 shallots, sliced

3 garlic cloves, minced

1 (3-inch) piece ginger, peeled and minced

3 stalks lemongrass, trimmed, smashed, and chopped (see page 28)

1 tablespoon coriander seeds

3 or 4 cilantro stems

2 or 3 mint stems

Coarse kosher salt

1 (28-ounce) can crushed tomatoes

4 cups vegetable stock or water

2 tablespoons apple cider vinegar

¼ cup juice from Pickled Cucumbers and Radishes (see Pickles at the Rooster, page 244)

Juice of 2 limes

1 teaspoon honey

FOR THE CEVICHE

2 garlic cloves, sliced thin

1 shallot, sliced thin

½ cup fresh orange juice

¼ cup fresh lemon juice

¼ cup fresh lime juice

¼ cup juice from Pickled Cucumbers and Radishes

3 tablespoons extra-virgin olive oil

2 teaspoons aji paste (see page 29); or 1 teaspoon adobo from a can of chipotles in adobo

2 teaspoons Aleppo pepper (see page 27)

1 teaspoon coarse kosher salt

1 tablespoon olive or grapeseed oil

1 pound extra-large (16–20 count) shrimp, peeled and deveined

1 cup chopped Pickled Cucumbers and Radishes

1 tablespoon chopped fresh cilantro

1 tablespoon chopped fresh mint

FOR THE CEVICHE

3 Whisk the garlic, shallot, citrus juices, pickle juice, olive oil, aji paste, Aleppo pepper, and salt in a mixing bowl. Leave the dressing on the counter for 30 minutes.

4 Heat the olive oil in a skillet over high heat. Add the shrimp and sauté for 15 seconds per side. You're just firming up the outside of the shrimp; you don't want them cooked through. Transfer immediately to a cutting board.

5 Cut the shrimp into ¼-inch slices and put into a bowl with the chopped pickles and herbs. Pour in the dressing and stir. Cover and refrigerate until cold.

6 Ladle the soup into bowls. Give the ceviche a stir and use a slotted spoon to lift some out and pile into the center of the soup. Serve.

COCONUT FLUKE CEVICHE

SERVES 4 AS AN APPETIZER

Say ceviche and a lot of people will think of Peru, but I've found it all along Mexico's Pacific Coast on down to South America. This version, with coconut milk and grapefruit segments and topped with fried oysters, is pretty sophisticated.

→ **Fluke is a firm fish; that makes it great for ceviche. You can substitute tuna or hamachi.**

2 jalapeño chiles

8 ounces fluke fillet (see headnote)

3 tablespoons olive oil

2 tablespoons soy sauce

2 tablespoons rice vinegar

1 teaspoon sugar

Segments from 1 grapefruit

1 avocado, pitted, peeled, and sliced

½ cup coconut milk

Peanut oil for frying

3 tablespoons all-purpose flour

1 tablespoon unsweetened coconut flakes

8 oysters, shucked

Coarse kosher salt

1 pickled aji amarillo (see page 29), sliced, or Aleppo pepper (see page 27)

1 Heat a large cast-iron skillet over high heat. Rub the jalapeños with oil (any kind will do) and char them in the hot skillet until blistered all over and blackened in spots, about 5 minutes. Transfer to a cutting board. Brush the fish well with oil and sear for 30 seconds per side. Transfer to the cutting board.

2 Mix the olive oil, soy sauce, rice vinegar, and sugar in a bowl to make a dressing. Stem and slice the jalapeños and add to the dressing along with the grapefruit. Let sit for 10 minutes. Slice the fish.

3 Divide the avocado between four plates. Arrange the fish over the avocado. Stir the coconut milk into the dressing, then spoon the dressing over the fish. Let it marinate while you fry the oysters.

4 Fill a small saucepan one-third full with oil. Heat the oil to 360°F over medium-high heat.

5 Mix the flour and coconut in a shallow bowl. Working in batches, dredge the oysters in the flour and coconut, then fry until golden, about 2½ minutes. Drain on a rack set over a rimmed baking sheet and season with salt while they're hot.

6 Top each serving of the ceviche with 2 fried oysters and some sliced aji pickles (or a sprinkling of Aleppo pepper).

Jicama and apple make a great slaw. The crunchy texture and mild flavor make it a perfect foil for sea bass—particularly when the fish has that tasty char that comes from grilling.

RÓBALO *a la* PARRILLA (GRILLED SEA BASS) *with* JICAMA SLAW

SERVES 4

FOR THE SLAW

1 Toast the pepitas in a small skillet over medium heat, about 3 minutes. Pour into a bowl. Add the jicama, apple, sesame seeds, sugar, and lime juice. Toss well. Cover with plastic wrap and refrigerate until cold, about 1 hour.

FOR THE FISH

2 Season the fillets with salt and half of the cilantro. Set aside while you make the sauce.

3 Heat a grill pan over medium-high heat. Rub the garlic and poblanos with olive oil and grill, turning, until the garlic is charred in spots (about 5 minutes) and the chiles are blistered all over (about 10 minutes). At the same time, grill the limes, cut side down, until charred, about 5 minutes.

4 When it's cool enough to handle, peel the garlic and drop it into a food processor. Stem and seed the poblanos and give them a rough chop. Add them to the food processor, along with the avocado and remaining cilantro. Squeeze in the lime juice. Process to make a fairly smooth sauce. Taste and season with salt.

5 Heat the grill pan over medium-high heat. Oil the pan. Brush the fish with oil and grill, skin side down, until the fish is almost cooked through, about 8 minutes. Turn the fish and grill for 1 minute.

6 Divide the slaw between four dinner plates. Top with the fish and spoon on the sauce.

FOR THE SLAW

2 tablespoons pepitas (shelled raw pumpkin seeds)

½ large jicama, peeled and grated (use the big holes on a box grater)

1 Granny Smith apple, cored and grated

2 teaspoons toasted sesame seeds

1 teaspoon sugar

Juice of 2 limes

FOR THE FISH

4 (6-ounce) skin-on striped bass or sea bass fillets

Coarse kosher salt

1 tablespoon chopped fresh cilantro

3 garlic cloves, unpeeled

2 poblano chiles

Olive oil

2 limes, halved across the equator

1 avocado, pitted and peeled

Coarse kosher salt

PESCADO WRAPPED in BANANA LEAVES with GREEN SAUCE

SERVES 4

Steaming fish in banana leaves is a technique that always works, so it's great for all home cooks who want juicy and delicious fish.

→ **Cilantro and dill make the sauce green, but it's got spice from chiles and ginger and just a hint of funk from miso. The banana leaves make attractive packaging for the fish and add a delicate flavor and aroma. This will be very juicy, so make some quinoa or rice to go alongside.**

3 tablespoons olive oil

Juice of 2 limes

2 teaspoons white miso

2 teaspoons Korean hot pepper paste (gochujang; see page 29)

2 serrano chiles, stemmed and chopped

4 garlic cloves, chopped

1 (2-inch) piece ginger, peeled and sliced

½ cup fresh cilantro

½ cup fresh dill

4 (6- to 8-ounce) skin-on snapper or sea bass fillets

4 (15-inch) squares of thawed frozen banana leaves

1 Put the olive oil, lime juice, miso, hot pepper paste, chiles, garlic, ginger, cilantro, and dill in a blender or food processor and puree to make a loose paste. Reserve ¼ cup for serving.

2 Put a fillet in the center of a banana leaf and rub generously on both sides with the green sauce. Fold the top and bottom of the leaf over the fish, then fold the sides under.

3 Put about 1 inch of water in a skillet or pot that will hold your steamer baskets snugly and bring to a boil. Put the fish packets in the steamer baskets, cover, and set over the boiling water. Turn the heat to medium-high and steam the fish for 10 minutes.

4 Divide the fish between four plates, open the packets, and drizzle each with 1 tablespoon of the remaining green sauce. Serve hot.

A set of stackable bamboo steamers is the way to go here. It's an inexpensive piece of equipment (two steamer baskets and a tight-fitting lid for about $25), and you'll find lots of uses for it.

CORDERO (LAMB) *and* GRITS *with* GRILLED CHILE VINAIGRETTE

SERVES 4 TO 6

After giving big cubes of lamb a long braise, you spread them out on a baking sheet and roast them. The result is meltingly tender lamb with a crisp exterior. The play of textures continues with the creamy grits, and the vinaigrette adds bright acidity and some gentle heat. This really is a great dish.

FOR THE LAMB

6 garlic cloves, chopped

½ cup olive oil

1 tablespoon coriander seeds

1½ teaspoons fenugreek

1 teaspoon cumin seeds

1 teaspoon caraway seeds

1 tablespoon coarse kosher salt

1 teaspoon chopped fresh thyme leaves

1 teaspoon hot smoked paprika

1 teaspoon ground turmeric

4 pounds boneless lamb shoulder, visible fat trimmed, cut into 2- to 3-inch chunks

2 cups beer (Tecate or Modelo Especial)

2 cups water

2 tablespoons rice vinegar

2 tablespoons soy sauce

2 tablespoons honey

FOR THE GRILLED CHILE VINAIGRETTE (MAKES ABOUT 2 CUPS)

1 small red bell pepper

1 poblano chile

1 jalapeño chile

1 garlic clove, unpeeled

1 plum tomato

1 small red onion, cut into ½-inch slices

1 scallion, chopped

1 tablespoon chopped fresh cilantro

½ teaspoon ancho chile powder

¼ teaspoon ground cumin

¼ teaspoon ground turmeric

Juice of 1 lime

2 tablespoons sherry vinegar

¼ cup olive oil

Coarse kosher salt

FOR SERVING

Creamy Grits (from Whole Fried Fish with Grits, page 180)

FOR THE LAMB

1 Put the garlic into a blender and add ¼ cup of the oil. Blend until smooth. Pour into a large bowl.

2 Grind the coriander seeds, fenugreek, cumin seeds, and caraway seeds to a powder in a spice grinder. Add to the bowl, along with the salt, thyme, paprika, and turmeric. Mix to make a paste. Add the lamb and toss, massaging the seasoning paste over all the meat. Cover with plastic wrap and refrigerate for 3 hours.

3 Preheat the oven to 325°F.

4 Heat the remaining ¼ cup olive oil in a Dutch oven over medium-high heat. Working

The play of textures continues with the creamy grits, and the vinaigrette adds bright acidity and some gentle heat.

in batches, brown the lamb, about 4 minutes per batch. Pour in the beer and water and add the vinegar, soy sauce, and honey. Return all the meat to the pot and bring to a simmer.

5 Cover the pot and slide it into the oven. Braise until the lamb is fork-tender, about 3 hours. You can make the lamb up to this point a day ahead. Refrigerate it in the braising liquid.

FOR THE GRILLED CHILE VINAIGRETTE

6 Heat a grill pan over medium heat. Rub the bell pepper, chiles, and garlic with oil (any kind will do) and grill, turning often, until the garlic is blackened in spots (about 5 minutes) and the bell pepper and chiles are blistered and blackened in spots (about 10 minutes for the chiles and 12 for the bell pepper). Cool on a cutting board. Grill the tomato, turning often, until the skin is blackened in spots and beginning to split, about 4 minutes. Cool on the cutting board. Brush the onion slices

with oil and grill until you get nice grill marks, about 90 seconds per side. Add them to the cutting board.

7 When the vegetables are cool enough to handle, peel the garlic and drop it into a food processor. Stem and seed the pepper and chiles, give them a coarse chop, and add to the processor. Chop the tomato and onion and add to the processor, along with the scallion, cilantro, ancho chile powder, cumin, turmeric, lime juice, and vinegar. Pulse until chunky, then turn the machine on and pour in the olive oil in a steady stream. Process until you have a fairly smooth

vinaigrette. Season with salt. Pour into a bowl, cover, and leave on the counter for an hour or so.

TO SERVE

8 Preheat the oven to 400°F. Line a rimmed baking sheet with parchment.

9 Take the lamb out of the braising liquid (if you've refrigerated it, bring it to a simmer first), pat it dry, and set it on the baking sheet. Roast for 20 minutes, to give the meat a crisp exterior. (Save the braising liquid and use it to make rice or quinoa.)

10 Serve the lamb with the grits and vinaigrette.

DAY-AFTER FRITTERS

Got leftovers? Shred the lamb and mix it well with the cold grits— use your hands. Season with soy sauce and honey (be generous). Then roll into balls and deep-fry until golden, about 3 minutes. Serve with the grilled chile vinaigrette.

PUERCO *en* CERVEZA (PORK *in* BEER), PLANTAINS *on* THE SIDE

SERVES 6

Since moving to New York, I have come to love plantains. They can be savory or sweet, crisp when you fry them or fluffy when you mash them. Summer weekends you'll find music and dancing on the streets around La Marqueta, the market that Mayor Fiorello La Guardia built in East Harlem, and vendors selling slabs of pork cooked Latin style with plantains. It's the perfect food.

FOR THE PORK

4 garlic cloves, chopped

2 tablespoons chopped fresh sage leaves

2 teaspoons ground cumin

1 teaspoon powdered ginger

2 tablespoons Dijon mustard

8 tablespoons olive oil

4 to 5 pounds boneless pork shoulder or Boston butt, in two pieces

1 pound small sunchokes, scrubbed

6 shallots, peeled and cut in half lengthwise

2 (12-ounce) bottles beer (Modelo Especial or Tecate)

3 tablespoons cider vinegar

2 cups pitted prunes

1 cup canned chestnuts, drained (optional)

1 cup bottled sauerkraut, rinsed and drained

FOR THE PLANTAINS

2 cups peanut oil

2 green plantains, peeled and cut into ⅓-inch rounds

Coarse kosher salt and freshly ground black pepper

4 slices bacon, chopped

2 poblano chiles, diced

1 cup bottled sauerkraut, rinsed and drained

2 garlic cloves, minced

½ cup water

1 tablespoon apple cider vinegar

Juice of 1 lime

FOR THE PORK

1 Put the garlic, sage, cumin, ginger, mustard, and 6 tablespoons of the olive oil in a blender and whir to make a paste. Rub the paste all over the pork and leave it on the counter for 30 minutes.

2 Preheat the oven to 325°F.

3 Heat a large Dutch oven over medium-high heat. Add the remaining 2 tablespoons oil, the sunchokes, and shallot halves and cook, stirring until the shallots take on some color, 2 to 3 minutes. Transfer to a bowl.

4 In batches, brown the pork in the Dutch oven, 2 to 3 minutes per side. Move them to a plate as they're browned.

5 Pour the beer into the pot and bring to a simmer, stirring and scraping to dissolve the brown bits on the bottom of the pot. Add the vinegar and the pork, cover, and slide into the oven. Braise for 45 minutes. Add the shallots and sunchokes, along with the prunes, chestnuts (if using), and sauerkraut, pushing down to make sure everything is submerged. Cover and braise until the pork and sunchokes are tender, about 1 hour.

6 Transfer the meat to a cutting board and let it rest for 10 minutes. Use a slotted spoon to transfer all the solids to a serving plate. Pour the braising liquid into a fat separator.

FOR THE PLANTAINS

7 While the pork is braising, pour the peanut oil into a large cast-iron skillet. Set it over medium-high heat and heat the oil to 350°F. The oil will be ready when you set the handle of a wooden spoon onto the center of the skillet and a ring of bubbles appears instantly. Fry the plantains in batches until golden, about 5 minutes. Drain on paper towels and season immediately with salt and pepper.

8 Put the bacon and half the diced poblanos into a large skillet. Set over medium heat and cook, stirring occasionally, until the fat has rendered and the bacon is beginning to brown, 7 to 8 minutes. Add the sauer-kraut, garlic, water, and vinegar and simmer for 5 minutes.

9 Put the remaining diced poblano into a mini food processor or high-power blender and puree.

10 Add the plantains and poblano puree to the skillet with the bacon and sauerkraut and cook, stirring, for 1 minute to marry the ingredients. Stir in the lime juice and scrape it all into a serving bowl. Leave it on the counter until you're ready to serve; the plantains are best warm or at room temperature.

11 To serve, carve the pork and pile it onto the serving platter with the sunchokes. Pour the defatted braising liquid into a pitcher. And put everything on the table.

The best sauerkraut you'll find in the grocery store will be in a bottle in the refrigerated section. Second best will be in a plastic bag, usually near the hot dogs. Never, ever use the stuff in cans.

CHARRED CHAR AREPAS

SERVES 4 TO 6

Arepas, the classic Venezuelan corn patties, could become the new taco. They're great with all kinds of fillings and toppings: meat, shrimp, cheese, tomatoes—even salad.

I've played with the recipe, adding potato to give my arepas more body, and jalapeños for some heat. And for the topping? Fatty delicious char—a fish I call the better version of salmon—along with herbs, avocado, and pickled ginger. A mash-up, to be sure, and fun!

Fatty delicious char—a fish I call the better version of salmon—along with herbs, avocado, and pickled ginger.

FOR THE AREPAS

½ cup corn kernels

4 tablespoons olive oil, plus additional for the skillet

2 (8-ounce) russet potatoes, scrubbed and halved lengthwise

2 garlic cloves, unpeeled

2 jalapeño chiles

½ cup cornmeal

¾ cup buttermilk

2 large eggs, separated

1 tablespoon chopped fresh dill

Coarse kosher salt

FOR THE CHAR

1¼ pounds skinless center-cut char fillet

1 tablespoon Swedish sweet mustard (see page 26)

1 tablespoon olive oil

2 tablespoons minced fresh cilantro

2 tablespoons minced fresh dill

FOR SERVING

2 avocados, pitted, peeled, and sliced

Pickled ginger

FOR THE AREPAS

1 Preheat the oven to 375°F. Line a small rimmed baking sheet with parchment.

2 Toss the corn with 1 tablespoon of the olive oil and spread it on a corner of the baking sheet. Rub the potatoes with 1 tablespoon of the olive oil and add them to the baking sheet (cut side down), along with the garlic and jalapeños. Roast for 20 minutes. Remove the garlic and jalapeño and continue to roast the corn and potatoes until the corn is a rich brown and potatoes are tender, another 20 minutes.

3 Peel the garlic and stem and chop the jalapeños and put in a mini food processor or blender. Add the corn and the remaining 2 tablespoons olive oil and process to a paste.

4 When the potatoes are cool enough to handle, peel them and mash the flesh with a fork in a mixing bowl. Mix in the cornmeal, buttermilk, egg yolks, and corn-chile paste.

5 In a separate bowl, whip the egg whites to stiff peaks. Fold into the batter. Season with the dill and salt.

6 Heat a griddle or cast-iron skillet over medium heat. Brush it with olive oil. Use ¼ cup of the batter for each pancake, spreading it into a 3-inch round. Cook until nicely browned and cooked through (they will feel firm to the touch), about 3 minutes per side. Pile them on a platter as they're cooked, and oil the skillet for each batch.

FOR THE CHAR

7 Heat a griddle over high heat. Rub the char liberally with oil on both sides. When the griddle's screaming hot, sear the char for 10 seconds per side. Transfer to a cutting board.

8 Whisk the mustard with the olive oil and brush it on the char. Sprinkle the cilantro and dill over the top and press them in.

9 Slice the char.

TO SERVE

10 Top each arepa with char, avocado, and a piece of pickled ginger. Or arrange the components on platters and let your guests serve themselves.

LA MARQUETA PORK TACK TACK

SERVES 6 TO 8

M exico meets Ethiopia here. I combine cornmeal and teff flour to make a wrap for jerk bacon. It may seem like overkill to shallow-fry the pancakes after cooking them on a griddle, but believe me—it's not. You get that crisp outside (especially the edges) and fluffy interior that you expect from the best French fry. Wrap it around beautifully fatty bacon, garnish with scallions and crumbled cheese, and you have a scrumptious twist on a taco. I've made it in honor of the constant street party around La Marqueta in East Harlem.

→ **You need some advance planning for this dish. The batter for the tack tack needs to ferment for 4 days.**

FOR THE TACK TACK (MAKES ABOUT 24)

1 cup teff flour (see page 26)

1½ cups water

½ cup beer

1½ cups corn flour

½ teaspoon berbere (see page 27)

½ teaspoon ground cumin

½ teaspoon coarse kosher salt

Peanut oil for the griddle and shallow-frying

FOR THE CRISPY SHALLOTS

3 or 4 shallots, sliced thin

Wondra flour

FOR THE "TACOS"

Jerk Bacon (with the Jerk Sauce, pineapple, and jalapeños; page 112)

2 scallions, sliced thin

1½ cups crumbled queso fresco or mild feta

FOR THE TACK TACK

1 Whisk the teff, ½ cup of the water, and the beer together in a large mixing bowl. Cover with plastic wrap and leave on the counter for 2 days. It will smell very sour; don't worry. Whisk in the remaining 1 cup water and the corn flour, cover with plastic wrap, and leave on the counter for another 2 days. Now the batter will have separated and it will smell fermented, almost like beer. Whisk in the berbere, cumin, and salt.

About the name. It's pure whimsy. Tack *is "thank you" in Swedish.*

2 Heat a cast-iron griddle over medium-high heat. Brush the griddle with peanut oil. For each tack tack, spoon 2 tablespoons of the batter onto the griddle. Cook until bubbles rise and burst on the surface and the edge is starting to dry, about 30 seconds. Flip and cook until the tack tack feels firm, about 30 seconds. They will be lightly browned on each side. Transfer them to a plate, stacking as you go. Oil the griddle between each batch.

3 Heat ¼ inch of peanut oil in a cast-iron skillet. The oil will be ready for frying when you press the handle of a wooden spoon into the bottom of the pan and a ring of bubbles immediately appears around the handle. Fry the tack tack in batches until browned and crisp, 30 seconds per side. Drain on paper towels. Keep the oil hot so you can make the shallots.

FOR THE CRISPY SHALLOTS

4 Separate the shallots into rings and toss them in Wondra. Transfer to a strainer and shake off excess flour. Fry in the cast-iron pan until richly browned and crisp, about 90 seconds. Drain on paper towels.

FOR THE "TACOS"

5 Cut the bacon into ⅓-inch slices then into 3-inch pieces.

6 Cook the bacon in a large skillet (or use two if you want) over medium heat, turning several times, until it's richly browned, about 15 minutes. Layer it on a platter as it's done and smear jerk sauce over each piece.

7 To serve, slice the pineapple and put it on the platter with the bacon. Slice the jalapeños and mix in a small bowl with the scallions. Put everything out with the tack tack and cheese, and let your guests play—making "tacos" to their hearts' delight.

"GOD PUT THE ORGAN AT MY DOOR"

Nate Lucas, jazz organist, plays at the Rooster at Sunday night jazz. A while back, he told me of his childhood in Spanish Harlem and how he found his musical passion.

I grew up in Wagner Projects at 120th between First and Pleasant Avenue. Rough place—a lot of things went on. It's Disneyland now, compared to what it was. They'd knock all the lights out, so when you went in there, if you didn't know the place, you didn't know how to get around. It was pitch dark. It was rough. When you got into the elevators, you had a three-inch area to stand in that wasn't piss.

There were people who had an apartment for three generations—their grandmothers, their parents, and now they had it. They were proud, saying this is *ours.*

But you know, when you have three hundred people in one building project, of course there's going to be chaos. It's a prison. That's why I snuck away to my Uncle George. He lived on the West Side. His kids had nice clothes, new bikes. Not that they were better off; they were hustlers. The East Side had a lot of muggers and thieves. The East Side was where the West Side kids went when they wanted to get someone stuck up or hurt. Harlem was divided in half at Fifth Avenue. Two completely different worlds. Literally, when you crossed the street.

I love my parents intensely. They gave me things that they didn't have resources for. My mother would park my baby carriage in the hallway of Smalls Paradise, where the big bands played. It planted the seeds of music in my subconscious. I learned classical piano as a child. I couldn't read music, but I could play what I heard.

We lived across the street in the tenement buildings, which were a part of Wagner. When I was a kid, we didn't have electricity for two years. My parents thought it would be better for me to get an education at Catholic school. So for two years, we were without lights. They made these sacrifices. We had kerosene lamps and did homework in the daytime.

My ultimate hero is my father. He was the greatest thing about everything—period. But some great musicians were also my heroes. I remember Dizzy Gillespie coming to the house. Because my Dad played on a lot of hits—Louis Armstrong, Nat King Cole . . . I didn't even know they were famous. I just thought they were my father's friends. So, when I went to City College, I took a music history class, the professor was talking about all these people. And I'm thinking, *Are you kidding me? That's Uncle Dizzy.*

I got away from music until I was twenty-two or twenty-three. My father was going to work at La Famille. I walked in there and there was a guy, Bernie, playing the Hammond organ. His feet were hitting the pedals, he was pulling the draws. The music sounded so good—it was pure. I was mesmerized and fell in love. When the band took a break, I just stood there staring at it. When I got in the car, I said, "That's what I want to do for the rest of my life." My dad said, "Son, I wish that you would."

His feet were hitting the pedals, he was pulling the draws. The music sounded so good—it was pure.

The next day, I'm asleep, and a guy knocks on my door—it's Jack, the neighborhood junkie. He had a keyboard he wanted to sell. It was an organ—God put the organ at my door. I didn't know how to turn it on, I didn't know how to draw; I didn't know nothing. But I had DJ'd for years. So, I did know something about setting electronics. So I hooked it up to an amplifier, and then I turned the radio on to WBGO, and Lou Dobson is playing with the organ behind him. So I taped it off of the radio. And I started practicing from that little snippet from Dobson. I started going to La Famille all the time—I just had to be around that instrument.

I want good soul music, I want grits and gravy and grease on it. That's how I want my music. Forget Juilliard, before you can play, you should spend two years in a juke joint.

BIG DAY WEDNESDAY

SO WE GOT THE CALL. Even now, I'm stunned. Yes, we had done the State Dinner at the White House, but when you get a call from the highest office in the land, it comes at you like a bolt of lightning. You don't say "no, thanks" to the opportunity of having a sitting president dine at your restaurant. Still, we had only been open for five months.

Ginny's wasn't Ginny's. Back then, we called it Downstairs at the Rooster. It was a stinky basement that needed spackle and paint and a zillion-dollar renovation. There wasn't any wood paneling, we hadn't put in the booths, no recessed lighting. We had faux lighting that we strung up. I had to beg Thelma Golden to bring some art from the Studio Museum. And she brought us stuff from her storage, and we put everything up on the walls. We painted two days before the event. So the room smelled of paint, yeah, a little bit. It was all very rushed to make it happen. But you know what they say. Go big or go home. And there was no denying this was a big day for the Rooster. It was a big day for Harlem.

Cooking at the White House is a different beast from hosting the president's fund-raiser at your place. We needed to accommodate him and that meant working with the Secret Service. I've worked in New York City restaurants, so I've been inspected by the Health Department. They are pretty hard core. But nothing compares to being vetted by the Secret Service. We had to undergo all this various channeling. They even checked out our venting and duct work. The police were brought in to make sure we were ready to host him.

Cooking at the White House is a different beast from hosting the president's fundraiser at your place.

But the worst part was that we couldn't tell anyone. And man, did I want to advertise. *Hey, everybody, President Obama is coming to my house; to Harlem!* But we couldn't. The only people who knew were the guests who were invited. And of course, our staff who were sworn to secrecy. I think they were as nervous as I was, so they didn't tell anyone either.

The day of the fundraising dinner, I remember my heart thudding in my throat: *Gotta make it special.* And right behind that thought: *Please don't let anything bad happen to Obama while he's having dinner at the Rooster.* The president came in, down the back stairwell. He stopped every now and again, to say hello to the kitchen staff. There were a couple of servers who looked as if they were about to cry. We had a little room set up for him and his crew. That's where we served him our braised beef short ribs. We had the music. One of our hostesses at the time, Roz, sang, and Rakiem played. My friend Derek and I were downstairs, making sure the music went perfectly. Derek had been vetted, so when it was time to serve Obama, Derek went upstairs and took the meal to the president. Afterward, we watched Obama move from table to table. He spoke to everyone. Didn't have a lick of paper. Just spoke off the cuff and people's faces lit up.

But looking back at that day, what I think I remember most is watching a big day unfold in Harlem. We really had kept Obama's fundraising dinner a secret. But somehow it had gotten out. His caravan had come, and it had been reported. Through wide Rooster windows, I saw a growing crowd. Police barricades blocked off the avenue. Without Twitter or Facebook, gossip jumps from one mouth to the next in my neighborhood, and it seemed like most of Harlem stood shoulder to shoulder on the sidewalk. By the time President Obama was getting ready to go, it was a frenzy. Thousands of people were outside, the snipers were on the roofs. Every once in a while, you are a part of something important, and you know it. No one needs to blog about it, you don't need proof from anyone else. This was one of those iconic moments. A sitting president had broken bread at our restaurant. We passed out coffee and donuts to folks waiting to sneak a peek at the first black president. His presence put the building on the map.

BIG DAY PLAYLIST

"AIN'T NO SUCH THING AS SUPERMAN"	Charenée Wade
"WAKE UP"	Run-D.M.C.
"ENGLISHMAN IN NEW YORK"	Sting
"I AM LIGHT"	India.Arie
"CHERRY WINE"	Nas featuring Amy Winehouse
"LOVE REARS ITS UGLY HEAD"	Living Colour
"YOU CAN'T STOP US NOW"	Marc Cary

OBAMA'S SHORT RIBS

SERVES 4

Short ribs marry with many flavor combinations, and they taste much more expensive than they are. I chose plum sauce as an accent to this super-delicious braise; it adds an elusive flavor. We served this as part of a special menu when President Obama came to the Red Rooster, and it's a hit every time we put it back on.

→ You'll have extra braising liquid. Freeze it in ice cube trays, and you'll have flavor bombs to use in pan sauces or pasta.

---

4 (8-ounce) boneless short ribs

Coarse kosher salt and freshly ground black pepper

2 tablespoons grapeseed oil

1 onion, chopped

1 carrot, chopped

2 celery ribs, chopped

1 lemongrass stalk, trimmed, smashed, and minced (see page 28)

3 garlic cloves, chopped

1 (1-inch) piece ginger, peeled and minced

½ cup dry red wine

3 cups beef or chicken broth

½ cup plum sauce

¼ cup soy sauce

2 sprigs thyme

2 sprigs flat-leaf parsley

2 bay leaves

Horseradish, preferably freshly grated, for serving

1 Preheat the oven to 325°F.

2 Pat the meat dry with paper towels and season all over with salt and pepper.

3 Heat the grapeseed oil in a large Dutch oven over medium-high heat. When it shimmers, add the short ribs and brown on all sides, about 2 minutes per side. Put them aside on a plate.

4 Add the onion, carrot, celery, lemongrass, garlic, and ginger to the pot. Season with salt and cook, stirring often, until the onion softens, about 5 minutes. Pour in the wine and cook, stirring to dissolve any of the brown bits that may still be on the bottom of the pot. Add the broth, plum sauce, soy sauce, thyme, parsley, and bay leaves and bring to a simmer. Return the short ribs to the pot, along with any of the juices, cover, and slide the pot into the oven. Braise until the meat is fork-tender, about 1½ hours.

5 Transfer the meat to a plate. Strain the braising liquid into a fat separator. Discard the bay leaves and put the vegetables into a food processor. Process until smooth. Add 1½ cups of the defatted braising liquid to the processor and pulse to combine. Return the sauce to the Dutch oven and check for salt and pepper. Bury the short ribs in the sauce, cover, and leave on the back of the stove until you're ready to serve.

6 Reheat the short ribs in the sauce.

7 Divide the short ribs between four shallow bowls. Top each with a spoonful of sauce. Put the rest of the sauce in a bowl for passing at the table, along with a bowl of horseradish if you'd like.

SPICY SWEETS *and* GREEN BEANS

SERVES 4 TO 6

Carrots make the sweet potatoes even sweeter, and the beans provide crunch and a great color contrast.

This is the side I cooked when President Obama came to dinner. It's great with the short ribs or any meat that has a lot of sauce.

---

2 pounds sweet potatoes, peeled and cut into ½-inch-thick slices

2 tablespoons grapeseed oil

6 garlic cloves, unpeeled

1 tablespoon berbere (see page 27)

½ pound green beans, trimmed and cut into 1-inch lengths

2 tablespoons Spiced Butter (page 62)

1 medium red onion, chopped

½ cup chopped (½-inch) carrot

1 (3-inch) piece ginger, peeled and minced

2 jalapeño chiles, seeded and minced

Coarse kosher salt

1½ cups water

1 tablespoon chopped fresh chives

1 Preheat the oven to 400°F. Line a rimmed baking sheet with parchment.

2 Toss the sweet potatoes with the grapeseed oil and spread out on the baking sheet. Add the garlic and roast until the garlic is tender, about 20 minutes. Remove the garlic and continue roasting the sweet potatoes until they're tender, another 20 minutes. Put the sweet potatoes in a bowl. Peel the garlic and add it to the sweets. Use a fork to make a chunky mash. Stir in the berbere.

3 While the potatoes are roasting, bring a saucepan of salted water to a boil and set up an ice bath. When the water is boiling, add the green beans. Bring back to a boil and blanch for 3 minutes. Drain the beans and plunge them into the ice bath. When they're cool, drain them.

4 Melt the spiced butter in a large skillet over medium heat. Add the onion, carrot, ginger, jalapeños, and a pinch of salt and cook, stirring occasionally, until the onion is softened, about 5 minutes. Add the water and bring to a simmer. Cover and simmer until the carrots are tender and the water has just about cooked away, 10 to 15 minutes. Stir in the mashed sweets and the green beans and cook, stirring, until heated through. Stir in the chives and taste for salt. Serve hot.

Neck could be considered a poverty cut or just something to make broth with, but treat it right and you're rewarded with flavorful, succulent meat. I've given it a gentle braise, with hints of lemongrass, allspice, and clove. You'll want to eat this with your fingers, and suck out every bit of the tender beef. Look for beef neck in grocery stores and butchers in black or Latino neighborhoods.

BRAISED BEEF NECK

SERVES 4

1 Trim the visible fat from the beef necks. Rinse the necks well, pat dry, and put in a bowl. Season with salt.

2 Mix the mustard and hot pepper paste with 3 tablespoons of the oil. Add to the neck pieces and toss with your hands to coat the beef. Cover with plastic and refrigerate for 2 hours.

3 Preheat the oven to 325°F.

4 Heat 2 tablespoons of the oil in a large Dutch oven over medium-high heat. Working in batches, brown the neck pieces well, 5 to 6 minutes per batch. Turn the heat down to medium, add the remaining 1 tablespoon oil and the onions, carrots, lemongrass, and ginger. Cook, stirring often, until the onion has softened, about 3 minutes. Add the beer, broth, soy sauce, honey, and bay leaves. Tie the allspice and cloves in a piece of cheesecloth and add the sachet to the pot. Bring to a simmer.

5 Cover the pot, slide into the oven, and braise until the meat is tender and falling off the bone, about 2 hours. Give it a stir once or twice while it braises.

6 Transfer the meat to a serving bowl. Discard the bay leaves and spice sachet and skim the fat from the top of the sauce. Set the pot over medium heat and simmer until the sauce is reduced by one third, about 7 minutes. Pour the sauce over the meat and serve.

12 (1- to 1½-inch) pieces beef neck (about 4 pounds)

Coarse kosher salt

1 tablespoon Dijon mustard

2 teaspoons Korean hot pepper paste (gochujang; see page 29)

6 tablespoons grapeseed oil

2 red onions, sliced thin

1½ cups sliced (¼-inch) carrots

1 stalk lemongrass, trimmed, smashed, and minced (see page 28)

1 (1-inch) piece ginger, peeled and chopped

2 cups dark beer

2 cups chicken broth

2 tablespoons soy sauce

1 tablespoon honey

2 bay leaves

2 teaspoons allspice berries

3 whole cloves

You'll want to eat this with your fingers, and suck out every bit of the tender beef.

SHOEBOX HAM

SERVES 8, WITH

PLENTY OF LEFTOVERS

It was difficult enough for Southern blacks just to get on trains during the Great Migration; but Jim Crow laws made getting something to eat impossible. The dining cars were closed to African-Americans. Their solution was simple. They packed up lunches in shoeboxes and ate in their seats. I like to think that this would be the kind of ham that would be perfect packed in a shoebox. The curing salt is a preservative so the ham's good for a long journey.

Think pastrami rather than smoked ham. Pastrami with deep pork flavor.

→ **Fresh ham can be hard to find. You may need to order it from your butcher, or you can substitute Boston butt. You need to start this ham 5 days ahead.**

FOR THE BRINE

6 quarts water

1 cup coarse kosher salt

1 packed cup dark brown sugar

3 tablespoons pink curing salt (see page 28)

4 poblano chiles, seeded and chopped

6 garlic cloves, peeled and smashed

2 tablespoons mustard seeds

1 tablespoon coriander seeds

6 juniper berries

2 bay leaves

6 black peppercorns

3 cardamom pods

5 star anise

1 (8- to 10-pound) bone-in fresh ham, skin removed

FOR BAKING

½ cup olive oil

4 garlic cloves, chopped

2 tablespoons Dijon mustard

1 tablespoon white miso

1 teaspoon ground cumin

1 teaspoon coriander seeds

1 teaspoon caraway seeds

Needles from 1 sprig rosemary

2 tablespoons honey

FOR THE BRINE

1 You'll need a pot large enough to hold the brine and the ham.

2 Bring 2 quarts of the water, the salt, brown sugar, pink salt, chiles, smashed garlic, and spices to a boil in a large pot over high heat. Stir to dissolve the salts and remove the pot from the heat. Pour in the remaining 4 quarts water and cool the brine to room temperature.

3 Put the ham in the brine, cover, and refrigerate for 4 days. Remove the ham from the brine, set it on a rack placed over a rimmed baking sheet, and refrigerate, uncovered, overnight to dry.

continued on page 174 →

FOR BAKING

4 Preheat the oven to 225°F. Put the ham fat side up in a roasting pan.

5 Put the olive oil, chopped garlic, mustard, miso, cumin, coriander and caraway seeds, and rosemary into a blender and puree. Pour over the ham, spreading it to cover the top completely. It will form a soft crust as the ham bakes.

6 Bake the ham for 7 hours.

7 Take the ham out of the oven and turn the temperature up to 375°F. Mix 2 tablespoons of the pan juices with the honey and brush half of it on the ham. Bake the ham until it reaches an internal temperature of 155°F, about 45 minutes. Brush it with the remaining glaze about halfway through.

8 Leave the ham to rest on a cutting board for 20 minutes before carving.

THINGS TO DO WITH LEFTOVERS

✓ make sandwiches

✓ make hash

✓ dice it up, heat it up, and scramble eggs into it

✓ use the bone when you cook greens

✓ use the bone when you cook beans

✓ add it to the lentil soup on page 343

You'll find this old-school classic in many restaurants in Sweden. In a way, it's glorified hash, but it's made fresh, with the most tender cut of beef. And the combination of mustard, tarragon, and horseradish with the beef and potatoes is addictive. Our customers love it.

AUNT GRETE'S BEEF

SERVES 4

1 Put the beef into a bowl. Add the miso and massage it into the beef. Spoon in 1 tablespoon of the oil and toss with your hands. Season with salt and pepper. Leave it on the counter.

2 Heat 1 tablespoon of the oil in a skillet over medium heat. Add the onions, mustard seeds, and a pinch of salt and cook, stirring, until the onions have softened, about 10 minutes. Add the vinegar and cook until the skillet is just about dry, about 30 seconds. Scrape the onions out into a bowl and wipe out the skillet.

3 Heat the remaining 3 tablespoons of the oil in the skillet over medium heat. Add the potatoes, season with salt and pepper, and cook, stirring occasionally, until the potatoes are beginning to brown, about 10 minutes. Cover the skillet and cook, shaking the pan occasionally, until the potatoes are tender, about 10 minutes. Add the butter and cook, stirring, until the potatoes drink up the butter, about 1 minute. Scrape the potatoes into the bowl with the onions.

4 Whisk the egg yolks, mustard, wasabi, and tarragon together.

5 Heat a large skillet over high heat. When it's hot (a few drops of water should skitter over the surface), add the beef in a single layer. Leave it alone for 1 minute, then stir and take off the heat. The beef will stick; don't worry. Add the potatoes and onions and stir well, scraping the bottom of the pan. The juices from the onions will release all the browned bits. Stir in the egg yolk and mustard dressing.

6 Divide among bowls, top with horseradish, and serve.

1 pound beef tenderloin, cut into ½-inch dice

1 tablespoon dark miso

5 tablespoons grapeseed oil

Coarse kosher salt and freshly ground black pepper

2 red onions, chopped medium

2 teaspoons mustard seeds

2 tablespoons sherry vinegar

1 pound Yukon gold potatoes, peeled and cut into ½-inch dice

1 tablespoon unsalted butter, softened

4 large egg yolks

1½ tablespoons Swedish sweet mustard (see page 26)

½ teaspoon wasabi powder

1 tablespoon chopped fresh tarragon leaves

2 tablespoons horseradish, preferably freshly grated

CRAB *in a* LETTUCE CUP

SERVES 4 AS AN APPETIZER

Sweet and tangy crab salad, fiery peanuts, some cucumber, pickles, and radish are all piled into a lettuce leaf. This is an old-style dish with a twist. It's equally comfortable in a restaurant as it is at Mom's dinner party.

FOR THE CHILE-LIME PEANUTS

1 cup peanuts

2 tablespoons chipotle chile powder

Grated zest of 2 limes

FOR THE CRAB SALAD

½ cup mayonnaise, preferably Kewpie

½ cup sour cream

2 teaspoons yuzu kosho (see page 30) or wasabi paste

2 tablespoons fresh lime juice

1 pound jumbo lump crab meat, gently picked over for cartilage and shell

FOR SERVING

Bibb lettuce leaves

¼ daikon radish, cut into thin matchsticks

1 cucumber, halved, seeded, and cut into thin matchsticks

Mint leaves

Pickled Cucumbers and Radishes (see Pickles at the Rooster, page 244)

FOR THE CHILE-LIME PEANUTS

1 Put the peanuts and chipotle chile powder into a food processor and pulse 5 or 6 times. Pour into a bowl and stir in the lime zest.

FOR THE CRAB SALAD

2 Whisk the mayonnaise, sour cream, yuzu kosho, and lime juice together in a mixing bowl. Fold in the crab meat, taking care not to break it up. Cover and chill for 20 minutes.

TO SERVE

3 Spoon the crab salad into a serving bowl. Put it out with a platter of the lettuce, radish, cucumber, and mint; a bowl of the pickles; and the bowl of peanuts. Let each guest fill the lettuce as desired.

CRAB MAN MIKE

For twenty-five years now, Crab Man Mike goes up to the Hunts Point market in the Bronx to pick up crabs and clams, lobsters and shrimp, then comes back to Harlem to set up his propane fire and the big pot. He drops in his own blend of herbs and spices, adds water, and cooks up batches of seafood to sell.

A couple of years back now, I walked by Mike's usual location at Fifth Avenue and 124th Street and found out that he'd moved. I tracked him down to 132nd and Seventh to ask why. He told me that all the new faces and big crowds and bustling sales were making him uncomfortable. He wanted a slower pace, selling his seafood to people he knew.

Crab Man Mike wanted to be part of his customers' lives, knowing their families, their troubles, their joys. I started learning about that kind of hospitality from the first days I visited Harlem as a young cook. And I wanted to share Mike's version of it with my customers at Rooster. So now, Crab Man Mike comes by once a year and sets up his magic pot in the bar. He boils up crabs, and we all talk and eat and listen to music. And enjoy each other.

Crab Man Mike wanted to be part of his customers' lives, knowing their families, their troubles, their joys. I started learning about that kind of hospitality from the first days I visited Harlem as a young cook.

TROUT *with* GINGER *and* CITRUS

SERVES 4

W ell, you won't find trout in the Harlem River, but you will find fishing there and in the Hudson. I see these guys with their fishing poles and ask where they're going and—as a joke—if they're going to eat what they catch (the Hudson is still a polluted river). They all know what the rules are for eating fish from the Hudson, and they tell me if they catch the right fish—some are safe to eat—they surely *are* going to eat it. The kids come to learn the tradition from Dad. And the city has programs every year to educate about fishing in New York City's waters.

This dish is a little Asian and a lot New York. It's got mushrooms, bok choy, and water chestnuts, and trout rubbed with ginger and garlic, all swimming in a citrusy broth.

---

4 ounces shiitake mushrooms

FOR THE BROTH

2 cups water

2 cups fresh orange juice

1 cup dry white wine

Juice of 2 limes

2 tablespoons soy sauce

1 tablespoon white miso

1 (3-inch) piece ginger, sliced and smashed

1 stalk lemongrass, trimmed and smashed (see page 28)

FOR THE VEGETABLES

2 tablespoons olive oil

2 garlic cloves, sliced

1 shallot, sliced thin

2 Thai bird chiles, sliced thin; or 1 teaspoon hot red pepper flakes

1 teaspoon white sesame seeds

1 (8-ounce) can water chestnuts, drained and sliced

4 baby bok choy, cut in ½-inch slices

1 tablespoon soy sauce

1 tablespoon chopped fresh dill

FOR THE TROUT

2 tablespoons plus 1 teaspoon olive oil

3 tablespoons soy sauce

2 teaspoons honey

1 (2-inch) piece ginger, peeled and grated on a rasp grater

2 garlic cloves, grated on a rasp grater

2 teaspoons chopped fresh dill

4 (6- to 8-ounce) trout fillets

1 Pull the stems from the shiitake caps. You'll use the stems for the broth. Slice the caps and save them for the vegetables.

FOR THE BROTH

2 Combine all the ingredients—including the shiitake stems—in a saucepan and bring to a simmer over medium-high heat. Stir to dissolve the miso. Turn the heat to low and simmer for 20 minutes. Strain and return the broth to the pot (discard the solids). Keep warm.

FOR THE VEGETABLES

3 Heat the oil in a skillet over medium heat. Add the garlic, shallot, chiles, and sesame seeds and cook until the shallot is soft, about 2 minutes. Add the shiitake caps and cook, stirring often, for 2 minutes. Add the water chestnuts, bok choy, and soy sauce and cook, stirring, until the bok choy is wilted and everything is hot, about 2 minutes. Stir in the dill.

FOR THE TROUT

4 Stir 2 tablespoons of the olive oil, the soy sauce, honey, ginger, garlic, and dill together. Rub it over both sides of the trout.

5 Heat the remaining 1 teaspoon olive oil in a large nonstick skillet over medium-high heat. Add the trout, skin side down, and cook for 3 minutes. Flip the fish and cook until just cooked through, about 90 seconds.

6 Divide the vegetables between four shallow bowls. Pour in the broth, dividing it equally. Top with the trout and serve.

Hold each water chestnut on its edge and cut down to make 2 thin slices.

WHOLE FRIED FISH *with* GRITS

SERVES 6

S picy, moist fish with a cornmeal crust paired with lush, cheesy grits has got to be one of my favorite combinations. Swedes would eat a dish like this with a knife and fork; Africans would eat it with their hands—pulling off a morsel of fish and swiping it through the grits with their fingers. All would be equally tidy at the table.

→ **Start soaking the grits the night before.**

FOR THE CREAMY GRITS

1½ cups stone-ground grits, soaked overnight in a large saucepan with 4½ cups water

2¼ cups milk

¾ cup heavy cream

1½ cups chicken broth

1 teaspoon white miso

2 tablespoons unsalted butter, softened

½ cup shredded cheddar cheese

½ cup freshly grated Parmesan cheese

¼ teaspoon freshly grated nutmeg

Coarse kosher salt and freshly ground black pepper

FOR THE DIPPING SAUCE

¼ cup olive oil

Juice of 2 lemons

1 tablespoon Korean hot pepper paste (gochujang; see page 29)

1 teaspoon fish sauce

1 tablespoon chopped fresh cilantro

1 teaspoon brown sugar

FOR THE FISH

3 (1½ pounds each) snappers or striped bass, scaled and gutted

1 (3-inch) piece ginger, peeled and grated

4½ teaspoons Korean hot pepper paste (see page 29)

1½ teaspoons toasted sesame oil

¾ cup cornstarch

¾ cup cornmeal

1 tablespoon coarse kosher salt

Peanut oil for frying

FOR THE CREAMY GRITS

1 Add the milk, cream, broth, and miso to the grits and their soaking water and bring to a simmer, stirring, over medium-high heat. Turn the heat down to low, cover, and simmer for 20 minutes. Give the grits a good stir every 5 minutes. Put the saucepan in a skillet of barely simmering water for at least 20 minutes. When you're ready to serve, stir in the butter and cheeses and season with the nutmeg and salt and pepper to taste.

FOR THE DIPPING SAUCE

2 Stir all the ingredients together.

FOR THE FISH

3 Cut several slashes to the bone on both sides of the fish. Mix the ginger, chili paste, and sesame oil. Rub over the fish—including inside the cavities.

continued on page 182 →

4 Put the cornstarch, cornmeal, and salt into a large shallow bowl and whisk to combine.

5 Fill a wok half full with peanut oil. Set over medium-high heat and heat the oil to 350°F. Dredge one of the snappers in the dry ingredients, pat off any excess, and fry for 5 minutes. Use two spatulas to turn the fish over and fry until cooked through, another 5 minutes (you can make a cut with a paring knife and peek; the fish should be barely translucent). Monitor the temperature of the oil and adjust the heat to keep it between 340° and 360°F. Transfer the fish to a rack set over a rimmed baking sheet. Fry the remaining fish.

6 To serve, divide the grits between six dinner plates. Cut off the fish heads and put them on their own plate for picking. Cut each fish through the bone into two portions. Set the fish on the grits and serve with little bowls of the dipping sauce.

If you don't have a wok, use a deep skillet. The tails will probably not fit. You can let them hang off the edge or cut them off. Fill the skillet with ½ inch of oil.

The lime juice melts the seasoning paste you've cooked the fish with and gives the halibut a glaze that looks like lacquer. And I like to think of the eggplant as a gentle pillow for the fish to lie down on.

LACQUERED HALIBUT *with* CHARRED EGGPLANT *and* SPINACH

SERVES 2

FOR THE EGGPLANT

1 Set a rack in the middle of the oven and preheat the broiler. Lightly crumple a piece of aluminum foil (it will keep the eggplant from rolling) and set it on a small rimmed baking sheet.

2 Rub the eggplant with olive oil and set it on the foil. Slide the pan into the oven and broil the eggplant, turning it several times, until the skin is charred and split in spots and the flesh feels soft, 15 to 20 minutes. Cool on a cutting board.

3 Meanwhile, heat a small cast-iron skillet over medium-high heat. Char the jalapeño and garlic until the chile is blistered and charred all over and the garlic is browned in spots, about 10 minutes. Cool on the cutting board.

4 When the vegetables are cool enough to handle, peel the eggplant, cut it into chunks and put it in a food processor. Stem, seed, and chop the jalapeño and add it to the processor. Peel the garlic and add to the processor. Spoon in 2 tablespoons olive oil and puree.

5 Heat a skillet over high heat. Add the water and spinach and cook, tossing with tongs, until the spinach wilts, 30 seconds to 1 minute. Turn off the heat, stir in the eggplant puree, and taste for salt and pepper.

FOR THE HALIBUT

6 Mix 2 tablespoons of the olive oil, the ketjap manis, minced garlic, and dill in a small bowl to make a seasoning sauce.

continued on page 185 →

FOR THE EGGPLANT

1 medium eggplant (about ¾ pound)

Olive oil

1 jalapeño chile

1 garlic clove, whole and unpeeled

2 tablespoons water

1 packed cup baby spinach

Coarse kosher salt and freshly ground black pepper

FOR THE HALIBUT

2 tablespoons plus 1 teaspoon olive oil

1 tablespoon ketjap manis (see page 29)

1 garlic clove, minced

2 teaspoons chopped fresh dill

2 (10-ounce) bone-in halibut steaks (about 1 inch thick)

2 tablespoons unsalted butter

Juice of ½ lime

7 Heat the remaining 1 teaspoon olive oil in a nonstick skillet over medium heat. When it's hot, brush the halibut liberally with the seasoning sauce and add to the skillet. Cook for 4 minutes. Turn the fish over and add the butter to the skillet. Cook, basting often, for another 4 minutes. Add the lime juice and cook, basting constantly, for another minute.

8 Divide the eggplant and spinach between two dinner plates. Top with a piece of halibut steak and serve.

There's a big advantage to cooking halibut—which doesn't have a lot of fat—on the bone. It helps keep the fish moist and juicy. And since it's just one big bone, it's easy to pull off; there are no pin bones to worry anyone.

ROOSTER DONUTS *with* SWEET POTATO CREAM

MAKES ABOUT 85 LITTLE DONUTS

We wanted a donut that would be ours, and one that had some ties to the South. The solution? The quintessentially Southern sweet potato, which we turned into a gently spiced sweet potato pastry cream. A little familiar and a little surprising, it's become a signature dessert.

This makes lots, so serve them to a crowd.

FOR THE SWEET POTATO CREAM

1 (12-ounce) sweet potato

1½ cups milk

3 large egg yolks

¼ cup granulated sugar

¼ cup cornstarch

Coarse kosher salt

2 packed tablespoons brown sugar

1 teaspoon vanilla extract

¼ teaspoon ground cinnamon

FOR THE DONUTS

⅓ cup warm water

1½ teaspoons active dry yeast

⅓ cup granulated sugar

5 large eggs, at room temperature, lightly beaten

3½ cups bread flour

1 teaspoon coarse kosher salt

2 sticks (½ pound) cold unsalted butter, cut into cubes

1 teaspoon vanilla extract

Safflower oil for frying

TO FINISH

1 cup granulated sugar

1 teaspoon ground cinnamon

FOR THE SWEET POTATO CREAM

1 Heat the oven to 400°F. Line a small rimmed baking sheet with parchment.

2 Prick the sweet potato all over with the tip of a paring knife. Set the potato on the baking sheet and bake until soft and any juices that have oozed out have started to caramelize, about 45 minutes. Cool completely.

3 Bring the milk to a boil in a saucepan over medium heat.

4 Meanwhile, whisk the egg yolks, granulated sugar, cornstarch, and a pinch of salt together in a bowl.

5 While whisking, pour the boiling milk into the beaten yolks. Return this pastry cream to the saucepan and cook, whisking, until it comes to a simmer and thickens. Scrape the pastry cream out into a bowl.

6 Peel the sweet potato and measure 1 cup of the flesh. Put it in a food processor with the brown sugar, vanilla, and cinnamon and process until smooth.

7 Scrape the sweet potato into the pastry cream and whisk. Cover with plastic wrap, pressing it onto the surface, and refrigerate until cold. You can make this a day ahead.

FOR THE DONUTS

8 Pour the water into the bowl of a stand mixer. Add the yeast and sugar, stir, and let sit until creamy, about 5 minutes.

9 Add the eggs, flour, and salt and beat with the hook attachment on medium speed for 15 minutes. The dough will be very tight. Scrape it down and continue to beat, adding the butter in several additions and scraping down before each addition. Add the vanilla and continue to beat on medium speed until the dough is glossy, about 15 minutes from when you start adding the butter.

10 Cover the bowl with a clean kitchen towel and set in a warm place to rise until doubled, about 1 hour.

11 Line three rimmed baking sheets with parchment and dust lightly with flour.

12 Turn the dough out onto a lightly floured surface (a cold surface is best) and roll out to ½ inch thick. The dough may seem greasy; don't worry. Use a 1-inch round cutter to cut out the donuts, setting them on the baking sheets with at least an inch between them. Gather the scraps together, knead, and roll out again and cut more donuts (they may not be as pretty as the first ones, but they'll be just as tasty). Cover with a kitchen towel and let rise until doubled in size, about 1 hour.

13 Fill a large saucepan one-third full with safflower oil. Set over medium-high heat and heat the oil to 360°F. Working in batches, fry the donuts until golden brown all over, 2 to 3 minutes. Drain on a rack set over a rimmed baking sheet.

TO FINISH

14 Mix the sugar and cinnamon in a shallow bowl.

15 Fill a pastry bag fitted with a ¼-inch plain tip with the sweet potato cream.

16 While the donuts are still warm, pierce them with the tip and pipe in the cream. Roll the donuts in the cinnamon sugar and serve warm. If you have leftover sweet potato cream, put it out in a bowl so your guests can dip the donuts in it.

When President Obama came to eat at Red Rooster, we had a lot of NYC cops on duty up and down Lenox Avenue. I sent some of the waitstaff out with trays of Rooster donuts. Their smiles told me Rooster had arrived in Harlem.

"NO IS NEVER NO"

Melba Wilson is a pioneer in the Harlem restaurant scene. Part of Sylvia Woods's family, she always had her own idea for success—wanting to have her own restaurant on the west side of Harlem before the idea was popular. She opened in 2005 with great food, great hospitality, and the same DNA that is the song of Harlem.

I'm born, bred, and buttered in Harlem. I was born in Harlem Hospital and raised on 137th between Lenox and 7th, and then we moved to 144th between Lenox and 7th. Growing up in Harlem for me was really an extension of the South. A lot of people migrated here from South Carolina and North Carolina in search of better paying jobs. My mom didn't want to string tobacco any more where she made literally pennies on the dollar. She was the youngest of eleven, and she knew that if she moved up north, she would be able to make more money. She was eighteen, nineteen when she moved. She had brothers and sisters and cousins who were already up here. And they all lived together. And that was quite common in Harlem.

My momma would often tell stories about how Saturday, that was their day. I have photographs of my mom from back then. When they hung out, they got dressed. There was always a photographer and you had on your black dress, and it was a time to let your hair down, hear some great music, and celebrate life. Today I think about how I provide an opportunity and an outlet to celebrate life.

Harlem when I was a kid: I remember going to the corner and seeing the Renaissance Ballroom. And just oohing and ahhing and watching people come down, and they were dressed in their fur stoles and their wraps, and they had on makeup and the red lipstick. And to me, seeing those people was like seeing movie stars, they were celebrities to me. I just remember thinking *okay, this is how you step out on your big day.* That's what being born and raised in Harlem has given me.

In the late sixties, Harlem was a place where you could get told on by your neighbor. I mean nowadays, they have child services, but back then, try getting to the phone before your neighbor told on you to your parents. Just try it. You had embarrassed your momma and daddy. You were in a bunch of trouble.

In the late sixties, Harlem was a place where you could get told on by your neighbor.

Harlem was a lot of love; it was a lot of sharing. When folks were sick, it was like, "Melba, go take a plate down the hall, take this plate down the street, down the block." Every weekend me and my cousins were together. Harlem was about family; Harlem was about community; Harlem was about unity.

You knew on Sunday, you were going to *church*. You were putting your white socks on, you were putting your Mary Janes on. And your momma wore a hat, and on Easter you got your purse and your bonnet. *That* was

"Momma, please don't burn me. Please, Lord." And Momma on the phone with her head cocked like this, and the cord running down. That was my Harlem, the Harlem I loved.

I was surrounded by the arts, by the culture, by the song, by the celebration. I grew up with a lot of food and a lot of church. To me, Harlem is a place that everybody came with a dream. Sometimes that dream was just to make a little bit of money. And you sent that money back down South, to your sisters and your cousins so they could make it.

You knew on Sunday, you were going to *church*. You were putting your white socks on, you were putting your Mary Jane's on. And your momma wore a hat, and on Easter you got your purse and your bonnet. That was Harlem.

Harlem. And every girl who went to Harlem looked like that. It was a time to pay respect, it was a time to give thanks. And it was also a time to eat. Every church had a basement, every church had a kitchen, and boy, those church mommas could throw down. We all partook. Let me just say, my mother was a stickler. She was like, "Girl, don't go in there like you haven't eaten a meal. Don't embarrass me like that. Don't go in there like we ain't got no food up in here."

Sundays in Harlem was my mother doing my hair with a hot comb, sitting between her legs, my head on a pillow and holding my ear. The sizzle of the straightening comb.

The blueprint of my life is from the people who dreamt. Being a kid from Harlem, we had to be very resilient. It's in our fiber, it's in our being; it's in our bones. We know how to survive. No is never no to me. I have to go around it; I have to go through it. No is I have to work that much harder to get what I want. And Harlem prepares you for that. You can live here and navigate the waters of the world. You live in Harlem and you can say, "Oh, Lord, don't move this mountain, just give me the strength to climb." That's the foundation of the people in Harlem. That's my family. That's me.

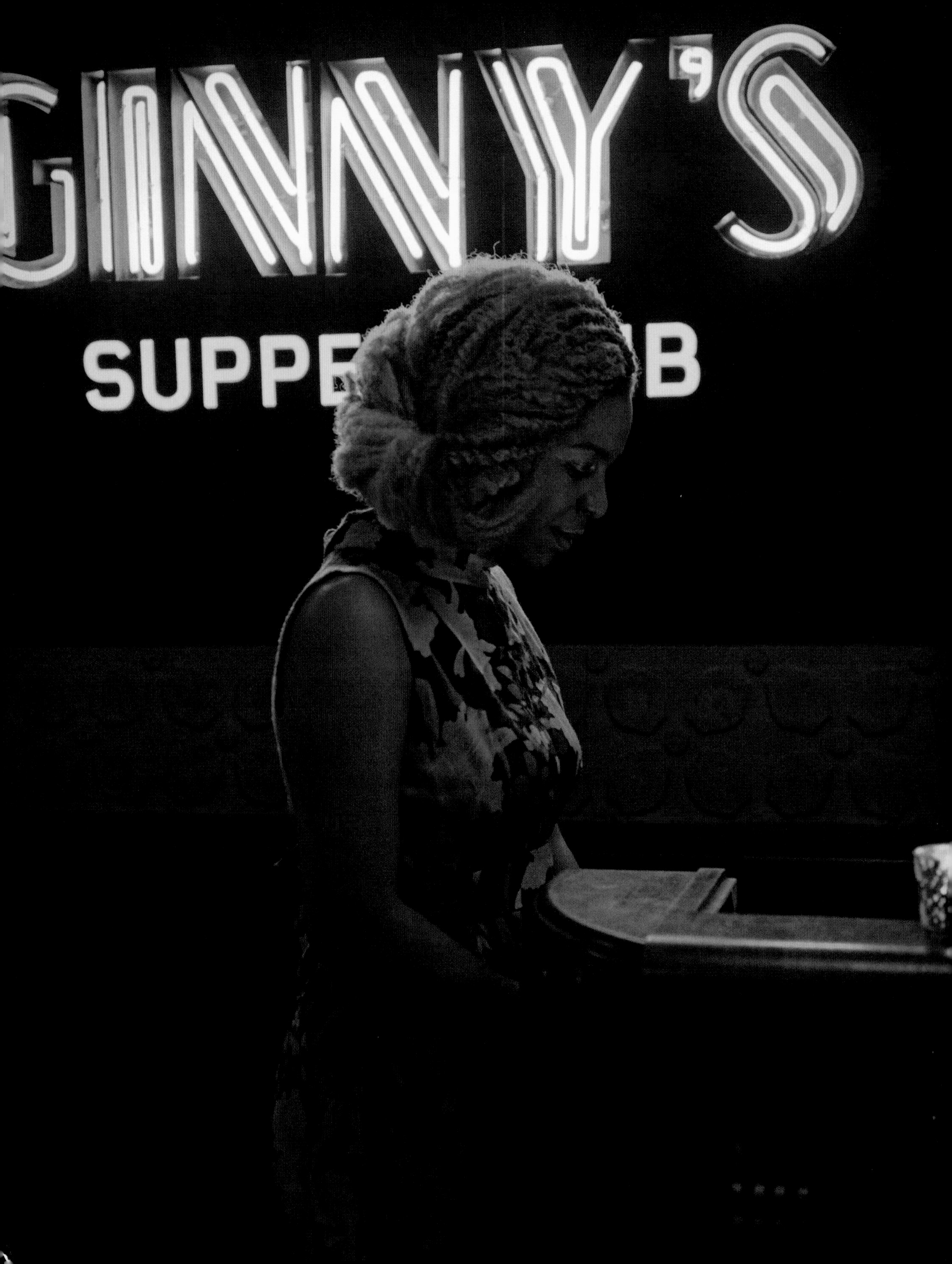
GINNY'S

FRIDAYS AT GINNY'S

IN THE BEGINNING, Ginny's was just a cement basement. A cavernous, near-empty space that stank. When the 2 and 3 subway trains roared beside us, the entire place shivered in response. Still, I fell in love with it. The space reminded me of the house parties I threw back in Sweden. My friends and I would find secret rooms, lit by a single light bulb that swayed back and forth to the music we had brought with us—Bob Marley, Prince, Michael Jackson. I would make platters of food and, in the winter, I would pass around pitchers of glögg. I loved those house parties. Every time I stepped inside the Rooster basement, I had visions of making the space a grown-up version of that time. That's what this room was meant to be. A place full of music, a sweaty crush of bodies dancing to song, where, when folks got hungry, they could eat the food they loved.

A place full of music, a sweaty crush of bodies dancing to song.

I didn't just draw on memories of my Swedish house parties; I also thought about Harlem's unique history. During the Great Migration, when black families had to think of creative ways to make money and pay their rent, there was always a rent party. And you didn't have to know the secret knock to get in. Aunts and uncles, mommas and daddies tore it up in the kitchen and in the parlor room. Candied yams, collard greens, neck bones and gravy were served alongside a three-man band. There was nothing amateurish about the culinary and musical performances. In fact, rent parties became so popular they began to hire professional musicians. Speckled Red, Willie "the Lion" Smith, and Fats Waller were just some of the musicians who were brought in to make rent. At their height, rent parties began to advertise:

If you're looking for a good time don't look no more
Just ring my bell and I'll answer the door
Southern Barbeque
Given by Charley Johnson and Joe Hot Boy and Oh How Hot!

Knowing that history gave us confidence. Yeah, the basement was smelly, but that didn't mean we couldn't throw a party. We still could give people good music, good food, and that unmistakable feeling that they had just stumbled upon the coolest family reunion ever. My business partner, Andrew Chapman, and I spent days picking out couches from a consignment shop called Housing Works, and we asked Scotty, an old craftsman from Harlem, to help us with as many finishing touches as we could afford. Sometimes we'd pick out items that he'd let us buy and other times, Scotty would look at the things we wanted and say, "Oh, I can't let you buy that. I love that thing." But the pièce de résistance was the disco ball I found at a second-hand shop on Frederick Douglass. I thought of it as my ball of hope. Bits of glass stuck to Styrofoam. When the lights hit it just so, it lit up our aspirations. A beautiful room, a state-of-the-art sound system for my friend Derek Fleming to book bands. With enough time and cash, we could pull that off. Derek, Andrew, and I had a long talk about our short money. We'll get there one day, we told each other. Just not today.

People would crowd in and move along to a shaking basement. We had a party for Sting. By the time Questlove said he would DJ with no A/C, I knew I could allow myself to start thinking about an entire overhaul. I thought about the speakeasies and supper clubs that flourished during the Harlem Renaissance, the furtive spaces so often found in New York City. All over Harlem, black people had created places where the music was exceptional, but not exclusive, where the food was familiar and exquisite. The invitations were for one and all. Come on. Come on by.

All over Harlem, black people had created places where the music was exceptional, but not exclusive, where the food was familiar and exquisite.

We were trying to tap into that vibe when we first opened Downstairs at the Rooster. It may have been a cement box, with divots in the wall and a little bar in the back corner, but it also was a place where we gathered and joked around at the staff's family meal before the evening shift; where musicians and a couple of neighbors could come in and fix themselves a plate. And after eating a little something, musicians asked if they could jam a little. I'd listen, amazed by how much I had in common with Braxton Cook, a terrific saxophonist, or Brianna Thomas, a wonderful great jazz vocalist (Bill Clinton is a fan). Musicians, like chefs, work crazy hours and love it. We'd trade stories about being "the entertainment," at fine dining establishments. I'd worked for a year at one of the top restaurants in Europe, but the first time I saw its dining room was the last day I worked there. Artists experienced something similar. They played their instruments, but they weren't invited to mingle.

Whatever we turned Downstairs at the Rooster into, it had to remain a place where my restaurant family felt comfortable. Where the musicians who played in Harlem could play on a stage *and* sit at a table. It had to remain true to our purpose: preserving and presenting great music. The first decision we made was to rename Downstairs at the Rooster "Ginny's," after the woman who had worked for Andrew's family and was a big part of his upbringing. She lived in Harlem, and we wanted to build a place where she could come and relax. And if Andrew, Derek, and I put our minds to it, we could turn the basement into a cultural space that had the thump and go of a rent party, the heart of a speakeasy, and the feel of home.

Whatever we turned Downstairs at the Rooster into, it had to remain a place where my restaurant family felt comfortable. Where the musicians who played in Harlem could play on a stage *and* sit at a table.

We threw ourselves into the project. Ginny's needed to possess the mood of Nina Simone, along with the African syncopation of Fela. We wanted a cool seventies' vibe; a telephone booth in the corner, the back wall like an old juke box. We wanted to replicate a certain New York and Harlem architecture: surprising and secret. The walls that created a smaller room in Ginny's were actually wide paneled doors. No one can see it, but we soundproofed the entire basement. So now, walking down the stairs and short hall meant our diners could move from the distinct vibe of the Rooster to an altogether different one at Ginny's.

Andrew handled the striking design details; Derek found the artwork, and I, of course, was in charge of the menu. Most supper clubs offer traditional American fare: steak and potatoes, shrimp cocktail. But I wanted to offer dishes beloved in Harlem. None is better known than chicken and waffles. You can always tell when a dish has reached iconic status. Suddenly folks argue about who invented it. The chicken and waffle dish that most folks know and love was born in Harlem, U.S.A., at the Wells Supper Club in 1938. It was first served to jazz musicians who had arrived at the supper club far too late for dinner, but way too early for breakfast. The fantastic crunch of the fried chicken along with the subtle sweet of the waffle is a perfect combination. I took my inspiration from musicians who thrill listeners with songs they think they know. So while I present a classic chicken and waffle, the surprise is the addition of chicken liver butter. As it melts over both the waffle and the chicken, it adds a deeply unctuous sweet taste to the entire dish.

Chicken and waffles were just the beginning. I put shrimp and grits, deviled eggs with chicken-skin mayo, and peanut-bacon pork chops on the menu. Dishes that may not be traditional American fare, but ones Harlemites knew were delicious.

We had the menu, we had the art, we had the details down cold. Along the way we even got lucky, and Ron Carter, the legendary jazz bassist, stopped in and gave us pointers about our sound system. All we needed now was the big opening act. Andrew, Derek, and I went round and round about who it should be. We weren't looking for the latest summer sensation. We wanted an icon. But what if an icon didn't want us? Never mind that. Who should it be? Andrew's dad gave us the answer.

Roberta Flack.

She was perfect. And she was so out of our league. Screw that. Go big or go home. Andrew's dad knew her, and though he couldn't promise she would do it, he would give us an introduction. We knew exactly what we were going to say to convince her. And really, what's the worst she could say?

She said no.

It wasn't one of those no's you get from people who are trying to let you down gently—it's not you, it's me; I would do it, but I'm washing my hair; I would love to but I have to start a brand new company. It was just no. I felt like Roberta had taken a chef's knife to my chest and carved out my heart.

"So what are we going to do now?" Derek said.

"We beg." I told them.

And we did. Please Ms. Roberta Flack, please. She was on tour, she told us. But can't you give us one night? Any night at all? I think she relented to save us from ourselves. And once she said yes, I got really scared.

Listen, she said, this is how this is going to work. I'm not going to raise my voice; you're not going to serve drinks and food while I sing.

There was no way Ginny's would have Roberta Flack as its first opening act and fourteen people show up. I opened my Rolodex and pleaded with everyone to come. Bring your mom. And your cousin. But making sure there was a full house was the least of my troubles. Of course everyone was coming; Roberta Flack was going to be there. The real problem was that I'm a chef and when I want to get things done, I cook it. Or I cook around it. I couldn't cook Roberta Flack. Her band showed up for the four o'clock rehearsal, tuning their instruments, looking relaxed. They had done this a thousand times. I realized this wasn't a situation where I could call my purveyor and ask him where the hell is my chicken? My fish? My Roberta Flack? Everything was out of my hands. The show started at eight o'clock.

She walked in the door at 7:59.

I'll always remember what she said as she settled on her stool. Listen, she said, this is how this is going to work. I'm not going to raise my voice; you're not going to serve drinks and food while I sing. And I want you to clap for my band. Let's enjoy the night.

It was magic. She tore it down.

A hundred and fifty people were held spellbound. When Andrew's dad whispered to me, "There's no way you can top this. You might think about closing the joint, now, " Andrew and I started laughing.

We tell everyone who will listen: You come on in; come on by.

Ginny's has changed since Roberta, April 2012. But so have we. Sometimes I feel as if we are reclaiming that original spirit of the Harlem rent party. We've had incredible jam sessions with Alicia Keyes and John Legend. And when the community needs to mourn or celebrate; when my neighborhood looks around and wonders how to make the ends meet, we gather to eat, drink, dance, and think at Ginny's. We tell everyone who will listen: You come on in; come on by. Come look at Derrick Adams' art; come listen to a Harlem gospel choir; come hear Wynton Marsalis share his gift; come celebrate Harlem EatUp! and watch me and Charleston chef Sean Brock play with good things to eat; come grieve and think about South Carolina. Come inside a place with big dreams and a disco ball. Come.

GINNY'S PLAYLIST

"THE IMPALER" Jeff "Tain" Watts

"HEART AND SOUL" Ron Carter/Cedar Walton Duo

"THE JOINT IS JUMPIN'" Fats Waller

"STARDUST" Brianna Thomas

"LOVE AND BROKEN HEARTS" Wynton Marsalis

"YOU ARE MY HEAVEN" Roberta Flack featuring
Donny Hathaway

"COFFY IS THE COLOR" Roy Ayers featuring
Dee Dee Bridgewater

"ENTERTAINER" Jonathon Batiste

"AFRO BLUE" Robert Glasper Experiment
featuring Erykah Badu

"WIDE OPEN" Braxton Cook

DEVILED EGGS *with* CHICKEN-SKIN MAYO

SERVES 6 AS AN APPETIZER

No gathering in the South would be complete without a platter of deviled eggs. What sets ours apart is the bed of rich chicken-skin mayonnaise we serve them on. Tradition has it that the best way to eat a deviled egg is in one bite, but with this mayo, you're going to want to double dip.

We make our own duck salumi, but you can purchase duck salumi from several vendors or from amazon.com.

FOR THE CHICKEN-SKIN MAYO (MAKES ABOUT 1 CUP)

2 fried chicken drumsticks (from Fried Yardbird, page 85)

¾ cup mayonnaise

Coarse kosher salt

FOR THE DEVILED EGGS

6 large eggs

¼ cup mayonnaise

½ teaspoon sweet paprika

Coarse kosher salt

Chopped fresh chives and duck salumi for garnish (optional)

FOR THE CHICKEN-SKIN MAYO

1 Pull the meat and skin off the chicken bones and put into a food processor. Process to a fine mince. Add the mayonnaise and process, scraping down the sides as needed, until very smooth, 5 to 6 minutes. Taste and season with salt. Scrape the mayo out into a bowl, cover, and refrigerate until you need it. It will keep for up to 2 days.

FOR THE DEVILED EGGS

2 Put the eggs in a saucepan in a single layer, cover with cold water by 2 inches, and bring to a boil over medium-high heat. Cover the pan, turn off the heat, and let the eggs sit for 12 minutes. Drain the water off the eggs, and shake the eggs in the pan, cracking the shells. Cover with cold running water. Pour the water off, and fill again with cold water. Then let the eggs cool for a few minutes.

3 Peel the eggs and slice them in half lengthwise.

4 Carefully pop the yolks out of the whites and put them in a mini food processor with the mayonnaise and paprika. Process until completely smooth. Taste and season with salt. (You can also do this in a bowl, mashing and stirring with a fork). Scrape the filling into a pastry bag.

5 Spread ½ cup chicken-skin mayo on a platter. Set the whites on the mayo, pipe in the filling, and garnish with chives and salumi if you want.

CORN-OYSTER SOUP

SERVES 4

There are some great high notes here. The natural sweetness of summer corn. The briny saltiness of oysters. Pureeing the oysters with the corn infuses this soup with more pure ocean flavor than you'd think possible from just four oysters.

2 ears corn, shucked

1 red onion, peeled and quartered

Olive oil

2 garlic cloves, unpeeled

½ teaspoon fresh thyme leaves

8 oysters

2 cups bottled clam juice

1 cup dry white wine

1 cup water

1 cup heavy cream

Juice of 2 limes

1 teaspoon Aleppo pepper (see page 27)

Coarse kosher salt and freshly ground white pepper

1 tablespoon chopped fresh dill

1 Preheat the oven to 350°F.

2 Rub the corn and onion with olive oil and place on a small rimmed baking sheet with the garlic. Roast until the garlic is tender and the onion is softened and browned at the tips, 25 minutes.

3 Cool slightly, then cut the kernels from the cobs (keep the cobs for later) and peel the garlic. Put into a food processor with the onion and thyme. Shuck 4 of the oysters and add them and their liquor to the processor and process until smooth, 1 to 2 minutes.

4 Put the clam juice, wine, water, cream, lime juice, Aleppo pepper, and the cobs into a saucepan and bring to a boil over medium-high heat. Turn the heat down to medium and cook at an active simmer until reduced by one third, about 30 minutes.

5 Take the pot off the heat and let the soup sit for 30 minutes. Stir in the corn puree and add salt and pepper to taste. Stir in the dill.

6 Divide the soup between four bowls and garnish each serving with a shucked oyster.

You're adding the puree when the soup is warm—not hot—so the oysters in the puree don't cook and change texture.

SHRIMP, BIRD, and GRITS

SERVES 4

There's a sense of discovery with jazz. Notes that surprise you; riffs that take a sudden turn. There's surprise and discovery in this dish, too. There's a play of textures with the snap of the shrimp, the creaminess of the grits, the little crunch from the bird powder, the tenderness of the chicken. Each bite is different.

→ **If you make your own pimiento cheese, use it. Otherwise, the grocery-store stuff is fine. You'll need to soak the grits overnight.**

FOR THE BIRD

Peanut oil for frying

2 bone-in, skin-on chicken thighs

All-purpose flour

3 saltine crackers

1 teaspoon freshly grated Parmesan cheese

FOR THE GRITS

1 cup chicken broth or fish stock

1 cup tomato juice

½ cup milk

½ cup heavy cream

1 teaspoon shrimp powder (see page 30) or white miso

1 cup grits, soaked overnight in a saucepan with 3 cups water

1 tablespoon unsalted butter, softened

4 to 6 tablespoons pimiento cheese

Coarse kosher salt and freshly ground white pepper

FOR THE SHRIMP

2 tablespoons olive oil

½ cup corn kernels

2 garlic cloves, minced

1 pound large (21–30 count) shrimp, peeled and deveined

Coarse kosher salt

1 cup tomato juice

Juice of ½ lemon

FOR THE POACHED EGGS

4 large eggs

¼ cup distilled white vinegar

FOR THE BIRD

1 Fill a small saucepan one-third full with peanut oil. Set the pan over medium-high heat and heat the oil to 360°F.

2 Dust the chicken thighs with flour, pat off excess, and deep-fry until the meat reaches an internal temperature of 165°F, about 10 minutes. Pull the skin off right away and drain the thighs and skin on a rack set over a rimmed baking sheet.

3 When the skin has cooled, chop it and put it in a mini food processor with the saltines and Parmesan. Grind to make the bird powder.

There's surprise and discovery in this dish, too.

FOR THE GRITS

4 Add the broth, tomato juice, milk, cream, and shrimp powder to the grits and soaking water and bring to a simmer, stirring, over medium-high heat. Turn the heat down to low, cover, and simmer for 20 minutes, giving the grits a good stir every 5 minutes. Put the saucepan in a skillet of barely simmering water for at least 20 minutes. When you're ready to serve, shred the chicken thigh meat and stir in into the grits with the butter and cheese. Season with salt and pepper to taste.

FOR THE SHRIMP

5 Heat the olive oil in a large skillet over medium-high heat. Add the corn and garlic and cook, stirring, until the garlic is fragrant, about 1 minute. Add the shrimp, season with salt, and sauté until the shrimp curl and start to turn pink, about 1 minute. Add the tomato juice and lemon juice and bring to a simmer. Simmer until the shrimp are just cooked through, about 2 minutes. Take off the heat.

FOR THE POACHED EGGS

6 Crack the eggs into four cups.

7 Fill a large saucepan about half full with water and bring to a simmer over medium-high heat. Add the vinegar and turn the heat down to low. Stir the water to create a vortex and drop in the eggs one by one. Poach the eggs for 4 minutes. Transfer to paper towels with a slotted spoon.

8 To serve, divide the grits between four shallow bowls. Make a well in the center of each and fill with a poached egg. Top with the shrimp and garnish with the bird powder.

PIMIENTO GRITTY CAKES

These are so good that you might just cook up a batch of grits so you can make a lot of them.

► Pack your leftover grits in a square or rectangular container— you'll want them about 1/2 inch thick—and refrigerate. The grits will set up.

► Heat 1/4 inch of grapeseed oil in a cast-iron skillet. Turn the grits out onto a cutting board and cut into squares or rectangles. Dredge them in corn flour, then beaten egg, then corn flour again. Fry the cakes until they're browned and crisp around the edges, maybe 5 minutes per side.

CATFISH *with* BLACKENING RUB, BEETS, *and* PEANUTS TOO

SERVES 4

The spice blend is everything here. There are only five ingredients, but the flavor is complex. Frying blooms the spices in a way that charring in a cast-iron skillet never can—and it won't set off your smoke alarm.

The last-minute sauce of lemon, soy, and dill adds a jolt of brightness. And the beets and peanuts will make your tongue smile.

FOR THE BLACKENING RUB

4 teaspoons tomato powder (see page 29)

4 teaspoons chipotle chile powder

4 teaspoons smoked paprika

4 teaspoons Wondra flour

1¼ teaspoons coarse kosher salt

FOR THE BEETS AND PEANUTS

1 lemon

3 tablespoons olive oil

2 cups diced (¼-inch) beets

1 cup diced (¼-inch) daikon radish

½ cup coarsely chopped peanuts

2 tablespoons soy sauce

1 tablespoon honey

1 tablespoon capers

1 tablespoon chopped fresh dill

FOR THE FISH

½ cup all-purpose flour

½ cup cornstarch

½ cup peanut oil

4 (6- to 7-ounce) catfish fillets

2 tablespoons unsalted butter, cut into small pieces

Juice of 2 lemons

2 tablespoons soy sauce

2 tablespoons chopped fresh dill

FOR THE BLACKENING RUB

1 Whisk all the ingredients together in a small bowl.

FOR THE BEETS AND PEANUTS

2 Cut the lemon into quarters lengthwise. Cut out the center membrane and nudge out the seeds. Dip the lemons into the blackening rub.

3 Heat the oil in a large skillet over medium heat. Set the lemon wedges around the edge of the skillet and place the beets and daikon in the center. Cook, turning the lemons once to sear both sides and stirring the beets and daikon often, for 5 minutes. Remove the lemon. Sprinkle the beets with 1 teaspoon of the rub and stir in the peanuts. Cook, stirring occasionally, until everything is golden brown, another 3 minutes. Turn the heat down to low and squeeze the juice from the lemon into the pan. Add the soy sauce, honey, and capers and cook, stirring constantly, until the vegetables and peanuts are nicely glazed, 1 to 2 minutes.

4 Spoon out into a serving bowl and garnish with the dill.

continued on page 208 →

FOR THE FISH

5 Preheat the oven to 375°F.

6 Mix the flour, cornstarch, and 2 tablespoons of the blackening rub in a shallow bowl.

7 Heat the oil in a large skillet over medium-high heat.

8 Dredge the fish fillets in the seasoned flour and lower them, skin side down, into the oil. Sprinkle the remaining blackening rub over the fish. Fry for 3 minutes. Flip the fish and fry for 2 minutes.

9 Transfer the fish, flipping it skin side down, to a rimmed baking sheet and dot with the butter. Bake until the fish is just cooked through, 2 to 3 minutes. Divide the fish between four dinner plates.

10 Stir the lemon juice, soy sauce, and dill together and spoon over the fish. Serve with the beets and peanuts.

YEP, CHICKEN *and* WAFFLES

SERVES 4 TO 6

Chicken and waffles, the story goes, was a dish that came about for the musicians who had played through dinner and on through the night, only sitting down to the table when the sun was coming up. They were missing dinner and wanting breakfast and made an ingenious compromise. There's music in this dish.

FOR THE CHICKEN

1 tablespoon grapeseed oil

1 shallot, minced

1 large garlic clove, minced

¼ cup Aleppo pepper (see page 27)

2 sprigs thyme

1 cup water

3 tablespoons coarse kosher salt

2 tablespoons sugar

2 cups buttermilk

8 boneless, skin-on chicken thighs

Peanut oil for frying

2 cups all-purpose flour

1½ teaspoons freshly ground black pepper

FOR THE WAFFLES

1½ cups all-purpose flour

½ cup cornstarch

1 teaspoon coarse kosher salt

1 teaspoon baking powder

½ teaspoon baking soda

1 teaspoon ground cinnamon

1½ cups buttermilk

½ cup milk

2 tablespoons grapeseed oil

2 large eggs, separated

1 teaspoon vanilla extract

2 tablespoons sugar

FOR SERVING

Mustard-Pickled Melon (optional; see Pickles at the Rooster, page 244)

Chicken Liver Butter (page 82)

FOR THE CHICKEN

1 Heat the grapeseed oil in a small saucepan over medium heat. Add the shallot and garlic and sauté until the shallot is translucent, about 2 minutes. Add the Aleppo pepper and thyme and cook, stirring, until very fragrant, 20 seconds. Don't let the pepper scorch. Add the water, 1 tablespoon of the salt, and the sugar and turn the heat up to medium-high. Bring to a boil, turn the heat down to medium-low, and simmer for 2 minutes.

2 Pour the seasoned water into the buttermilk and cool to room temperature.

3 Put the chicken into a 1-gallon zip-top bag and pour in the buttermilk marinade. Squeeze out the air, seal the bag, and massage to make sure all the thighs are coated in marinade. Refrigerate for at least 2 hours, or up to 24 hours.

4 Fill a large saucepan one-third full with peanut oil, set over medium-high heat and heat the oil to 360°F. Preheat the oven to 225°F.

5 Whisk the flour, the remaining 2 tablespoons salt, and the black pepper together in a bowl. Lift the chicken out of the marinade, let excess drip off, and dredge in the flour, packing it on.

continued on page 212 →

Set on a rack set over a rimmed baking sheet.

6 Working in batches, fry the chicken until it is a rich golden brown and has an internal temperature of 165°F, 5 to 7 minutes. Keep an eye on the heat and adjust it to keep the oil between 350° and 375°F. Drain the chicken on a rack set over a rimmed baking sheet. Slide the chicken into the oven to keep it warm. If the coating on the remaining chicken looks gummy, roll it in the flour again before frying.

FOR THE WAFFLES

7 Set a rack on a rimmed baking sheet and place in the oven.

8 Preheat the waffle iron to high.

9 Whisk the flour, cornstarch, salt, baking powder, baking soda, and cinnamon together in a bowl.

10 Whisk the buttermilk, milk, grapeseed oil, egg yolks, and vanilla together in another bowl.

11 Beat the egg whites to soft peaks with an electric mixer. Add the sugar gradually, beating all the while, and continue to beat until stiff peaks form.

12 Pour the wet ingredients into the dry and stir until just combined—some lumps are fine. Fold in the egg whites until just incorporated.

13 Spray the waffle iron with pan spray and pour in 1/2 cup of the batter. Follow the manufacturer's instructions to cook the waffle. But if

you have an iron that tells you when the waffle is done, cook for 1 minute more for a crisper waffle. Continue making waffles, setting the finished waffles on the rack in the oven to keep them warm and crisp until you're ready to serve. Leftover batter will keep, tightly covered in the refrigerator, for 1 day.

TO SERVE

14 Pile the chicken and waffles on platters and put them out with a bowl of pickles and the chicken liver butter. If you want a little sweetness with an edge, serve with the Spiced Maple Syrup (recipe follows) with a half shot of bourbon stirred in.

SPICED MAPLE SYRUP

> 1 cup maple syrup
> 3 or 4 dried red chiles

Bring the syrup and chiles to a boil in a small saucepan. Pour into a pitcher and let it sit until you're ready to serve.

PEANUT-BACON PORK CHOPS

SERVES 4

When in doubt, add bacon to pork. Then add peanuts for a smoky crunch. "Now you has jazz, jazz, jazz, jazz, jazz." (Thank you, Cole Porter.) Serve with Spicy Sweets and Green Beans (page 170).

"Now you has jazz, jazz, jazz, jazz, jazz."

FOR THE PEANUT-BACON SAUCE

½ pound bacon, chopped

½ cup roasted peanuts

2 shallots, minced

2 garlic cloves, minced

1 teaspoon mustard seeds

½ cup dry red wine

1 cup chicken broth

¼ cup juice from Pickled Cucumbers and Radishes (see Pickles at the Rooster, page 244) or pickled gherkins, plus 1 tablespoon chopped pickled cucumber or pickled gherkins

½ teaspoon fresh thyme leaves

1 tablespoon peanut butter

1 tablespoon unsalted butter

Coarse kosher salt and freshly ground black pepper

FOR THE PORK CHOPS

3 tablespoons olive oil

2 tablespoons Jerk Sauce (page 112)

4 (12-ounce) center-cut pork chops (1½ inches thick)

FOR THE PEANUT-BACON SAUCE

1 Cook the bacon and peanuts in a skillet over medium heat until the fat has rendered and the bacon is crisp, 12 to 14 minutes. Use a slotted spoon to transfer the bacon and peanuts to a bowl. Pour off all but about 1 tablespoon of the bacon grease. Add the shallots, garlic, and mustard seeds and cook, stirring, until the shallots have softened, about 2 minutes.

2 Add the wine and bring it to a simmer, stirring to dissolve the brown stuff in the skillet. Add the chicken broth, pickle juice, and thyme and bring to a simmer. Turn the heat down to medium-low and cook at a simmer until reduced by two thirds, about 25 minutes. Stir in the chopped pickle, peanut butter, butter, and the bacon and peanuts. Season to taste with salt and pepper. Keep warm.

FOR THE PORK CHOPS

3 While you're working on the sauce, mix 2 tablespoons of the olive oil with the jerk sauce. Rub over both sides of the pork chops.

4 Heat the remaining 1 tablespoon oil in a cast-iron skillet over medium heat. Add the pork chops and cook until they reach an internal temperature of 140°F, 6 to 7 minutes per side.

5 Let the chops rest on a cutting board for 5 minutes before serving with the sauce.

B- CRUSTED RACK *of* LAMB

SERVES 4

B, as in berbere, is the Ethiopian spice mix you combine with oil to make awase. Lamb is a very popular meat in Ethiopia for festive occasions; it's the first thing that disappears from the meat markets. Its slightly gamey flavor and delicious fat make it the perfect canvas to paint with awase.

2 racks of lamb, frenched

Coarse kosher salt and freshly ground black pepper

4 tablespoons Awase (page 61)

2 tablespoons Dijon mustard

Olive oil

4 garlic cloves, peeled

2 sprigs rosemary

2 tablespoons bread crumbs

1 tablespoon freshly grated Parmesan cheese

1 Preheat the oven to 375°F.

2 Season the lamb with salt and pepper and leave on the counter for 30 minutes.

3 Mix 2 tablespoons of the awase with 1 tablespoon of the mustard.

4 Heat a large cast-iron skillet over high heat. Add a slick of olive oil to the skillet and when it's smoking, sear the racks for 1 minute per side, starting with the fat side. Turn off the heat and slather the racks, still in the skillet, with the awase and mustard paste. Add the garlic and rosemary to the skillet, slide it into the oven and roast for 10 minutes.

5 Mix the bread crumbs and Parmesan and pack onto the lamb. Slide the skillet back into the oven and roast for 5 minutes. Use an instant-read thermometer to check for an internal temperature of 120° to 125°F for medium-rare. If your racks are large, you may need to roast them for another 5 minutes. Transfer the lamb to a cutting board, tent with foil, and let them rest for 10 minutes.

6 Pull the rosemary needles off the stems and crumble them into a small bowl. Smash the garlic with the side of a chef's knife and mince. Add the garlic to the rosemary, along with 2 tablespoons olive oil and the remaining 2 tablespoons awase and 1 tablespoon mustard.

7 Slice the chops between the bones and pile them onto a platter. Pass the bowl of sauce.

All across the South, cooks head out to their kitchen gardens as soon as there are big tomatoes on the vine. No, they don't wait for them to ripen; they pick them green, slice them, and shallow-fry them with a cornmeal crust. Cooling, tangy buttermilk dressing is my ideal complement to fried green tomatoes. You get two levels of sour playing off each other and off my spicy cornmeal and panko coating.

When I'm down at Ginny's listening to music, I often get the feeling I'm in a roadhouse down South. And I want fried green tomatoes to complete the picture.

FRIED GREEN TOMATOES *with* BUTTERMILK DRESSING

SERVES 4 TO 6 AS AN APPETIZER OR A SIDE

FOR THE DRESSING

1 Whisk all the ingredients together with a grind or two of pepper. Cover and refrigerate until you're ready for it.

FOR THE TOMATOES

2 Put the panko, cornmeal, Aleppo pepper, paprika, and salt and pepper to taste into a food processor and pulse until ground fine. Pour into a shallow bowl.

3 Heat 1/2 inch of oil in a large cast-iron skillet over medium-high heat. Dredge the tomato slices in the coating, patting it on. The oil will be ready when you press the handle of a wooden spoon down in the center of the skillet and a ring of bubbles forms around it immediately. In batches, fry the tomatoes until the coating is crisp and golden brown, about 2 minutes per side. Drain on a rack set over a rimmed baking sheet. Use a spider or slotted spoon to remove any of the coating that's fallen off between batches, and add more oil if necessary.

4 Serve with the buttermilk dressing.

FOR THE DRESSING

1 cup buttermilk

1 cup mayonnaise

1/2 cup sour cream

1 1/2 teaspoons chopped fresh chives

1 teaspoon minced garlic

1 teaspoon coarse kosher salt

Freshly ground black pepper

FOR THE TOMATOES

1 cup panko bread crumbs

1 cup cornmeal

2 tablespoons Aleppo pepper (see page 27)

1 tablespoon smoked paprika

Coarse kosher salt and freshly ground black pepper

Peanut oil or bacon grease for frying

4 green tomatoes, cored and sliced 1/3 inch thick

CHARRED SUMMER SUCCOTASH *with* COOLING YOGURT

SERVES 6 TO 8

A dish like this tastes better and better as summer heightens and produce comes into its own. Search out the best tomatoes, peppers, and fava beans in your area when you make this.

FOR THE YOGURT

1 tablespoon sesame seeds

1 teaspoon berbere
(see page 27)

1 cup Greek yogurt

1 tablespoon tahini

Grated zest of 1 lime

Juice of ½ lime

FOR THE SUCCOTASH

3 ripe tomatoes (preferably heirloom), cored and cut into ¾-inch dice

2 cups corn kernels

1 tablespoon olive oil

1 teaspoon paprika

Coarse kosher salt

4 slices bacon, chopped

4 tablespoons (½ stick) unsalted butter

1 tablespoon berbere

1 red bell pepper, seeded and diced

2 shallots, chopped

2 tablespoons diced poblano chile

1 tablespoon thinly sliced garlic

2 sprigs thyme

3 tablespoons apple cider vinegar

½ cup chicken broth

1 cup peeled fava beans (see opposite)

2 tablespoons chopped fresh mint

2 tablespoons chopped fresh basil

Freshly ground black pepper

Juice of ½ lime

FOR THE YOGURT

1 Toast the sesame seeds and berbere in a small skillet over low heat until fragrant, about 2 minutes. Add to the yogurt along with the tahini, lime zest, and lime juice. Stir well, cover, and refrigerate for at least 1 hour before serving.

FOR THE SUCCOTASH

2 Set a rack in the top position and preheat the broiler. Line a rimmed baking sheet with parchment.

3 Toss the tomatoes and corn with the olive oil, paprika, and salt to taste. Spread out on the baking sheet. Broil until the tomatoes and corn are charred, 5 to 8 minutes.

4 Cook the bacon in a large skillet over medium heat, stirring occasionally, until browned, about 6 minutes. Add the butter, berbere, bell pepper, shallots, poblano, garlic, and thyme and cook, giving it a stir once in a while, until the peppers begin to soften, about 5 minutes.

5 Pour in the vinegar and cook, scraping the bottom of the pan to dissolve any browned bits, until reduced by half, about 5 minutes. Add the broth and fava beans and simmer for 5 minutes.

6 Fold in the tomatoes and corn, the mint, and the basil and season with salt, pepper, and lime juice. Transfer to a serving bowl and serve with the yogurt on the side.

PREPPING FAVA BEANS

This is a three-step process.

- ► Shell the favas.

- ► Put the beans in a heatproof bowl and cover with boiling water.

- ► When the water has cooled to room temperature, make a nick with your thumbnail and pop the beans out of their skin.

You'll need 1 pound favas in the pod to get 1 cup prepped beans.

"MAKE A MARK"

Andrew Chapman opened Red Rooster Harlem and Ginny's Supper Club with Marcus. He is a co-founder of FoodRepublic.com, a food and lifestyle website. Here, he remembers the beginnings of the Rooster, the creation of Ginny's, and the woman who inspired him.

Initially, we were looking for a tiny place. I remember talking everything over with Marcus and we both thought, well let's do something that has ten to twelve tables. But we couldn't find anything that fit that bill. Then one day Derek showed us eighty-five-hundred square feet of Lenox Avenue real estate. I was more than a little intimidated by what it would mean to invest in a restaurant of that size, to sustain it. But then Marcus and I had a talk with my father.

He's old enough that he remembers Harlem in the nineteen-forties and when we told him about the space, he said, "Do it. The Cotton Club, Wells Supper Club, Minton's. Harlem was big. Make a mark." The more he spoke about a Harlem full of music and food and dance, the more convinced Marcus and I were that that's what the Rooster should aspire to.

We knew, almost from the beginning, that we wanted downstairs to be a space dedicated to music—jazz, blues, hip-hop, Motown. But because we lacked the money, we had to go slow. People came and sat on our hand-me-down couches and crummy chairs and had a great time because the food and music were so good. Even back then you could see the potential. At every step, we were making sure that our interests aligned with the neighborhood's.

Finally, we got the money together to do a major renovation. I remember being really nervous. Partly because, when you make a move like that, you think, well, let's not ruin it, but at the same time I also thought, let's create a space that honors the music we play and the

> **People came and sat on our hand-me-down couches and crummy chairs and had a great time because the food and music were so good.**

people who come. I think ultimately it was going to work out because the core of what we were doing wasn't going to change. Marcus would still be creating this wonderful soulful food every night; we still would be offering jazz and blues and live music.

We wanted Harlem artists represented, we were devoted to creating a space with great food and music; we wanted the downstairs to have the feel of a supper club, but we weren't building a relic. Basically, we wanted a lot. Because of our relationship with the community, a lot of artists came in and gave us invaluable advice. From that, we were able to build a state-of-the-art sound system. The works of art on the walls are from our friends in the neighborhood. All the details of the room create a funky but relaxed space. One of the questions Marcus and I kept asking ourselves is: But will it be fun?

The last piece of the puzzle was finding a name. For such a long time, we called downstairs what it was: Downstairs at the Rooster. Some people called it the Basement. But we wanted to re-open downstairs with a name that would be remembered. Everyone knows the Cotton Club or the Apollo. We wanted to stand out like that. Marcus, Derek, and I went around and around. Then one day it just knocked me on the head—Ginny's.

Ginny Streater, the woman who helped raise me. She was from Harlem. All of my childhood memories have her there. I love Motown and gospel because that's what she set the radio to when we were in the kitchen together. She introduced me to Southern food. In a strange way, she led me to Marcus. When he started talking to me about the Rooster menu, I knew what he was talking about. I know what grits are. I love grits.

I can't quite put into words how it makes me feel that I helped make a place that played the music she loved and served the food she introduced me to. She lived for a long time, and one of my happiest days was when I brought her here. I couldn't tell who was more pleased—her or me.

SATURDAY ON MY BLOCK

SATURDAY MORNINGS I wake up and want to follow my nose. In the summer with the windows thrown open, I can smell the preparations happening in the morning. Marcus Garvey Park is right outside; its jagged bedrock fills my window. I can't see the charred meat, the plantains in crates, the not-yet-fondled mangoes stacked and ready, but I can smell it all. I want to get outside, where there's music and food and aunties counting the number of hotdogs they've bought for a favored nephew's birthday.

Most days I run or bike, but on Saturdays I walk. If I leave my house early enough, I'm greeted by a quiet city. On the piers, fathers and sons fish for crab and perch, while they whisper about the need for patience and quiet. That's the secret to getting a bite on your line. The silence doesn't last for very long. Already the city is waking up. Inside Garvey Park, families are setting up celebrations. There's no cooking allowed in city parks, but as long as I've lived in Harlem, it's been a rule the officials don't want to enforce. There's a birthday party happening in the shadow of the cliff, and next to them, parents and friends are setting up a blue canopy for a kid's high school graduation party. Out come the folding chairs and tables. A grandfather dozes in one of them. Aluminum trays filled with Caribbean rice with pigeon peas or empanadas or potato salad are hefted out of beach bags. Balloons float and mingle with the leaves of birch trees. Around the grill, men and women are serious. "Don't put it like that, Papi."

"Put the ribs on that side."

"Not like that! Sth. Let me do this." The scold sounds harsh but when the guy next to her suddenly bows and hands her the tongs, they both start laughing. "Alright, alright. Fuck you." I can smell the ribs from where I stand. Cumin, paprika, garlic, and onion powder. The tang of lemon sizzling on fire fills my nose and follows me all the way to the basketball court, where I see guys my age playing pickup ball. "Yo, Man, you in?" The invitation makes me smile. I'm tempted, but the sharp ascent of the stone stairway beyond the court beckons. On it, a couple, unmindful of their audience, is making out. There's a whole park I haven't gotten to, never mind the neighborhood surrounding it.

The tang of lemon sizzling on fire fills my nose and follows me all the way to the basketball court, where I see guys my age playing pickup ball. "Yo, Man, you in?"

"Nah, Man. Maybe later." I walk away, but the smell of sweet, spicy, and salt on the ribs follows me.

There's a little farmers' market set up on the other side of the park. Rain or shine, this little band of farmers and cooks are out there, hawking their wares. Muffins and sandwiches, piles of watermelon and corn are stashed next to crates. These folks are selling more than fruits and vegetables, they're selling goodwill and good news. The guy making sandwiches is also running a cooking school for men newly released from prison and helps them find work on the outside. I want to know how many people he has helped get a job so far; does he follow up with the guys he's placed in restaurants? How are they doing? Are they making it work on the outside? Does he work with their families? Stop by the Rooster, I tell him. He looks surprised. "Are they hiring?"

"Yeah. Probably."

I wander over to the Jamaicans who are placing jerk-seasoned chicken and shrimp on their grill. "Rooster Man!"

"Morning, Chef!"

"I knew it was you." It's a family affair: a son and his wife, a twin brother, a cousin, a father and mother. "Now you gotta try this." I can smell the heat of the cayenne pepper, but also the allspice, sage, and a whiff of nutmeg. There's a half a dozen food stands I want to get to before I leave the park, but the father insists I stay. "Try the shrimp, Chef? You gonna love the banana bread, Chef. Try it, Chef." I'm licking my fingers, while the son tells me about his plans to go to culinary school.

"But what you think about this cooking school? He need to go, you think?" his mother asks, and I give them all my opinion. He should intern in a kitchen at a restaurant. Opening your own business is more than learning the mother sauces. If I know nothing else, I know cooking is not a formula; it's a way. What does it taste like to you, what's your stove doing, what's the weather like right outside your door? Cooking, the love of it, forces you ask those kinds of questions. And you do have to love it, love cooking, love making people happy with your food in this embarrassing, almost irrational way. Can you talk about chicken and carrots and vinegar all day long and never get bored? Can you work well under pressure? Can you deliver dishes with love and care for fifty people at the same time? His mother is nodding and smiling. "See? You see there? That's what I been saying. He can work with you, right?" I trade looks with her son, there's no way I'm saying no. She rewards me with another piece of banana bread. It's delicious.

Can you talk about chicken and carrots and vinegar all day long and never get bored? Can you work well under pressure?

There's a row of brownstones I walk past almost every day to get to the avenue and on Saturdays they are crowded with my neighbors. Music from the Commodores floats out of an open window and does battle with Lil Wayne whose rhymes thump out of a beatbox on the sidewalk. Everybody wins. It's midday but no one wants to shake loose of the good vibes of the morning. Old men pull up folding chairs and look ready to settle in. There'll be news and gossip to pass along. Some mother will stop by, set her groceries on the stoop, and tell everyone about the block party happening three blocks over. "You coming?" "Hell, yeah. They got BBQ." All throughout the summer, most of Harlem tumbles out of their apartments to escape the heat and dance, sing, and cook on their street. Guys selling their CDs out of their car trunks get up the nerve to grab the mike and rap a hook and a verse of their latest. They're praying they're good enough for a block of their neighbors to sing along. That their beats get little Darnell to do his impersonation of Michael Jackson, that the three hundred or so people morph into a choir and sing out, "Go; go; go; go; go." An hour or two from now all that might happen, but only if the men and women I'm standing with spread the word. They are good at it. Drinking coffee, the *Amsterdam News* tucked under their arms, they move from conversations about block parties to the state of the neighborhood.

Old men whose eyes are blue with cataract reminisce about their parents who fled the South and settled in Harlem, who witnessed race riots and lived to tell about them, who survived the crack epidemic. Those stories may not sound like happy ones, but they are. On the stoop, drinking bodega coffee, we swap stories about the progress of our neighborhood. How we love the ups and the downs. How what's important is that we bear witness. When I add to the conversation that on my block we used to have four methadone clinics and four jails, and now we are down to one and one, a man on the stoop throws his head back and laughs. Everyone joins in.

"Alright then. See, Chef? If that ain't progress what is?" We talk more, about what we have seen and what we have been told about the neighborhood. But all of that dialogue is derailed when a mother and her little six-year-old girl walk past us. She's practicing her pigeon-toed walk and loving it. One, two, three. We all watch her marching to the Kendrick Lamar album blaring out of a car half a block away. She's headed toward Lenox, arms out, her nodding head keeping the beat. She pays no attention to us. The wondrous architecture of the brownstone where we are all gathered—the projecting stone window lintels, the projecting cornices, embellished with moldings, replicated for an entire block—doesn't faze her. At six years old, she's got more important things to do. She's working on a strut all her own.

Spirituality, hope, pride, and despair all come together in my neighborhood.

It takes a minute to wind down the conversation, but soon I'm heading for the avenue, too. When I hit Lenox, I look around and am reminded of the enormity that is Harlem. It's a neighborhood that's almost sixty city blocks with a jagged southern border, a community that straddles the island, from river to river. There are so many people walking the avenue, it feels like a parade. Lenox is like an Africanized version of a Parisian boulevard. Everyone has their hustle on. Folks are pulling T-shirts and hats and purses out of vans to drape them on the racks they have set up on the sidewalk. Jamaican patties and kebobs are being arranged on warming platters. Business is afoot, but so is play. In the middle of the sidewalk, there's a guy with a saxophone. His music leaps from "My Funny Valentine" to "A View to a Kill." The tourists pause to listen and throw dollars, while my neighbors scowl at all the room he and his impromptu audience take up on the sidewalk. Still, they snap their fingers to the beat. Anything you want or need can magically appear out of a bag and you can buy it at half price. Watching the haggling over incense or ties reminds me of Africa. And it's not because Harlem has a big black community, it's because on display is a constant intersection of culture and mystique. Spirituality, hope, pride, and despair all come together in my neighborhood. And if you are here long enough, you can't help but become a part of it. The only other place I can compare it to is Africa.

Lenox is like an Africanized version of a Parisian boulevard. Everyone has their hustle on.

I watch the traffic on the sidewalk, unsure where I want to get to next. Past conversations float in my head. David Dinkins in his bow tie and linen suit told me all about tennis games in West Harlem. Go there. Or stop by the Hotel Theresa, just to see it, the former mayor told me. Charlie Rangel used to be the doorman. I think about that, but I could visit the Senegalese bakery in Little Senegal, or maybe I'll stop by and pick up peaches at the farmers' market. I could head east and go to La Marqueta, where I can listen to a mariachi band and buy fresh summer tomatoes at the same time. Or maybe I'll get lucky and somebody I work with will walk by with their kids in tow. Lo and behold, I see Angela with several bags in both hands. She's been with the Rooster since we opened and lived on 125th for eleven years. I grin as I see her coming my way. "Hey."

"Hey, Chef." We find an empty bench. We talk about everything, her kids, her mom, my wife, the Rooster. But mainly our conversation circles around the neighborhood. I'm excited about the tiny boutiques. We both talk about the young people, how they give a certain patina to the neighborhood. Angela's got a bag full of fruit from the famers' market and we both note how Harlem's farmers' market is a little

different from the others found in the city. We have live music. "And that guy in purple."

I know who she's talking about. There's this guy, dressed all in purple with white sunglasses, who sings with the band even though he's not a part of the act. Or maybe he is. "He was there, Chef. He was killing it." We chuckle and I'm reminded again of how Harlem works on a different grid. Even when a chain-store outlet pops up in our neighborhood, the way the neighborhood interacts with it makes it altogether unique. It's the only place I know that, when I walk around, I'm forever moving in and out of pockets of music. From a marching band that clearly feels like they don't need a holiday to play, to some woman singing gospel who has found the perfect acoustics in the subway station. Harlem's changed, yes, but I can't help but think for the better. We've become a neighborhood where folks can shop at Target, not be a target.

We've become a neighborhood where folks can shop at Target, not be a target.

I've got to go, I tell Angela. I want to pick up some shea butter on 125th; she wants to peek in on a baby yoga center and watch toddlers do a downward facing dog and dream. Mostly I want to walk a little more. Watch the sunset. Smell Harlem summertime. It's this odd potpourri of grilled meat, roasted nuts, the sweat of bodies, and piss. When I'm in a certain frame of mind, I think it smells like ambition.

Angela and I have talked longer than I realize. The setting sun—the kind I've only seen in New York City—is bathing everything in a Broadway glow. I head back home, passing the brownstone where Maya Angelou lived. I miss her all over again. But I feel lucky, too. She invited me into her kitchen and we cooked liver and onions. The memory of eating that inexpensive luxury is sharp. We talked about a lot of things, but mainly about the Rooster. Did I understand that

I was a part of the community now? Did I know what that meant? Standing on the sidewalk, her words float to me: "I've learned that people will forget what you said, people will forget what you did, but people will never forget how you made them feel."

BLOCK PLAYLIST

"NO ONE WILL DO"   Mary J. Blige

"HARLEM'S NOCTURNE"   Alicia Keys

"NOT JUST A SONG"   Debo Band

"21ST CENTURY"   Dion Parson & 21st Century Band

"BIG WHEEL"   Saun & Starr

"CHANGE THE BEAT"   Fab 5 Freddy

"FOREVER SPRING"   Kris Bowers

"THE DREAMER"   Common featuring Maya Angelou

"EVERYTHING SCATTER"   Fela Kuti

"THE THORN"   Willie Jones III

"UMMAH"   Winard Harper and Jeli Posse

BLOCK-PARTY RIBS *with* SWEET Q SAUCE

SERVES 8 TO 12

A proper block party always has ribs, and proper ribs should be sweet, spicy, and salty. The three essentials, and you've got them here. You eat them with your hands and get really messy.

→ **You'll have extra Q sauce. If you want, make another couple of racks of ribs, or put the sauce out for whoever wants more.**

→ **Start the ribs the day before.**

FOR THE RUB AND RIBS

½ cup ketjap manis (see page 29)

½ packed cup dark brown sugar

3 tablespoons smoked paprika

2 teaspoons coarse kosher salt

2 teaspoons freshly ground black pepper

1 teaspoon cayenne

1 teaspoon ground allspice

1 teaspoon powdered ginger

1 teaspoon garlic powder

1 teaspoon onion powder

1 teaspoon celery seeds

Leaves from 4 sprigs thyme

Grated zest of 2 lemons

4 slabs baby back ribs (about 3 pounds each)

FOR THE SAUCE

2 tablespoons grapeseed oil

3 poblano chiles, chopped

2 red onions, chopped

4 garlic cloves, chopped

1 (2-inch) piece ginger, peeled and chopped

Coarse kosher salt

2½ cups chicken broth

2 cups ketchup

1 (12-ounce) bottle beer (Negra Modelo is a good choice)

1 cup brewed coffee

¾ cup apple cider vinegar

½ cup molasses

½ cup ketjap manis

Juice of 2 lemons

2 teaspoons XO sauce (see page 30)

2 teaspoons mustard seeds

2 teaspoons celery seeds

1 teaspoon cayenne

TO FINISH

4 cups water

FOR THE RUB AND RIBS

1 Mix all the rub ingredients together.

2 Divide the rub between the ribs, rubbing it onto both sides. Put the ribs, meat side up, on two rimmed baking sheets, cover with plastic wrap, and refrigerate overnight.

FOR THE SAUCE

3 Heat the oil in a large saucepan over medium heat. Add the chiles, onions, garlic, ginger, and a big pinch of salt and cook, stirring occasionally, until the onions

soften, about 10 minutes. Add the remaining ingredients and bring to a simmer. Turn the heat down to medium-low and cook at an active simmer until reduced by about half, 30 minutes to 2 hours.

4 Let the sauce cool, then puree it in batches in a blender. Taste for salt.

TO FINISH

5 Preheat the oven to 225°F. Line two rimmed baking sheets with aluminum foil and set baking racks in both.

6 Set the ribs, meat side up, on the racks and pour 2 cups of water into each of the baking sheets. Bake the ribs for 2 hours. Spread 1 cup of the sauce over each rack and bake for another 2 hours.

7 Turn the heat up to 400°F and roast until the sauce the caramelizes, 15 to 20 minutes. Switch the baking sheets from top to bottom about halfway through.

8 Cut into individual ribs, heap onto a couple of platters, and serve.

CURRIED GOAT STEW

SERVES 4 TO 6

There's always a Caribbean family that seems to take over the farmers' market on my block each weekend. They usually serve something curried—sometimes goat, sometimes chicken—with roti flatbread. It's rustic and lip-smacking good. Perfect block-party food. Like any stew, this will be even better the next day, so make it in advance if you can.

2 tablespoons grapeseed oil

4 red onions, roughly chopped

4 garlic cloves, crushed

1 (⅓-inch) piece ginger, peeled and smashed

1 lemongrass stalk, trimmed, smashed, and minced (see page 28)

1 cinnamon stick

4 green cardamom pods, crushed

2 or 3 fresh curry leaves (see page 27)

2 teaspoons garam masala

2 large ripe tomatoes, chopped

1 (28-ounce) can crushed tomatoes

2 cups chicken broth

1 cup coconut milk (Goya is best here)

2 yellow plantains, cut into ⅓-inch dice

1½ cups chopped carrots

1 teaspoon ground turmeric

1 tablespoon Indian curry paste (hot or mild)

3½ pounds bone-in goat stew meat

¼ cup water

Coarse kosher salt

2 tablespoons chopped fresh cilantro

FOR SERVING

Rice

Roti (page 239)

Picklz (see Pickles at the Rooster, page 244)

1 Heat the oil in a Dutch oven over medium heat. Add the onions, garlic, ginger, lemongrass, cinnamon, cardamom pods, and curry leaves. Cook, stirring occasionally, until the onion is turning golden, about 15 minutes. Add the garam masala and cook, stirring, for 1 minute.

2 Add the chopped and crushed tomatoes, the chicken broth, coconut milk, plantains, carrots, turmeric, and curry paste. Bring to a simmer and cook, stirring occasionally, for 10 minutes to start developing the flavors.

3 Stir in the goat meat, bring back to a simmer, and cook for 10 minutes. Stir in the water, turn the heat down to low, and cover the pot partway. Simmer, stirring and scraping the bottom of the pot occasionally, until the meat is tender, about 1½ hours. Season with salt.

4 Spoon the stew into a serving bowl and garnish with the cilantro. Serve with rice, roti, and Picklz.

Perfect block-party food.

FRIED LIVER *and* ONIONS *with* MUSTARD-PICKLED MELON *for* MAYA ANGELOU

SERVES 4

I grew up eating liver, and my mother always served something sweet on the side. Usually lingonberries. These chicken livers get a great crunchy exterior from the panko. I love the contrast with the meltingly soft onions. And the pickled melon is my nod to Mom's lingonberries.

1 cup buttermilk

1 tablespoon Dijon mustard

1 pound chicken livers, halved and trimmed

2 sprigs tarragon

2 tablespoons olive oil

2 red onions, sliced thin

Coarse kosher salt

1 cup panko bread crumbs, powdered in a food processor

2 tablespoons cornstarch

½ teaspoon garlic salt

Peanut oil for frying

Freshly ground black pepper

Mustard-Pickled Melon (optional; see Pickles at the Rooster, page 244)

1 Mix the buttermilk and mustard together in a bowl. Add the livers and tarragon and let sit for 30 minutes.

2 Heat the olive oil in a large skillet over medium heat. Add the onions and a big pinch of salt and cook, stirring occasionally, until the onions are very soft and turning golden, 18 to 20 minutes.

3 Mix the panko, cornstarch, and garlic salt in bowl.

4 Fill a saucepan about one-third full with peanut oil. Set over medium-high heat and heat to 360°F.

5 Lift the livers out of the buttermilk and dredge in the seasoned panko.

6 Working in batches, fry the livers until the breading is golden, about 1 minute. Keep an eye on the heat and adjust it to keep the oil between 350° and 375°F. Use a spider or slotted spoon to remove any breading that's fallen off. Drain the livers on a rack set over a rimmed baking sheet and season with salt and pepper while they're hot.

7 Put the livers on a platter, cover with the onions, and serve right away. Pass the pickles.

Maya Angelou was a major motivating force behind my move to Harlem, and the house I bought is eight doors down from hers. So I am reminded of her every day, and I think of the times she cooked for me and when I cooked for her. This liver and onions dish was just the kind of food she loved.

These flatbreads came to the West Indies with workers from India and South Asia in the 1800s and were quickly and happily adopted into Caribbean cuisine—particularly in Trinidad. It's just the right bread when you're eating soup or stew and want something to sop it up.

Our master roti maker is our Guyanese friend IJ. Her formal job is server, but she has made flags and banners for Rooster, helped build tables, performed in talent shows. She's a marvel.

ROTI

MAKES 8

1 Melt 1 tablespoon of the spiced butter in a small saucepan or skillet over medium heat. Add the chickpeas, garlic, cumin, and turmeric. Cook for 5 minutes to meld the flavors. Transfer to a bowl, mash coarse with a fork, and stir in the cilantro.

2 Put the flour in a bowl with a good pinch of salt. Add the remaining 2 tablespoons spiced butter and work together with your fingers until no lumps of butter remain. Add the water and knead it in the bowl until you form a shaggy dough that cleans the bowl. Cover with plastic wrap and rest for 15 minutes.

3 Turn the dough out onto a work surface and roll it into a log. Cut into 8 equal pieces, then roll each piece into a ball. Flatten a ball on one palm, add about 2 teaspoons of the chickpeas, and gather up the sides—pinching them together to enclose the chickpeas. Flatten into a disk. Repeat with the remaining balls. Then cover with plastic wrap and rest for 15 minutes.

4 Roll each disk into a 6-inch round. Heat a cast-iron skillet or griddle over medium-high heat. Rub the skillet with a little spiced butter and cook the roti in batches until blistered and browned, about 40 seconds. Flip and cook for 30 seconds. Stack and wrap in a kitchen towel or napkin to keep warm.

3 tablespoons Spiced Butter (page 62), plus additional for cooking

½ cup canned chickpeas, rinsed and drained

1 garlic clove, minced

1 teaspoon ground cumin

½ teaspoon ground turmeric

1 tablespoon chopped fresh cilantro

2 cups all-purpose flour

Coarse kosher salt

½ cup water

FRIED OYSTERS AND ALBERT MAYSLES

We love frying oysters at the Red Rooster, even if we don't have them on the menu often. They might be a special, paired with Wild Wild Wings (page 80). Or maybe we're in a New Orleans mood, so we'll make oyster po' boys with Scallion Sauce (page 90) and shredded cabbage piled onto a potato roll.

Because there are so many ways to approach frying oysters, you can have a lot of fun and make them your own. Maybe you soak them first. Milk, buttermilk, an egg beaten with pickle juice, all are great options. But nobody says you have to soak them at all. For coating, you've got flour with some cornstarch mixed in, cornmeal (white, blue, or yellow), panko. Season the coating or not.

However you prep them, just make sure to fry them in plenty of hot oil until the coating is crisp. It won't take long, maybe 3 minutes. But you can't beat that contrast of crunch and briny ocean sweetness. Sprinkle them with salt as soon as you take them out of the fryer.

Condiments are up to you. Have some lemon wedges ready. Keep the Red Rooster Hot Sauce (page 243) in mind. And Green Mayonnaise (page 57). The Green Harissa on page 94 would make a great dip, too.

I can't think about oysters without remembering my neighbor, filmmaker Albert Maysles. He loved oysters. Loved them. Toward the end of his illness, I stopped by with a pot of soup. He was happy enough to drink soup, but he smiled and asked me to bring oysters next time.

Business took me out of town, and when I came home, Albert was gone. I miss my friend. He touched so many lives and was always eager to talk about food and film. And to eat oysters.

You can't have a block party or a cookout or any big gathering without some meaningful and seriously delicious filler. It could be a potato salad, but black-eyed peas and rice—with some chiles and ginger, coconut milk and tomatoes, and a hint of curry to make things right—is even better. What's more, it's equally good hot or at room temperature.

→ **Soak the peas the night before.**

PEAS *and* RICE, GOOD *for* A CROWD

SERVES 10 TO 16

---

1 Melt the butter in a large, deep pan over medium heat. Add the onion, chiles, garlic, ginger, thyme, bay leaf, curry, cumin, and a big pinch of salt and cook, stirring occasionally, until the onion is softened, 6 to 7 minutes. Drain the peas and add them to the pot, along with the 5 cups fresh water. Turn the heat up to medium-high and bring to a simmer. Turn the heat down to medium-low and simmer until the peas are tender, about 30 minutes. Taste and season well with salt.

2 Wash the rice in several changes of cold water until the water runs clear. Drain. Stir the rice, tomatoes, coconut milk, and tomato juice into the peas. Turn the heat up to medium-high and bring to a simmer. Stir, cover, turn the heat down to medium-low, and simmer for 15 minutes. Turn off the heat, stir, and leave it at the back of the stove for 15 minutes. The rice will be very tender. Stir in the lemon juice and cilantro and taste for salt.

3 Serve hot or at room temperature.

2 tablespoons unsalted butter

1 red onion, chopped

2 poblano chiles, chopped

4 garlic cloves, chopped

1 (3-inch) piece ginger, peeled and minced

1 sprig thyme

1 bay leaf

1 tablespoon Madras curry powder

1 teaspoon ground cumin

Coarse kosher salt

1 pound black-eyed peas, soaked overnight

5 cups water

2 cups jasmine rice

1 (28-ounce) can crushed tomatoes

1 (14-ounce) can coconut milk

1 cup tomato juice

Juice of 1 lemon

¼ cup chopped fresh cilantro or mint

TOMATO-WATERMELON SALAD *with* BURRATA *and* TOMATO SEED VINAIGRETTE

SERVES 4

When it's summertime in New York City and it's hot and humid and you're making a salad for a lot people who'll be eating in the backyard, nothing is better than something that starts with cold, juicy watermelon. Add tomatoes and the sly heat of jalapeños, and you'll have some happy eaters. Double this, triple this, go wild.

4 wedges watermelon

Grapeseed oil

6 ripe tomatoes, preferably heirloom

2 tablespoons balsamic vinegar

1 teaspoon sugar

1 teaspoon freshly ground black pepper

¼ cup olive oil

Coarse kosher salt

1 cup chopped arugula

8 fresh basil leaves, torn

2 garlic cloves, sliced thin

2 jalapeño chiles, stemmed and sliced thin

8 ounces burrata, at room temperature

1 Heat a cast-iron skillet over high heat.

2 Brush the watermelon with grapeseed oil and sear it in the skillet for 30 seconds per side. Transfer to a plate.

3 Put the tomatoes into the skillet and char until the skin is blistered all over and blackened in spots. Cut the tomatoes through the equator. Nudge the seeds out of half the tomatoes, using your finger and squeezing gently, into a bowl. Core and dice all the tomatoes and put in a salad bowl.

4 Mix the tomato seeds with the vinegar, sugar, and pepper. Whisk in the olive oil to make a vinaigrette. Taste for salt.

5 Add the arugula, basil, garlic, and jalapeños to the tomatoes and toss. Chop the burrata and add it to the bowl with some of the vinaigrette and toss again. Taste and add more vinaigrette if you need it.

6 Divide the tomato salad between four plates. Add a wedge of watermelon to each, for dipping and eating.

Seriously, there can't ever be only one hot sauce. You need to be able to pick a level of heat depending on your mood and what you're eating. You decide how much heat you want and then figure out if you go for the extra shake or two, or if you up the ante even more. I'm giving you three levels here. Hot, Spicy, and Devil. Maybe you'll want some on catfish, or peas and rice. Could be you want some on your fried chicken or an oyster. Or maybe you're like me and want hot sauce on your pickles.

→ **When in doubt, travel with your own hot sauce. Then you can be sure you can turn any meal into something fantastic.**

RED ROOSTER HOT SAUCE

MAKES ABOUT 4 CUPS

---

1 Preheat the oven to 450° F.

2 Put the bell peppers and garlic on a rimmed baking sheet. Roast, turning several times, until the peppers are blistered all over and slightly charred and the garlic is soft, 20 to 25 minutes. Put the peppers into a bowl, cover with plastic wrap, and steam for about 15 minutes. Peel the garlic.

3 Peel, stem, and seed the peppers and give them a coarse chop. Put the peppers and any juices in the bowl of a food processor along with the garlic, jalapeño, shallots, tomato powder, paprika, cayenne, mustard, cumin, sugar, salt, and vinegar. Process to a coarse puree. With the motor running, pour in the oil in a slow, steady stream and process, scraping down the sides if necessary, until completely smooth.

4 Transfer the hot sauce to jars and refrigerate for up to 3 weeks.

SPICY HOT SAUCE

Roast just 1 bell pepper and 4 garlic cloves. Replace the jalapeño with half a seeded habanero chile and 4 seeded Thai bird chiles. Finally, replace the smoked paprika with 1 tablespoon berbere (see page 27).

DEVIL HOT SAUCE

No bell peppers in this version. Roast 2 habanero chiles and 4 garlic cloves. You don't need to peel the habanero after roasting, but do remove the seeds. Add 2 seeded Thai bird chiles and 1/4 teaspoon wasabi powder.

3 red bell peppers

2 garlic cloves, unpeeled

1 jalapeño chile, stemmed, seeded, and chopped

2 shallots, sliced

1 tablespoon tomato powder (see page 29)

1 tablespoon smoked paprika

1 tablespoon cayenne

1½ teaspoons mustard powder

1½ teaspoons ground cumin

1½ teaspoons sugar

1½ teaspoons coarse kosher salt

½ cup apple cider vinegar

1½ cups olive oil

PICKLES AT THE ROOSTER

These are all small-batch recipes, quick to make and great to have in the refrigerator. They'll keep better if you pack them in small jars as you won't keep opening a bigger jar and exposing the pickles to air. And never, never stick your fingers into the jar. Use a fork or a spoon.

▶ **House Pickles.** Make a brine by simmering 3 cups water, 2 cups distilled white vinegar, 1 cup sugar, 1 sliced onion, 1 sliced carrot, a 1½-inch piece ginger (peeled, sliced, and smashed), a cinnamon stick, 1½ teaspoons black peppercorns, 8 juniper berries, 4 whole cloves, and half a star anise in a saucepan for 15 minutes. Take the pot off the heat and add ½ cup baby carrots, ½ cup small cauliflower florets, ½ cup trimmed okra (use small pods), and ½ cup peeled pearl onions. Cover with a small plate to keep the vegetables submerged in the brine and leave the pickles on the counter for 1 hour.

You can serve the pickles now, but they'll be better if you pack them in a few small jars and refrigerate overnight. This pickle will keep for about 2 weeks.

▶ **Pickled Fresno Chiles.** Bring 3 cups water, ½ cup red wine vinegar, ½ cup sherry vinegar, ½ cup coarse kosher salt, ½ cup sugar, 2 teaspoons fish sauce, 2 smashed garlic cloves, a 1-inch piece ginger (peeled, sliced, and smashed), and a bay leaf to a boil. Remove from the heat. Add 1 cup sliced Fresno chiles and a tablespoon roughly chopped fresh cilantro. Cover with a small plate to keep the chiles submerged in the brine, and leave them on the counter for 1 hour.

You can serve the pickles now, but they'll be better if you pack them in a few small jars and refrigerate overnight. They'll keep for about 1 week.

▶ **Pickled Cherry Tomatoes.** For this brine, combine 1½ cups water, 1 cup white wine vinegar, ½ cup kosher salt, ½ cup sugar, 4 black peppercorns, 1 sprig thyme, a bay leaf, and a jalapeño cut in half lengthwise in a saucepan. Bring to a boil, then take the pot off the heat and cool to room temperature (the brine needs to cool so the tomatoes don't get mushy). Pour the brine over 1 pint peeled cherry tomatoes. Cover with a small plate to keep the tomatoes submerged in the brine, and leave them on the counter for 1 hour.

You can serve the pickles now, but they'll be better if you pack them in a few small jars and refrigerate overnight. The tomatoes will keep for about 1 week.

▶ **Picklz (Spicy Haitian Cabbage).** Bring 2 cups water, ½ cup apple cider vinegar, ¼ cup distilled white vinegar, ¼ cup sugar, ¼ cup honey, 1 tablespoon grated ginger, half a habenero or Scotch bonnet chile, 3 sprigs thyme, and a bay leaf to a boil over high heat. Turn the heat down to low and simmer for 5 minutes.

Toss 1 cup shredded red cabbage, 1 cup shredded green cabbage, and ½ cup grated carrots together in a mixing bowl. Pour in the hot brine. Cover with a small plate to keep the vegetables submerged, and leave on the counter for 1 hour. Pack into small jars, cover, and refrigerate. It will keep for about 1 month.

► **Pickled Cucumber and Radishes.** Use your fingers to make a paste of 1 tablespoon Korean hot pepper paste (gochujang; see page 29), 3 tablespoons sugar, and 3 tablespoons coarse kosher salt in a bowl. Quarter a cucumber lengthwise, then cut into 2-inch pieces. Add the cucumber to the bowl and keep tossing it with your hands until it is coated with the paste. The cukes will start to release water as you toss, so you'll be able to coat them well. Leave on the counter for 20 minutes. Pour off the liquid that's been drawn from the cukes.

Quarter 6 radishes and add them to the bowl, along with 1 cup rice vinegar, ³/₄ cup soy sauce, 1 teaspoon sesame oil, and 1 teaspoon fish sauce. Cover with a small plate to keep the vegetables submerged and leave on the counter for 2 hours. Pack into small jars and refrigerate until cold. These will keep for about 5 days.

► **Mustard-Pickled Melon.** Bring 2 cups water, 1 cup apple juice, 1 cup apple cider vinegar, ¹/₄ cup sugar, ¹/₄ cup coarse kosher salt, 1 tablespoon mustard oil, 1 tablespoon Dijon mustard, 2 teaspoons mustard seeds, 2 bay leaves, 2 allspice berries, and 2 star anise to a boil.

Peel half a cantaloupe and cut into 2-inch cubes. Put the cantaloupe in a bowl and pour in the brine. Cover with a small plate to keep the melon submerged and leave on the counter for 1 hour. Pack into jars and refrigerate for at least 3 hours before serving. These keep for about 4 days.

► **Pickled Eggs.** Stir 4 cups soy sauce and 1 cup mirin together with 3 garlic cloves, 3 halved Thai bird chiles, a 3-inch piece of ginger (peeled, sliced, and smashed), and a third of a lemongrass stalk (trimmed, smashed, and chopped; see page 28).

Peel 8 hard-boiled eggs and pack them into a half-gallon jar. Pour in the pickling liquid, cover, and refrigerate for 24 hours. They'll keep for about a week.

"BE A GOOD NEIGHBOR"

Rebekah Maysles calls herself a collector—of photographs, conversations on the corner of 125th Street, notes that fall out of people's pockets. She also is a New York City–based artist and the managing director of Maysles Films, Inc.

I was at some weird event, and an aristocratic woman came up to me and said, "Oh, you live up in Harlem—Harlem has changed so much." I said, "Dude, New York has changed." I hardly get called Snowflake anymore. There are hustles that I used to watch that I don't see anymore.

One of the reasons my parents like the neighborhood is it's a place where people say hi to you on the street and make eye contact with you. Now, though, there is no middle ground: I don't want a Whole Foods, I just want a nice grocery store. I don't want the most expensive one. Why can't I get something that is in between?

I try to contribute as much as I can. I don't live in Brooklyn, but I do think that there are neighborhoods in Brooklyn that are being gentrified so rapidly people just don't give a fuck. They don't go to community board meetings, they don't have to get in good. In Harlem, you have to put a lot of work in.

My mom first met Marcus when he was moving to Harlem. He was thinking hard about opening the Red Rooster and what that meant, and he talked to her a lot about it. I think there are some things he thought would be easy that were much harder and probably some things that he thought would be harder that were much easier. But you know, Harlem

has an amazing history that you have to respect. And you know things are changing, but you can be a part of it in a positive way.

Maysles Documentary Center initially started off with the mission that everyone has a voice and everyone has a story to be told. We give people tools to be able to tell that story. It's very democratic, with the idea that telling your story should be something that everyone has access to. So we do educational programming and show films, primarily documentaries.

Most of the films have social justice backgrounds. Jessica Green does the programming, and she did a series early on called *Rent Control*, about gentrification in every borough. The idea is to have more films that open a discussion. My dad used to film a lot of the Q&As, and that was always really fun. And we'd have parties and we'd have receptions and that was also nice because you'd show the film and everyone could continue the conversation downstairs. A few years ago, we did a big Black Panther film festival, which was a collaboration between Black Panthers and Jessica, and they helped figure out what films made sense to show. Basically, Maysles Films is trying to be a good neighbor. That's what it's all about in Harlem.

SUNDAY BRUNCH

EVERY SUNDAY I can find a slice of church at Ginny's. We don't have a pastor or an army of deacons; we don't have ushers or a scripture; we're not one of the four hundred—yes, I said four hundred—places of worship to be found in Harlem. What we have are busboys, cooks, severs, the singer Boncella Lewis upstairs at the Rooster, and then downstairs we have a dozen teenagers who transform Ginny's into a church basement by singing gospel. Vy Higginsen, director of Gospel for Teens, leads them and me and anyone else who wants to eat good food while being moved by music. It's Easter Sunday. I talked to Vy on the phone a couple of days ago. "Are you doing something special?" I asked her. There's a swollen pause on the phone.

"Always."

Maya, my wife, picks out my best tie, the one with the purple dots, and I drape the scarf she just got from Ethiopia around her neck. She takes my hand just as we step out the door. We walk around the weekend trash—half-drunk beer bottles and Styrofoam containers heavy with fried fish bones and half-eaten hushpuppies that are a feast for pigeons, and for the sparrows who fight them for their fair share. "Look," Maya says and points up to Harlem on a spring Sunday. Cherry trees, crab apples, and pear trees take turns, flashing their blossoms. Even that beauty is forced to compete with lilacs and tulips in bloom, and on display, in planter pots sitting at the bottom of brownstone stoops. We turn the corner together and join hundreds of Harlem families walking the avenue, making the trek to praise Him, to sing, to rejoice.

Not every family is headed for Mother A.M.E or the Abyssinian Baptist. There are women and men standing on a food line that stretches all the way to the six-dollar latte shop. Every Sunday and Wednesday when I pass those good people, I wonder if those of us in Harlem who can help are doing enough. Are we making sure everybody is a part of the conversation? Every day, folks are struggling in Harlem; every day, I ask myself, *Am I doing all I can?* Cooking, eating, feeding, *hiring* based on a spiritual compass never felt more relevant than right now. Because one thing is certain: That line is getting longer and longer.

There are women and men standing on a food line that stretches all the way to the six-dollar latte shop.

When we walk past the Rooster, Maya asks if we should stop in for a second to say hi to Kingsley. We're going to be late if we do, but her suggestion makes me start texting my chef: *Easter's not a pork day. Is the leg of lamb out of the oven; are the beef roasts rested? We need lots of vegetable sides. How's Teniesha's arm? Little sister burned herself, yesterday. She okay?* We're chefs and holidays are our biggest days. Those are the days when it's hard to think about yourself, when you think about who's eating and who's not, when you don't make family plans because there's no time. *What's cooking* isn't a pickup line, it's a real question. Everything is about what are you cooking and who is coming to eat it. Kingsley texts back, *We're all good.*

A block away from the Abyssinian, we are shoulder to shoulder with neighbors in their Sunday best. Little boys in bow ties yawn and hold their mothers' hands. "Morning, Food Dude."

"Happy Easter, Little Man," I call back to him. I watch little girls with pigtails tied in ribbons stare at their feet, so careful not to scuff their church shoes. "That's a pretty scarf. Where'd you get that at?" Fathers nod their heads in approval of their children's good behavior, then add their own hellos. Women in pastel walk with us, and I'm mesmerized by the artful creations made of plumage and toile perched on their heads. Like me, I think they are held spellbound by how the Abyssinian carves a striking skyline. It's a wonderful service. I head for the restaurant as soon as we're done with the final prayer. Maya says she wants to stay, catch up with her girlfriends. "Try to get home soon, Marcus." I smile when she rubs an imagined stain on my collar. Damn, I'm lucky.

The original Red Rooster was half a block away from the Abyssinian. Close enough that I can't help but wonder what kind of party its owner, George Woods, would have thrown back in the day on an Easter Sunday night. Big L's beats thumping out of a window frame my imagination. At the old Rooster, there must have been music, and the women would have danced with their church hats on. I hit Lenox and, next to the Schomburg Center, four kids are well on their way to becoming a marching band. The one with the trumpet isn't holding up his end, at least according to the little boy at the end of the line with the snare drum. He can't be more than nine years old, but he sounds like he's forty. "Yo, Man, you're messing us up! Come on." They sound good to me, but I tell them they need to get hats. People need a place to drop their tips. Two blocks away from the Rooster, I start to see the familiar faces of the street vendors. Aretha Franklin and Mahalia Jackson CDs, Tupac perfume, Obama candles. It's all there for sale right outside Sylvia's and the Rooster. Easter's a big day in Harlem.

A woman in white hums loud enough for me to hear her as we pass each other on the sidewalk. Her tune is full of yearning. I

wonder how a melody can sound both inviting and secret. I watch the feather in her hat that seems to say hello to me before she does.

Twelve teenagers are checking their shirts and the state of their dress when I step into the dressing room. Vy's looking them over. She's part mother, part teacher, part wise aunt, part general. Their excitement is palpable. All except for one young woman, whose eyes are fastened to the cuffs of her sleeves. A lot of the teenagers who sing in Vy's choir come from homes with supportive families, but just as many come from homes where to come to rehearsal, never mind showing up for a performance, is a triumph. I'm not sure which circumstance matches the young woman. "Hey. I'm Marcus." My hand is out to shake hers but she doesn't want to take it. She takes a step back from me and contemplates the floor between us. Vy watches our exchange and steps in.

"Tell Marcus your name. Look him in the eye. Tell him where you are from." Vy's warm voice has the familiar ring of a command. The young woman frowns, and Vy places her hand on the girl's shoulder. This girl begins to shake her head slowly, and I realize she's not saying no, she's just looking around, trying to find a safe place to land her gaze. For a moment, she looks at me. Her eyes are big and brown, and as much as she may think otherwise, they're innocent. Her gaze touches my cheek, moves to my forehead. She tilts her head high to the ceiling. What does she see up there, I wonder. Her name in capital letters, her courage, her voice? All of that must be right above us, in a spot that she can't quite reach. She looks scared. I'm sorry I ever asked. Her eyes climb down from the ceiling and rest on the slope of my shoulder. Her voice is delicate, breathless.

"Tonya."

When I leave the dressing room, I head upstairs to listen to Boncella and check on the racks of lamb in the kitchen. At the top of the stairs, I pause to take in my diners. Damn, everybody looks so good in their Sunday best. Then I go back downstairs to check on the buffet table one last time. The selection of dishes looks like a potluck found in a church basement. We've got our best on display: fried chicken, Swedish meatballs, cheese grits, creamed mashed potatoes with a tower of fried shallots on top. Then there's the array of what we hope our guests will want: mustard greens with a roasted garlic vinaigrette, quinoa with beets and oranges, home fries, scrambled eggs. Our pastry chef Charlene Johnson's cakes look better than ever. Corn bread. In one corner, we've set up a station for sliced steak. On the table we have a platter of my father's smoked salmon, surrounded by capers, thinly sliced onions, and fresh tomatoes. Taken altogether, the dishes make you wonder how they all belong on the same table. But that's a question easily answered. My chefs, Kingsley and IJ, and I spend more time than I would like to admit discussing what dishes should be served during the gospel hour. We're in Harlem; it matters.

"Hey, Jamie. Happy Easter." Jamie, who has worked for me for more than three years, who despite having two sons and being a single mother I think of as my kid sister, is hovering around our potluck table. She gives me one of those smiles that holds an entire conversation. Seeing her reminds me of the particular ecosystem that is Harlem. I don't find the people who work at the Rooster from ads in the *Times*. Word of mouth runs rampant all over the neighborhood. That's how Jamie heard about us. Her mother, who was getting her hair done at the beauty salon, had heard from a church sister that Rooster was hiring. Barber shops and church basements and corner bodegas hum with news, with advice.

"How's your mom? And the boys?"

"You know? Pretty good." There's more to say, a larger conversation we'll probably have later, but we both see Vy come out from the back. The show's starting, even though the kids are still in the dressing

room. Every Sunday, Vy walks around Ginny's introducing herself and making small talk with the guests waiting for the performance. To watch her is to be humbled. *And how are you, Darling? Where are you from? That is a beautiful hat. Where did you find that?* She does more than tell our guests what she is about, she points out they have more in common than they think. Did the Tim and Matthew who are sitting at the bar know that there's a whole group of twentysomethings who are from London, too? Say hello, now. Don't be strangers. That kind of introduction gets repeated over and over. Here I am and here you are and quiet as it's kept, you have so much in common with that nice lady over there, that wonderful man over here, that family sitting there. It takes half an hour to turn a room full of strangers into something that looks like a congregation. You may not know everyone, but you want to. By the time they're lined up at the potluck table, a hundred or so people are fearless enough to make small talk. I can't help but feel satisfied.

Twelve teenage gospel singers, a drummer, a bass player, and a pianist can create a roar of music. *Go down . . . Moses. Way down in Egypt's land. Tell ole Pharaoh to let my people go.* I'm huddled in the far corner of the bar, next to the telephone booth, swaying to song. I know it's just my imagination, but I think I can hear Tonya's voice. She sings with her head bowed. And even when she's courageous enough to look up and out, her eyes are shut tight. Voices teeming with yearning and struggle make me think about how the original Red Rooster was around the corner from the Abyssinian, how our Red Rooster's success is in part based on the church. The New Orleans chef Leah Chase taught me that a restaurant shows its soul in its community. That I should always ask myself: *Who feels invited?* I look around. There's black folks from New Orleans, a bunch of Londoners, the passel of church ladies, their hats bobbing to the music. But most importantly there's Tonya, standing in front of us all, giving herself permission to succeed or fail. Her eyes are closed but I can see her courage.

Red Rooster's success is in part based on the church.

The choir sings its last song, "Oh, Happy Day." Twelve kids are dancing in the aisles. They clap and strut in and out of the crowd, inviting our guests to sing the chorus. Some guests are shy and their voices crack, others are bold and give everything they've got. Watching it all makes me realize we are all a part of a piece, an intricate theater that requires all of us to pull it off. The Swedish tourists, the church ladies, my chefs, Jamie, the Sunday parade that happens on the way to church. It's not just the choir standing on a stage. The thought brings a small smile to my face.

The standing ovation lasts long enough that there's a second encore. "Happy Easter, everybody. Thank you for coming out!" Every member of the choir introduces themselves to the beat of a drum. First and last names, where they live. Tonya is swaying left to right. She's the third one from the end of the line. When it's her turn, she looks at the ceiling again. But this time instead of the ceiling her eyes land on the disco ball. Her smile feels private. "Tonya," she almost shouts, but then she mangles her last name. Whatever Tonya's trying to say is a jumble and no one can hear it. But the choir is still clapping and so is the audience. The drummer's beat hasn't faltered. Vy is sitting on a stool nearby, clapping the beat and mouthing the words, "Come. On. Come. On." Tonya stares at the disco ball and takes a deep breath. What she says next sounds like a battle cry.

"Harlem!"

SUNDAY BRUNCH PLAYLIST

"DOWN BY THE RIVERSIDE"   Lawrence Brownlee and Damien Sneed

"WE SHALL OVERCOME"   Bruce Springsteen

"GLORY HALLELUJAH"   Wycliffe Gordon

"YOU MUST HAVE THAT TRUE RELIGION"   Abyssinian Baptist Church Concert Chorale

"A PLACE CALLED THERE"   Damien Sneed featuring Djore Nance and Tiffany Stevenson

"COME SUNDAY"   Duke Ellington featuring Mahalia Jackson

ANDOUILLE BREAD PUDDING

SERVES 4

The perfect brunch casserole: sausage, eggs, greens, cheese. And bacon. Everything's better with bacon.

4 slices bacon, chopped

1 cup diced (¼-inch) andouille sausage

1 packed cup stemmed and chopped collard greens

1 red onion, chopped

¼ cup dry-roasted peanuts, chopped

½ teaspoon hot smoked paprika

Coarse kosher salt

3 large eggs

½ cup milk

½ cup heavy cream

3 tablespoons raisins

½ cup shredded cheddar cheese

2 cups cubed (½-inch) Chicken-Fat Challah (page 97) or leftover country bread

1 Preheat the oven to 375°F. Generously butter an 8-inch square baking dish.

2 Put the bacon and andouille into a skillet and cook over medium heat, stirring occasionally, until the bacon is browned, about 13 minutes. Use a spider or slotted spoon to transfer the meat to a bowl.

3 Add the collards, onion, peanuts, paprika, and salt to taste to the fat in the skillet and cook over medium heat until the onion has softened, 5 to 6 minutes. Scrape the vegetables into the bowl with the meat.

4 Whisk the eggs, milk, and cream in a large bowl until smooth. Stir in the raisins, cheese, and bread and let it sit for 5 minutes. Stir in the cooked meat and vegetables, then scrape it all into the baking dish.

5 Bake until the bread pudding has puffed up and is lightly browned, about 30 minutes.

6 Divide the pudding between four plates and serve.

A flat omelet (we call them farmer's omelets in Sweden) and a spoonful of stew—topped with an egg fried sunny side up. It's an egg lover's paradise.

EGG ON EGG

SERVES 1

1 Beat 2 of the eggs with the milk. Stir in the scallion and season with salt and pepper.

2 Heat 1½ teaspoons of the butter in a small nonstick skillet over medium heat. Pour in the egg mixture and cook, shaking the pan and stirring with the back of a fork, to make a soft omelet. Without folding it, slide it out onto a plate. Sprinkle with the cheese and spoon the stew on top.

3 Melt the remaining 1½ teaspoons butter in the same skillet over medium heat. Crack in the last egg and cook it sunny side up. Slide the egg on top of the stew.

4 Garnish with the sour cream and serve with hot sauce.

3 large eggs

¼ cup milk

1 whole scallion, chopped

Coarse kosher salt and freshly ground black pepper

3 teaspoons unsalted butter

1½ teaspoons freshly grated Parmesan cheese

2 tablespoons leftover stew (or more, if you want), reheated

1 tablespoon sour cream

Red Rooster Hot Sauce (page 243), or your favorite

SUNDAY TOMATO EGGS

SERVES 4

Tomatoes, celery, capers, horseradish—these ingredients remind me of a Bloody Mary. And that would not be a bad choice to accompany these eggs.

→ **If you can find soft chorizo in a Mexican grocery store, you won't need to chop it. But the commercial stuff comes in casings, which need to be removed, and the sausage will have to be chopped.**

→ **Think about who you're cooking for here. If your guests aren't fans of very runny yolks, cover the skillet while you cook the eggs.**

---

1 tablespoon olive oil

½ cup chopped Mexican (soft) chorizo

1 onion, chopped

2 tablespoons minced celery

2 garlic cloves, chopped

1 (14.5-ounce) can crushed tomatoes

1 tablespoon capers, drained

3 Kalamata olives, pitted and chopped

1 chipotle in adobo, minced

¼ cup water

1½ teaspoons horseradish, preferably freshly grated

Coarse kosher salt and freshly ground black pepper

8 large eggs

4 slices country bread, toasted

8 ounces burrata, at room temperature, cut into pieces (optional)

Extra-virgin olive oil

4 fresh basil leaves

1 Heat the olive oil in a large cast-iron skillet over medium heat. Add the chorizo, onion, celery, and garlic and cook, stirring occasionally, until the onion starts to soften, about 5 minutes. Stir in the tomatoes, capers, olives, chipotle, and water and bring to a simmer. Simmer until the sauce is thick, 5 to 7 minutes. Stir in the horseradish and season with salt and pepper.

2 Crack each egg into the sauce and cook until the whites are set, 5 to 6 minutes.

3 Put a piece of toast on each of four plates. Spoon 2 eggs onto each piece of toast, and divide any sauce left in the skillet. Top the eggs with burrata if using, drizzle with extra-virgin olive oil, tear the basil leaves and drop on top, and serve.

"We just know inside that we're queens. And these are the crowns we wear."

—Felecia McMillan, journalist, From *Crowns: Portraits of Black Women in Church Hats* by Michael Cunningham and Craig Marberry

THE BREAKFAST

SERVES 4

Save this for the weekend, when you have time to spend in the kitchen and time to spend with friends and family. Everything is flavorful here, the shiro (an Ethiopian stew made with chickpea flour), the candied bacon, the grits; and you have a poached egg with a golden yolk to run into everything. Put it all out on the table so everyone can make a plate.

FOR THE SHIRO

2 medium white onions, chopped

1 (15.5-ounce) can white beans, rinsed and drained

2 garlic cloves, chopped

4 tablespoons olive oil

1 teaspoon tomato paste

1 tablespoon berbere (see page 27)

1 cup canned crushed tomatoes

½ cup chickpea flour

1 cup tomato juice

1 cup diced plum tomatoes

1 tablespoon chopped fresh cilantro

1½ cups water

2 teaspoons Spiced Butter (page 62)

Coarse kosher salt and freshly ground black pepper

FOR THE CANDIED BACON

8 slices thick-cut bacon

3 tablespoons maple syrup

1 tablespoon unsalted butter, softened

Cayenne

Freshly ground black pepper

FOR THE EGGS

4 large eggs

¼ cup distilled white vinegar

FOR SERVING

Creamy Grits (from Whole Fried Fish with Grits, page 180)

FOR THE SHIRO

1 Puree the onions, beans, and garlic in a food processor.

2 Heat 1 tablespoon of the olive oil in a large skillet over medium-high heat. Add the onion puree and cook, stirring and scraping the bottom of the pan frequently, until the puree is light brown, about 8 minutes. Don't let it scorch, and be sure to scrape the pan thoroughly. Stir in the remaining 3 tablespoons olive oil, the tomato paste, and the berbere and cook, stirring and scraping, for 1 minute to meld the flavors. Stir in the crushed tomatoes.

3 Sprinkle the chickpea flour over the top and stir it in quickly, so it doesn't clump. Whisk in the tomato juice, plum tomatoes, cilantro, and 1 cup of the water. Turn the heat down to low and simmer, stirring and scraping frequently, for 30 minutes.

continued on page 268 →

Add the remaining ½ cup water and simmer for 15 minutes. Stir in the spiced butter. Taste and season with salt and pepper. Keep warm at the back of the stove.

FOR THE CANDIED BACON

4 Preheat the oven to 375°F.

5 Arrange the bacon on a large rimmed baking sheet. Bake until crisp, 15 to 18 minutes. Take the baking sheet out of the oven and tilt it so the fat gathers in one corner. Add the syrup, butter, and ½ teaspoon cayenne to the fat and stir to melt the butter. Use this to baste the bacon. Bake for 2 minutes and baste again. Bake until the glaze is frothy, another 2 minutes. Drain the bacon on a rack set over waxed paper. Grind on some black pepper and sprinkle with more cayenne.

FOR THE EGGS

6 Crack the eggs into four cups.

7 Fill a large saucepan about half full with water and bring to a simmer over medium-high heat. Add the vinegar and turn the heat down to low. Stir the water to create a vortex and drop in the eggs one by one. Poach the eggs for 4 minutes. Transfer to paper towels with a slotted spoon.

TO SERVE

8 Put out bowls of the shiro and grits and a platter of bacon, and hand everyone a plate with a poached egg on it.

After my Sunday morning run, I make breakfast for me and Maya. We'll read the paper, talk about who may be visiting, make plans for the coming week. We'll sit down at eight o'clock, and we may not get up until one-thirty.

This satisfying dish—slabs of toast topped with leftover stew and fried eggs—is just what we want on those lazy mornings.

FAVORITE SUNDAY TOAST

SERVES 2

1 Shred the stew meat, add the collards, and reheat.

2 Heat a griddle over medium heat. Spread the bread lightly with spiced butter and toast it on the griddle. Divide the toast between two plates and sprinkle with salt and berbere.

3 Melt a teaspoon or two of the spiced butter in a nonstick skillet and fry the eggs to your liking.

4 Top the toasts with the cheese and stew, and then the eggs, and serve.

1 cup leftover Curried Goat Stew (page 236)

2 tablespoons leftover Killer Collards (page 123)

4 thick slices sourdough bread

Spiced Butter (page 62), softened

Coarse kosher salt

Berbere (see page 27)

4 large eggs

4 tablespoons cottage cheese

AUNT MAYBEL'S HAM BUNS *with* CHOCOLATE GRAVY

MAKES 10 BUNS AND PLENTY OF GRAVY

Come Sunday, if Elvis was home at Graceland, chances are he'd be eating biscuits and chocolate gravy for breakfast. Biscuits are good, but these ham buns are even better. The tender dough is filled with tiny bombs of flavorful ham (yes, leftovers) with a hint of honey and sage. You rip off a piece of the bun, spoon on some chocolate gravy, and damn. Savory and sweet like you've never experienced it. We named it after a friend's grandma.

→ **Down in the Appalachians, chocolate gravy is often called "soppin' chocolate," but it's closer to chocolate pudding than anything else. Pile it onto those buns.**

FOR THE BUNS

½ cup warm water

2¼ teaspoons (1 packet) dry active yeast

⅓ cup sugar

5 large eggs, at room temperature, lightly beaten

4 cups bread flour

1 teaspoon coarse kosher salt

10 tablespoons plus 2 teaspoons (⅔ cup; 1⅓ sticks) cold unsalted butter, cut into cubes

FOR THE FILLING

½ pound Big Baked Ham (page 341) or Shoebox Ham (page 172) or other cooked ham, cut into chunks

2 tablespoons unsalted butter

2 tablespoons honey

2 tablespoons chopped fresh sage

FOR THE GLAZE

2 tablespoons unsalted butter

½ teaspoon brown sugar

2 tablespoons bourbon

¾ teaspoon coarse kosher salt

¼ teaspoon ground cinnamon

¼ teaspoon ground cardamom

FOR THE CHOCOLATE GRAVY

1 cup milk

1 cup heavy cream

1 (1-inch) piece ginger, peeled, sliced, and smashed

2 whole cloves

1 cinnamon stick

1 Thai bird chile, whole

2 tablespoons unsalted butter

2 tablespoons all-purpose flour

1¼ cups confectioners' sugar

⅔ cup cocoa powder

Coarse kosher salt

1 cup semisweet chocolate chips

Savory and sweet like you've never experienced it.

FOR THE BUNS

1 Pour the warm water into the bowl of a stand mixer. Add the yeast and sugar, stir, and let sit until creamy, about 5 minutes.

2 Add the eggs, flour, and salt and beat with the hook attachment on medium speed until you have a smooth dough, about 5 minutes. Scrape it down and add the butter in several additions, scraping the dough off the hook before each addition. Continue to beat on medium speed until the dough is very smooth, about 15 minutes from when you started adding the butter.

3 Cover with plastic wrap and refrigerate until doubled, about 2 hours.

FOR THE FILLING

4 Put the ham into a food processor and pulse until the ham is minced. Transfer to a bowl.

5 Melt the butter with the honey and sage in a small saucepan over medium heat. Stir and let it sizzle for about 30 seconds. Add to the ham and stir.

FOR THE GLAZE

6 Melt the butter and brown sugar in a small saucepan. Add the bourbon, salt, cinnamon, and cardamom and stir.

FOR THE GRAVY

7 Bring the milk, cream, ginger, cloves, cinnamon stick, and chile to a simmer in a small saucepan over medium heat. Turn off the heat and infuse for 20 minutes.

8 Melt the butter in another saucepan over medium heat. Add the flour and cook, stirring, for 2 minutes. Strain in the infused milk and cook, whisking, until the gravy comes to a simmer. Add the confectioners' sugar, cocoa, and a pinch of salt and whisk until smooth. Turn off the heat, add the chocolate chips, and whisk until they melt.

TO ASSEMBLE

9 Turn the dough out onto a floured work surface and roll out into a 10-x-20-inch rectangle. Scatter the filling over the dough, leaving a 1-inch rim on the long sides. Starting with a long side, roll the dough up into a log, brushing off any excess flour as you roll. Pinch the seam closed. Cut into 10 buns, each 2 inches wide, and set, seam side down, on a rimmed baking sheet.

10 Cover the buns with a kitchen towel and let them rise for 30 minutes, while you preheat the oven to 375°F.

11 Stir the glaze and brush the buns with half of it. Bake the buns for 30 minutes. Brush the buns with the rest of the glaze and bake until the buns are a rich brown and sound hollow when you tap their bottoms, about 5 minutes. Cool on a rack.

12 Pile the buns on a platter and give each guest a big bowl of gravy.

Food historian Sara Camp Arnold spent some time looking into chocolate gravy. She says it "probably originated somewhere in the Mountain South and spread through the so-called hillbilly diaspora." I have to agree with her when she says it's more than likely that some mama or aunty started playing with what she had on the pantry shelves to make something sweet for breakfast.

DIGGING UP THE TRUTH

Billy Mitchell, "Mr. Apollo," has worked for the Apollo Theater for over fifty years. This is his story about reclaiming history.

It started in 1934, when Mayor La Guardia banned burlesque—he was such a hard-nosed guy. Burlesque was becoming too vulgar, too risqué, promoting prostitution. They shut every burlesque house in Manhattan. In 1934 new owners bought our building and renamed it the Apollo Theater, based on the Greek god. Here's the reason why they bought this building: 1934 was right at the very end of the era called the Harlem Renaissance, when a lot of black entertainers were being discovered—black theater, literature, comedy, dance, fashion, activism. And white people coming here to see burlesque started hearing about Cab Calloway, Eubie Blake, Fats Waller, Duke Ellington. And they wanted to see them in this theater. But then again, blacks weren't allowed in the theaters in Harlem. So the owners who bought the building and named it the Apollo said, since no other theaters in Harlem allow colored folk in, we're going to be the first. This was the first theater in Harlem to allow blacks not only to perform on stage, but also to work behind the stage. And the guys who bought the building—they were Jewish brothers. Not brothers by birth, but, you know, Jewish brothers. And they started presenting what they called Colored Revues, shows featuring black performers.

Marcus knows we have to respect our past. We have to *know* it. Everyone thinks blacks have always been in Harlem. Originally, they were downtown, where the World Trade Center is—that's how they found our bodies down there. They found out that as the Dutch would bring us here to sell us as slaves, far back as 1655 , they made us live down there—near where Wall Street, World Trade, and South Street Seaport are now—and when we died, that's where they buried us. And over time, the people who ran New York didn't want future generations to know that slavery was done up here in the North.

And over time, the people who ran New York didn't want future generations to know that slavery was done up here in the North.

See, in American history, slavery was just done down in the South. To hide the bodies, they built streets on top of the cemetery—and buildings, big buildings, all over that six-acre cemetery.

And in 1991 when they were digging up that area to build a government building, that's when they stumbled upon what they called the Colored Cemetery, the Negro Cemetery. They found the bodies of twenty-thousand people. They were going to build a government building there, and we said, "What a minute. Our ancestors are buried there. Are you out of your damned mind? Are you crazy? And now you're going to build a government building for the General Services on top of them?"

And we went off—and we formed a committee and went to the White House—every house, green house, blue house. "What the hell you all doing? Stop them. And if you can't stop them, at least let us take our ancestors' bodies and ship them back to Africa. But we want a tract of land." And now we have a burial ground called the African Burial Ground. It's down at Duane and Broadway.

I go down there every Sunday to pray. Sometimes, I stop by Rooster for them chicken and waffles, then I head down. I've been wearing this—a bracelet—inscribed "African Burial Ground," and it represents the shackles worn on the wrists of our ancestors.

I'm very proud of this, I'm very humbled by this. I know it can be snatched away, just like that. I'm at the age of sixty-five and still working and loving what I do. I can't wait to get here every day. To share the truth about the Apollo. Not *his*-story, but the truth. I always tell people on the tours, there's a thing called *his*-story. And they say, "You mean 'history.'" And I say, "No, there's *his*-story and then there's the truth." Harlem is changing. And if we're not careful, the history will be changed right in front of our face, without us even knowing it. Without us even knowing it.

Harlem is changing. And if we're not careful, the history will be changed right in front of our face, without us even knowing it.

SUNDAY JAZZ

"NATE!"

"S'up, Man." Nate Lucas and I trade a brothers' hug—our palms slap, then make a two-handed fist, our chests touch for a second. I've been friends with Nate for almost ten years. Now that he plays at the Rooster on Sunday, we often meet up before his set and talk about jazz. Who's playing where, who tore it up on a Wednesday, who stumbled on stage and needed a forgiving audience to eat up the shame. Standing on the corner of 126th and Lenox, next to his van, Nate and I are having one of those conversations.

"You hit Paris Blues?"

"Hit it? I hurt it. Tuesday. Late, late. I thought Maya was going to kill me."

Nate opens the back of his van and pulls out a dolly. "Don't tell me you took the bike."

"I took the bike." I walk. I run. But in my opinion the best way to see Harlem is on a bike. You may see the boutiques, the restaurants, and the bars from the sidewalk; you can witness the chaos of street walkers from the safety of a cab; but only on a bike can you see it all: the sharp lines of project housing, church steeples made of copper or stone that look like they want to pierce the sky, four-story buildings that house all walks of life. Those of us who get around the neighborhood on two wheels don't do it for the exercise—I've never seen anybody in head-to-toe Spandex and sweating—most of us bike to see avenue views: Frederick Douglass Boulevard, Adam Clayton Powell Jr. Boulevard, Lenox Avenue: Traveling north on two wheels, I notice women leaning out of their windows with their chins out, waiting for a city breeze, or little kids bold enough to wave to me because they think I'm not watching. When I'm on my bike, I don't lean in, I lean back. And I'm not alone. Guys, bare-chested, ride the streets with their shirts tucked in their belt loops and beat boxes strapped to the back of their bikes. Some of us wear suits and ties. Whistles on strings sway back and forth on our chests. I can ride around and make business phone calls. For the most part, I bike around Harlem to a soundtrack. Miles Davis, John Coltrane, Jimmy Smith come out of my headphones and color my view. On my bike, in the earliest hours of the morning, I can follow a rising sun, east to west, my hands don't touch the handle bars, and I never leave the neighborhood. When I'm in Harlem, I don't have to pedal though; in Harlem I can glide.

For the most part, I bike around Harlem to a soundtrack. Miles Davis, John Coltrane, Jimmy Smith come out of my headphones and color my view.

"—trouble."

"What?"

"I said if you don't stay off that bike, you're gonna be in trouble with your lady." I don't bother to comment. I just shrug. Nate's my friend and a man; he can read the lift of my shoulder. "Alright, alright, I'll let it go. Bike your bike. You hear the keyboardist cooking at Showmans?"

"Yeah. You?"

"Hell, ya." If you think of yourself as a jazz head and you live in Harlem, you go to Showmans. At Paris Blues, you cackle in your seat at some overheard joke. The whole place is movement. People are gliding around the tables calling out hellos to friends they only see at the club. They sell everything from behind the bar: cigarettes and aspirin and postage stamps. The chicken and the black-eyed peas are free, but you pay for the booze. It's the kind of place where a musician grows a skin. Can you play through the din of laughter, forks clattering on plates? In a room full of folks as interesting as you, can you arrest their play and make them hear your own? Maybe it's because I'm a chef, but I can guess what musicians chant when they play Paris Blues: *Shake it off; concentrate.* It's the same song I sing to myself when I'm cooking at the restaurant.

But Showmans? At Showmans the audience is as serious as the musicians who play there. They have snacks there, too, but nobody eats them. How can you, when you're holding your breath? Sarah Vaughan, Duke Ellington, Pearl Bailey, Eartha Kitt were just a few legends who played Showmans. I once heard a saxophonist dive into "My Favorite Things," and just when I thought I knew where the music would go next, "John the Revelator" floated from his horn. European harmony complicated by African syncopation. At Showmans I watch musicians earn their swagger. You begin to understand why France and Japan lust after Harlem jazz musicians. Though it still makes my head hurt that jazz doesn't get that kind of adoration here in the States.

Whether Paris Blue or Showmans, I've seen magic happen. Men in their church suits with their legs braced apart are holding onto a note for dear mercy. There's an attitude, a mystique about it all, but there's also a wonderful intelligence on display. Playing with musical principles, understanding just how far you can manipulate what you've been told is fundamental—that feels familiar to me. And every time I witness it, I'm reminded about the power of ownership. Right or wrong, good or bad—own it. When Nate and I aren't catching up on where we've been, we're down at Ginny's drinking beers and having this conversation. Who owns this art? And more importantly, what are we all supposed to do with it?

Experiencing this music makes me think about the connections between jazz and Southern food. Both traveled north and were transformed. Both come from a deep tradition of what it means to riff on what you think you know. I listen to "Bitches Brew" and think gumbo. It's a dish that can be a fridge cleaner or can break your piggy bank if you let it. Onions, bell peppers, shrimp, tripe stirred into the patience of a whiskey-colored roux. Nate keeps telling me my mind goes sideways, but he grins when he says it. Like me, Nate knows what it feels like to play and improvise; to feel scared and arrogant at the same time. Catching Coltrane, that's what we call being deadly serious about our play. Well before nose-to-tail was cool, there were people standing over a stove thinking of what to do with what the well-heeled threw away. And the point wasn't just to make it edible. The point is to see how desire can shape a meal, how "not quite enough" can push your creativity. Beef hearts, tripe, pig feet. With enough skill, these odds and ends are delicious. They're so good, you feel like a chump when you eat a loin.

Onions, bell peppers, shrimp, tripe stirred into the patience of a whiskey-colored roux.

Nate grins when he hears me go over this familiar territory. He gets it. "Help me with my babies." We peer inside his van. There's his Hammond B3 and his XK, he's even got an Everett tucked in the back. Every time I see them, Nate points them out as if it's the first time. I don't say a word. He's got his instruments; I've got my knives. We're lifting his Hammond onto the dolly when a young guy with a horn case strapped to his back walks up to us.

"Yo, Nate!"

"Hey, Brother, what's up." Daryl's my age. His mother used to spoon and measure coke in her underwear for Nicky Barnes,

Harlem's famous drug lord. He didn't want part of that life and instead picked up the saxophone.

"Yo, I'm ready, Man."

"All right. Cool. Play." Nate and I had moved the Hammond to the sidewalk. Without looking at the time, we both knew he had to go in to the Rooster soon.

"What? Like now?"

"Yeah. Like right now. Play." It's not as if Nate and I had been talking in a dark corner somewhere, but I swear, Daryl and I notice the roar of the avenue when Nate tells him to play a little something. I can feel the curiosity of the couple leaning against the building on the corner, smoking cigarettes.

If I want to eat outside, then I cook outside. The same is true for music made in Harlem. You make your bones outside.

"Man, you want me to play out here?" We all look at the tourists walking past us, at our neighbors who wave hello. I know what Nate's up to. Those of us who live in Harlem create outside. Our stage is the sidewalk, the park. We don't make sandwiches in the privacy of our kitchens and then step out with baskets full of wine and olives to picnic. If I want to eat outside, then I cook outside. The same is true for music made in Harlem. You make your bones outside. Are you brave enough to play what you love in front of everybody—your neighbors and strangers? Because if you can give yourself that kind of reckless permission and be good to boot, maybe you can graduate to play at 449 LA, aka SCAT, where Sandy will become your musical aunty. She'll give you a meal when you need one or hold on to your instrument when you don't have any place safe to put it. You can become a part of a family.

Daryl fiddles with his saxophone case for a moment and then looks at me. I say the first thing that comes to mind. "You should play. Now."

"Man, I can't play out here."

"That's cool." Nate doesn't look disappointed; he looks patient. "Help me and Marcus with my babies. Grab those speakers, too."

As we bring all of Nate's equipment inside the Rooster, the conversation turns to what it means to be an official artist, playing unofficial music. Somehow the sidewalk, the streets, are a part of that negotiation. Are you making it? The answer is hard to get a hold on. Real music feels like real food. There's the rush of it, the immediacy, and then it's gone. The memory of eating well, listening well, trumps all the pictures or videos you can take of it. You can't put a price on that. Once we start talking about an artist's worth, we inevitably talk about that special brand of Harlem currency. Where does that kind of money spend?

"At Marjorie's," I tell them. I go to Marjorie's Parlor Jazz for my sanity, my dignity, when I feel an ache to make connections. Going to Marjorie's isn't about a transaction. Marjorie is our grandmother. Every Sunday in her living room, she shows anyone who wants to know that music is how you can restore neighborhood; music is how you wrestle with grief and not succumb to it. Sitting on folding chairs, we discover jazz. One Sunday we hear a new voice; the next, a new trumpet player.

Maybe it's the granola bars and orange juice, maybe it's because Marjorie sounds like a poet, but whatever the reason I keep thinking good food and good music shouldn't be like the division of church and state. When I first moved to Harlem it was hard to find the two together. It's a little better now. We at the Rooster are trying to hold up our end. Improvisation can happen on a plate or with a snare drum. Some days I'm lucky and witness artistic triumphs and sometimes we invite those who stumble due to nerves. Marjorie says keep on nurturing the art of jazz, because if we don't . . . Lord, look what happens. She doesn't have to complete her thought.

Good food and good music shouldn't be like the division of church and state.

There's the empty Lenox Lounge, a block away from Rooster. And when it closed, lives flew apart. Big Boy's was one of them. He's one of those guys who looks like his nickname: 6-foot-4, 220 pounds, cornrows, gold teeth, his neck is as big as my thigh. You think he's trouble until he smiles. He can tell you who's a misunderstood genius and who's smoking K2. Everybody knew Big Boy worked the door on Lenox. Everybody was worried what would happen to him when the Lenox Lounge shut its doors. He was the kind of guy who could just disappear. He told me he wanted to hang tight, maybe the owners would come back. Still he was nervous. Two kids, no resumé, and a kind of savvy that only works in the hood. So come work at the Rooster, I told him. We need you. Nine months later, he did. Sometimes, late at night, we both walk past the Lounge and try not to notice how it looks like a punched eye. Music used to anchor that block. I always hear Marjorie's advice when I make that trek. *Careful,* she tells everyone who comes to her parlor for a listen. *Own your art. No one else will. It's my job to help any way I can.* The last time Marjorie was here at the Rooster, we served her a bowl of gumbo. The spoon she held looked enormous in her small hand. She took a bite and smiled. "Look at you, Marcus. Making music."

Nate's getting ready to go on and Daryl's not sure what to do. Too scared to ask questions or for favors, he heads for the door. "Daryl, Man, where you going?" Nate, his guitarist, and his drummer start up a tune that I can only describe as *come here.* I rarely shout but it feels too good to do anything else. "You're invited!"

SUNDAY JAZZ PLAYLIST

"FLUX CAPACITOR" Aaron Diehl

"JUNCTION" Benny Golson

"LOOK AT ME" Cecile McLorin Salvant

"WHAT'S HAPPENING" Cyrus Chestnut

"BIG STUFF" Jason Moran

"SOMEONE TO WATCH OVER ME" Jimmy Scott

"OBSERVE" Tivon Pennicott

"THE RED ROOSTER" Christian Scott

"THE MORE I SEE YOU" Johnny O'Neal

HOT GUMBO
with TRIPE
and RICE

SERVES 6

H arlem and New Orleans are sisters, united by their love of music and food. They're two of the few places around where you routinely see musicians walking the streets with their instruments, and cooks commute back and forth. So chicken and shrimp gumbo thickened with filé powder (the powdered leaves of the sassafras tree) makes everyone feel at home. Tripe makes this gumbo extra special.

FOR THE ROUX

½ cup peanut oil

1 cup all-purpose flour

FOR THE TRIPE

2 pounds beef honeycomb tripe, cut into 3-x-4-inch pieces

4 cups water

1 red onion, sliced thin

2 garlic cloves, chopped

2 sprigs thyme

Coarse kosher salt

FOR THE SHRIMP STOCK

1 pound large (21–30 count) shrimp

1 teaspoon peanut oil

1 tablespoon tomato paste

2 cups water

1 cup dry white wine

1 cup clam juice

1 sprig thyme

FOR THE GUMBO

2 red onions, chopped

2 green bell peppers, cored and cut into ¼-inch dice

1 celery rib, cut into ¼-inch dice

1 carrot, cut into ¼-inch dice

2 garlic cloves, chopped

1 pound boneless, skinless chicken thighs, cut into bite-sized pieces

1 pound andouille sausage, cut into ½-inch slices

¼ pound okra, trimmed and cut into ¼-inch slices

1 tablespoon filé powder (see headnote)

2 teaspoons shrimp powder (see page 30)

1 teaspoon dried oregano

1 teaspoon cayenne

1 sprig thyme

Juice of 1 lemon

FOR SERVING

4 cups cooked jasmine rice

Chopped fresh cilantro

FOR THE ROUX

1 Preheat the oven to 350°F.

2 Pour the oil into a medium cast-iron skillet. Stir in the flour. Slide the skillet into the oven and cook the roux, stirring every 20 minutes, until it's chestnut brown, about 2 hours. You can make this roux days, weeks, or months ahead. Keep it in a glass jar in the refrigerator.

FOR THE TRIPE

3 Put all the ingredients into a pressure cooker. Lock the lid in place and bring to full pressure over high heat. Turn the heat down enough to keep high pressure and cook for 40 minutes. Turn off the heat and allow the pressure

Harlem and New Orleans are sisters, united by their love of music and food.

to drop naturally. Unlock the lid, open, and set the pot aside. Or, if you're making this ahead, pour everything into a bowl, cover, and refrigerate. If you don't have a pressure cooker, you can simmer the tripe in a covered Dutch oven over low heat until tender, about 4 hours.

FOR THE STOCK

4 Peel the shrimp, saving the shells. Put the shrimp into a bowl, cover, and refrigerate until you need them.

5 Heat a saucepan over medium-high heat. Add the oil and shrimp shells and cook, stirring, until the shells color, about 30 seconds. Add the tomato paste and cook, stirring, until the paste starts to turn brick red, about 30 seconds. Add the water, wine, clam juice, and thyme and bring to a simmer. Turn the heat to medium-low and simmer for 20 minutes. Turn off the heat, cover, and let the stock infuse for 20 minutes.

6 Strain the stock, pushing down on the shells to get out every last drop.

FOR THE GUMBO

7 Heat the roux in a Dutch oven over medium-high heat. When it's bubbling, add the onions, bell peppers, celery, and carrot and cook, stirring often, until the onions soften, about 10 minutes. Add the garlic, chicken, and sausage and cook, stirring often, until the chicken is no longer pink, about 5 minutes. Pour in the shrimp stock and bring to a simmer. Turn the heat down to low and simmer for 20 minutes. Add the okra, filé powder, shrimp powder, oregano, cayenne, and thyme and simmer for another 20 minutes.

8 Take the tripe out of its cooking liquid with a slotted spoon and slice it thin. Add it to the pot and simmer until the tripe is hot. Add the lemon juice and shrimp you saved when you were making the stock and simmer until the shrimp is cooked through, about 3 minutes.

TO SERVE

9 Spoon the rice into six pasta plates. Top with the gumbo and garnish with cilantro. And serve.

This recipe may look like a lot of work, but you can break it up over a couple of days and be rewarded by even deeper flavor.

► The roux will keep for months.

► You can make the tripe and stock a day or two ahead. Keep the tripe in its juices.

► And you could make the gumbo up to adding the shrimp a day ahead, too. Just bring it back to an active simmer before adding the shrimp.

SPRING PEA PASTA

SERVES 4 TO 6

When Nate Lucas plays every Sunday—which he has since we opened our doors—he does a great job of introducing people to jazz classics. We use this bright pasta to introduce spring on our menu.

Every time I want to cook something Italian, I check in with Leo Marino (who's now working in my restaurant in Bermuda); Leo checks in with his mother; and we get the perfect Italian-American dish.

→ **Thin asparagus are best here. And we use Rustichella d'Abruzzo pasta at the Rooster.**

---

3 tablespoons olive oil

1 shallot, minced

4 garlic cloves, sliced very thin

1 cup chopped (1-inch) asparagus

2 tablespoons yuzu kosho (see page 30)

2 cups vegetable stock

2 tablespoons coarse kosher salt

1 pound spaghetti

1 cup peas (fresh or thawed frozen)

1 cup peeled fava beans (see page 219)

4 tablespoons (½ stick) unsalted butter, softened

½ cup grated pecorino cheese

8 ounces jumbo lump crabmeat

1 lemon, cut into wedges

1 Bring a large pot of water to a boil.

2 Heat the oil in a large skillet over medium-high heat. Add the shallot, garlic, asparagus, and yuzu kosho and cook, stirring, until the shallot has softened, about 2 minutes. Pour in the stock.

3 Add the salt and spaghetti to the boiling water and cook until the pasta is 2 minutes shy of being cooked al dente.

4 Drain the spaghetti and add it to the skillet, along with the peas and favas. Cook, tossing with tongs, until the spaghetti has absorbed most of the stock, about 90 seconds. Toss in the butter. Turn off the heat and toss in the cheese and crabmeat.

5 Divide among pasta bowls or plates and serve with the lemon wedges.

Add a handful or two of sliced mushrooms with the asparagus if you want to.

BRUSSELS SPROUTS *with* BACON DIP

SERVES 4

The smokiness of bacon is an ideal foil for the bitterness of Brussels sprouts, plus you've got that pairing of creamy and crunchy. This is a perfect side for a pork chop or ham.

1 Put the bacon into a large skillet. Turn the heat to medium and cook, stirring, until it is crisp, about 10 minutes. Use a slotted spoon or a spider to transfer it to paper towels. Pour ¼ cup of the bacon grease into a bowl and reserve.

2 If you need to, add enough grapeseed oil to the skillet so there's about 2 tablespoons fat. Turn the heat up to medium-high and add the Brussels sprouts. Turn them so they're all cut side down and leave for about 3 minutes to caramelize. Then stir and sauté for another 2 minutes to get some brown on the other sides. Clear a space in the center of the skillet. If it's dry, add a slick of oil. Add half of the garlic to the center of the pan and cook until it's starting to color, about

45 seconds. Turn off the heat and stir. Add the oyster sauce, honey, and Aleppo pepper and stir until the Brussels sprouts are coated. Add the lime juice and stir until it's reduced to a syrup (residual heat does the cooking).

3 Put the egg and a good pinch of salt into a food processor. Turn the machine on and drop in the remaining garlic. With the processor running, drizzle in the olive oil in a slow, steady stream, then drizzle in the reserved ¼ cup bacon grease. Scrape out into a bowl and fold in the bacon.

4 Pile the Brussels sprouts onto a platter and serve at room temperature with the bowl of bacon dip.

6 slices bacon, chopped

Grapeseed oil, if necessary

1 pound Brussels sprouts, each trimmed and halved through the core

4 garlic cloves, sliced thin

1 tablespoon oyster sauce

1 tablespoon honey

1 teaspoon Aleppo pepper (see page 27)

Juice of 1 lime

1 large egg

Coarse kosher salt

¼ cup olive oil

ROASTED TURNIPS DDUK

SERVES 4

I love turnips, but I think they're weird. Jazz weird. They get spongy soft—almost like marshmallows—when you roast them, but they're bitter. The miso adds a low note of fermented earthiness. The something new is sliced Korean rice cakes (*dduk*): They're really chewy and bland, so they're a foil for all kinds of flavor. And if you're like me, you're going to love the challenge of that chewiness.

More jazz.

5 tablespoons olive oil

4 garlic cloves, chopped

1 tablespoon Korean hot pepper paste (gochujang; see page 29)

1 tablespoon white miso

1 pound turnips, peeled and cut into ½-inch wedges

1½ cups sliced Korean rice cakes (dduk, see page 31), thawed

1 scallion, cut into 2-inch lengths

2 tablespoons soy sauce

2 teaspoons honey

1 Preheat the oven to 400°F. Line a small rimmed baking sheet with parchment.

2 Mix 2 tablespoons of the olive oil with the garlic, hot pepper paste, and miso in a bowl. Add the turnips and toss well.

3 Spread the turnips on the baking sheet and roast until tender and starting to brown, about 20 minutes.

4 Heat the remaining 3 tablespoons olive oil in a heavy skillet over medium-high heat. Add the rice cakes and cook, stirring often, until hot, about 4 minutes. Stir in the turnips, scallion, soy sauce, and honey and stir-fry until everything is glossy, 2 to 3 minutes. Scrape into a serving bowl and serve warm.

SAVING LIVES, ONE SUNDAY AT A TIME

Marjorie Eliot has invited the world into her living room to listen to her play jazz on her piano every Sunday afternoon for over thirty years. She is Harlem's best-kept secret. Here she ruminates on jazz.

So. I do believe jazz is God's plan for black people. Truly. To understand it is to understand where black people go to find comfort for their grief. You have to understand that, before you understand anything else. Jazz saves. It's that simple. I know you think, *Well, it can't be that simple.* But truly when black people approach art, it's not merely an act of celebration. It is an act of revelation. It is an act of atonement. It is an act of salvation. When I lost my sons, I didn't know where to

You never lose your grief, but jazz—to listen to it, to create it—makes all bearable.

I was very lucky as a child. Very early, I took piano lessons. And when I was a child, my parents would invite over our neighbors and our friends, and I would play for them in our living room. Now, you know, a lot of us did that growing up. You took music lessons. You did! And you learned how to play piano or the clarinet. But most importantly you learned how to share your art. You learned you

You never lose your grief, but jazz—to listen to it, to create it—makes all bearable.

go. Philip passed away in 1992, and then I lost another son. They were the most important people in my life. Ah, so much grief on Sundays. I felt it coming, all this sorrow. I just dreaded Sundays. But then God said, "Go on. Face the day . . . with music." And suddenly my sorrow became manageable. Music chases the sadness; it enriches the sadness and the people who listen to what we do are critical. They embrace us, they understand us, in the most loving way. It's a miracle, really. When we engage in music and art, we are allowed to define ourselves in another way. That is a delegation that God gives us. I wanted to celebrate my sons' lives with what I do, and that's music and theater. Well, here's the thing:

are capable of creating something beautiful, and that's such an important lesson for black people to learn. You learned how to connect with others through your art. And if I may, this is what I worry about most for our young people. Are we teaching them about this connection? Ah, it is so convenient to lay blame at our youth's feet. To stand back and pronounce: *Why is it that you lack this connection, why don't you possess an art?* But shouldn't we also wonder who is passing this gift along? Jazz must be passed along. Music must be passed along. The theater must be passed along. And if we don't do that, who will?

So part of what I do on Sunday is pass along the gift of music, but I also teach. That is equally important. And I teach and play American classical music. And that's jazz. Now, I call jazz *American classical music* because, well, it is our musical history. America's musical history. It's also a history black people birthed. So it's very important that we claim this history. And what is so fantastic is when you understand it's not a static art. American classical music is growing and changing. Songs move in and move out. I do believe that this movement, this ability to move, is what makes jazz uniquely American.

Jazz is fearless and so are we. We are unafraid of change, but I think that's a necessity. But you must also remember that it is glorious. You can't forget that. That as much as I want people to know that playing music is the most humble piece of my life—that it has given me shelter from my loss—it also is

glorious. I've been very fortunate in my life, not only do I have jazz, I have a house for it. Living at 555 Edgecombe for so long really shaped me. This is just a building that loves art and music and dance. You feel a part of history when you live here: Count Basie, Paul Robeson, Max Roach, Joe Louis. For a very long time, the fifth floor was called the musical hall. People would leave their doors open and move from apartment to apartment. All kinds of jazz was being played. Beebop and cool jazz and free jazz. I have no idea what one of my neighbors was up to, but it sounded fantastic. So for those of us who love American classical music, those of us who find ourselves from time to time lamenting its place in America's musical hierarchy, you must ask yourself: What are *you* doing to ensure that this gift is shared and passed on? Well?

FAMILY MEALS

"FIRE MEATBALL. Fire funky. Fire catfish. Order Yardbird. Order shrimp and grits, 101. Wings rush, 304. Coco, two pork, burger rare and she's blue, 304. Steak, 702. Chowder, 51. Ribs, gravlax, 42, all for the table!" Tristen Epps sings out and five chefs leap. Sizzle plates clatter like cymbals, black steel pans thump on fire. It's hot in the kitchen. Heat licks Kone's face as he takes a pork chop from the drawer and slaps it on the grill. Fire sputters up, but he doesn't snatch his hand back.

"Get the baby a paci!" Tristen says, mocking him from the order box. Tristen is the expo man tonight, coordinating all the orders that come to the kitchen, our culinary conductor who lifts his voice instead of a baton. He calls out every order taken at the restaurant; he is the one who decides when we cook to a furious tempo and when we pause for breath. Kone laughs at the good-natured ribbing then adds a steak, a coco chicken.

I'm watching him from the window, when CJ bellows out, "Behind! Behind you!" She marches through the galley kitchen carrying a twenty-quart sauce pot full of boiled eggs. No one rubbernecks or stops the frenetic motions of their hands. Almost as one they step closer to the heat in front of them. For a second everything pauses, steam bathes five chefs as CJ passes them one by one. Johnny stops building the confetti of sliced radishes and takes a small step to stand flush against the sauté station. For one beat, then two, no one moves. Then Tristen shakes his head at the silence and picks up his song again.

"Fire ribs. Fire devil eggs. Fire chowder. Fire, kitfo, 22, 63," has a syncopated hook. "Order catfish, 803. Order mac and greens. Order Yardbird. Order Royale. Order meatball, 400!" We all dance to the reggae beat in the kitchen. When Adrienne stands at the box, her calls slip into Spanglish, "Fire Bacon! Fire waffle! ¡Y rápido, eh!"

Kingsley sounds like the islands, with a heavy sonata tone, and when he thinks no one is watching, he sings out the orders with his eyes closed. Right now he's strutting like the leader of a marching band, back and forth down the line, holding a bouquet of plastic spoons. He's tonight's taster. He dips a spoon into the funk sauce and then scowls. Tasting a sauce or a dish is like tuning an instrument. What's that off note? Where's my sour; where's my heat; where's my umami; where's my sweet? The point is to find harmony and contrast at the end of a spoon. The chicken liver butter, the buttermilk blue cheese, the lemon dressing. Is it there, yet? Johnny, standing at the sauté station, shakes his head. "Oh, baby, I'm cooking it, now. They're so tasty and delicious." All the guys on the line chuckle.

Tasting a sauce or a dish is like tuning an instrument. What's that off note? Where's my sour; where's my heat; where's my umami; where's my sweet?

"Yeah. Yeah. Shut up, Romeo."

Before they can start cursing each other or playing the dozens, Tristen looks down and then hollers, "Boogie time." It's a moment you brace for, and because we're all adrenaline junkies, we crave it. Ticket orders are flying out of the box like confetti, and when you walk down the line you can feel the intensity. Every man is playing his tune, fearlessly, flawlessly. Plates slide to the counter in twos and threes, "Service, where's service?" Tristen calls out and then in what he thinks is sotto voce says, "Where's the service?" Jamie and Ava appear at the window, and they can see Tristen's mild-mannered version of frustration. There are fourteen plates on the counter, and we need servers to run them to our diners. That's called service. "Long time, no see, Ava."

"Sorry, cocktails," she says and then picks up and balances four dishes in the crook of her arm.

Kone is on a tear. "Where's my sexy? I need two sexy." That's what we call our French fries. Jeanette hears him down the line, and pulls out a pile of fries straight from the fryer. She puts them in a boat and hands them off to Johnny who sprinkles chives, Parmesan, and fresh ground pepper over them. Sexy, right? Next to me, the servers pluck one dish, then two, then three. The jokes have dwindled down to nothing—all you can feel is the tension doubling and re-doubling. Cooks are working separately at their stations, but they are also working collectively. Five chefs cutting, chopping, cooking, each one bent over in concentration because it matters, the tiniest thing matters.

There's purpose on that plate. And music. And grace. And a hidden paycheck.

We're not about the monster menu or some famous or infamous somebody huddled in the corner booth. Nothing is more important than the plate of food in front of us. And to make that dish perfect, every scrap of discipline comes to the forefront. You hear the order for mac and greens, and the sneaking suspicion that you are onto something bigger moves you. There's purpose on that plate. And music. And grace. And a hidden paycheck. Five cooks hunched over liver butter and au jus like their lives depend on it aren't just earning weekly dollars, they're learning a skill and a language to express it. They're learning how to improvise when the ingredients have changed, how to coordinate with a dozen other people while still keeping their minds focused on the knife in their hands. The hidden paycheck is an introduction to a culture that crosses race and gender. It has no borders. It's a tradition that was birthed in the twentieth century, but is perfect for the twenty-first. It's a lifestyle. It asks you to test your commitment, to dive in now, because you're hungry for what comes next. But most importantly, it flows both ways. I guess I'm the boss man, but more importantly I'm a mentor. Am I giving opportunities to my guys? I feel a tremendous responsibility to do that. My whole journey—as a chef, as a man—is based on the hidden paycheck. It's literally an unwritten rule. Break that trust at your own peril. I was given a chance when I didn't think it would happen. Am I passing that on? The currency isn't dollars; but it spends. It forces you to ask what comes out of that transaction. How do you value cooking for the president of the United States? Or setting up a buffet at the First Corinthian Baptist Church? What's the value in doing a royal dinner for the kids at P.S. 76? How do you value cooking at a soup kitchen one day and then traveling to Europe the next? The hidden paycheck is an explanation as to why we take this work so seriously. Yes, you might be a misfit. But you are not alone. You can become a part of a band of misfits.

Yes, you might be a misfit. But you are not alone. You can become a part of a band of misfits.

That sense of a larger purpose, of curiosity and seriousness, that we bring into play has always reminded me of a jazz band. I don't have to squint to see the connective tissue between the two. My kitchen is like a stage and we jam in there. Let's play with beef heart, pig ears, and the catch of the day. Let's listen to what we can do with ceviche and pork tack tack. Both musicians and chefs need discipline, knowledge, sincerity, all of which are used in celebration. I'm not sure how anyone can look at what we do at the Rooster and fail to see its festivity, its creativity, its drive.

And like the best jazz quintet, our kitchen is proof that talent can come from anywhere. Nils, who's Swedish, passes along all that he knows to the Korean intern, who relates it to the runner from Ecuador, who can mix it up with my sous chef from Mexico, who can get down with Hannah, my hostess, who is a Columbia University student.

Like the best jazz quintet, our kitchen is proof that talent can come from anywhere.

Tristen might be panicking; Kingsley might be yelling that someone has messed up his stew, but it's humbling to witness my chefs seriously getting swept up in getting it right. Watching them work makes me want to call out, "Ladies and gentlemen, introducing, the chefs: Kone on the Grill; Jeanette on Fry; Adrienne on the Cold Station; Johnny on Sauté, Kingsley, the executive, riding hard with a Saint Lucian accent; and, in the box, singing his song, is Tristen Epps."

I'm still watching the orders come in as a wave when Zee and Nicolette, my hostesses, catch my eye. They give me knowing nods. I need to say my hellos not only to a full dining room, but to the fifty or so people standing near the bar, waiting and hungry. It's always strange for me to walk the length of the Rooster. I feel this urge to straighten everything. Is Thornton Dial's *The Lady and Red Rooster* hanging right? Art at the Rooster isn't some inert pretty thing, it's a way to honor my friends and my extended family: Lana Turner, Philip

Maysles, Lorna Simpson, Gordon Parks. Everything is just so, but still I want to touch the art. Maybe to remind myself it's there.

I'm saying hello to everyone when I still feel Nicolette's eyes on me. When I turn around, she gives me this exaggerated stare and crooks a finger. Next to the hostess's stand is a guy, maybe in his forties, dressed in a tan linen short suit and purple checkered dress shirt. He's over six feet tall and thin as a rail. His black bow tie looks like the real deal and not the kind you clip on. It's askew. And he's drunk. He's very, very drunk. Nicolette and Zee don't have to tell me what's the problem; as soon as I'm in earshot, he tells me. "I want a table. Do you know who I am? I want a table, now."

I look at Zee and state the obvious, "Get him a table." And that's when I learn the real problem. This gentleman has a table. In the middle of eating dinner, he stood up, started to stagger toward the bathroom, and then, when he was almost there, he forgot where he was going. Zee and Nicolette have been trying to convince him he has a table and they'll walk him to it if he'll let them. Right now, he just wants to sway. "I got it, guys," I tell them. He puts his hand on my shoulder and I can see the outline of a flask under his jacket lapel.

"Man, I killed it. It was all like, 'go, go, go, go.' My whole life in this neighborhood. And I brought the house down. Hear me? It's about to get real, Baby. I am Harlem." Thin as he is, his hand is heavy on my shoulder.

"Okay. I understand." I don't walk him to his table, I point the way to the bathroom, the place he wanted to go before he got lost. He titters and sways on the way, humming something bluesy.

When I think about that moment, I find myself thinking about the four ingredients of Rooster: Harlem, its staff, its customers, and its aspirations. That gentleman may have been a little boozy, but he hadn't forgotten that he belongs. He's a part of a tradition. He's a part of a migration of jazz and blues and food. And the thing is, swaying or not, drunk or not, if we are smart, we should let that man be. Harlem is changing, yes. But at its core, it still sings a gutbucket blues. Give this neighborhood a string and a washtub, and we can still make music and turn heads. I've begun thinking about gutbucket as a state of mind. The gutbucket is the Senegalese woman wearing Nikes standing next to a Japanese tourist on 125th. It's fermented shrimp and beef hearts and sucking the marrow from chicken bones. It's the Dancing Man who looks like Bootsy and Versace's love child and grooves outside the Rooster to our music; come closer and he'll whisper secrets about Harlem's history. It's being forty-something years old, wasted, and lost in a sea of people at the Red Rooster, but knowing you belong. You know you can instigate a roar of applause. You know you are the grit. You know you are Harlem.

Harlem is changing, yes. But at its core, it still sings a gutbucket blues.

It's Thursday and at twelve-thirty, Adrienne, Kingsley, Tristen, Kone, and Jeanette walk into a bar that feels like a crisp fall when compared to the hot summer of a kitchen. Five chefs pull off the towel bandanas they've worn all night. I spend more time with these guys than with anyone else. More than with my close friends. Or my sisters. Or my wife. This is my family. No chef would tell you different. I've got beers for all of them. We talk about what went wrong in the kitchen—where did the fluke go, we almost eighty-sixed the chowder when we had all that lobster—but mainly we murmur about food and Rooster family. Is the new guy going to work out? You think he's down? Butternut squashes are coming in; I've got an idea for them. Something's funky with the grill. "'Night, Chef."

"'Night." Our goodbyes sound like promises we'll keep.

"*Mañana*, Chef."

"Tomorrow."

FAMILY MEAL PLAYLIST

"AYNOTCHÉ TÈRABU"   Mahmoud Ahmed

"BREAD AND BUTTER"   The Roots

"JUNGLE"   Nina Persson

"MY JAMAICAN GUY"   Grace Jones

"THINKING OF YOU"   Lenny Kravitz

"BETTER DAYS"   Anthony Hamilton

"LADY DAY"   Lou Reed

Eggs scrambled with tortilla chips, served with a simple tomato salsa and some pickled onions and chiles. That's our migas. It's a very popular brunch item, but someone will make it at least once a week for Rooster family meal.

I can't imagine Rooster without a Latin beat. It comes from our staff. Our musicians. Our guests. And I love it!

MIGAS

SERVES 4

FOR THE PICKLED ONIONS AND JALAPEÑO

1 Bring the water, vinegar, sugar, cinnamon, allspice, and salt to a boil in a small saucepan.

2 Put the onion and jalapeño in separate bowls. Pour in the pickling liquid, dividing it between the bowls. Cover and refrigerate for at least 20 minutes before serving.

FOR THE SALSA ROJA

3 Put the tomato, onion, jalapeño, garlic, and cilantro into a blender and puree until smooth. Add a little water if you need to adjust the consistency. Pour into a bowl and season with salt.

FOR THE MIGAS

4 Melt the butter in a large skillet over medium-low heat. Add the eggs, season with salt and pepper, and cook, stirring constantly, until the eggs are almost scrambled but still runny. Stir in the tortilla chips.

5 Divide the eggs between four plates and top with queso fresco, pickled onions, pickled jalapeño, and salsa roja.

FOR THE PICKLED ONIONS

1 cup water

¼ cup sherry vinegar

2 tablespoons sugar

1 teaspoon ground cinnamon

½ teaspoon ground allspice

2 teaspoons coarse kosher salt

½ cup thinly sliced red onion

⅓ cup thinly sliced jalapeño

FOR THE SALSA ROJA

1 cup chopped ripe tomato

½ cup chopped onion

¼ cup chopped jalapeño

1 tablespoon sliced garlic

¼ cup fresh cilantro (small stems are fine)

Coarse kosher salt

FOR THE MIGAS

2 tablespoons unsalted butter

8 large eggs, beaten

Coarse kosher salt and freshly ground black pepper

2 cups tortilla chips, slightly crushed

½ cup crumbled queso fresco or mild feta

SCRAPPY FISH CHOWDER

SERVES 6 TO 8

Nothing better than a chowder to feed a lot of hungry people. We butcher our fish at Rooster, so we always have a lot of scraps to throw in the pot. When you make this at home, look for the cheapest fillets the fishmonger has that day. If you can find it, try paiche, a very meaty fish from the Amazon. It holds up well in chowder.

The chicken broth mayo is a Harlem riff on rouille—the garlicky saffron sauce from Provence that's spread on toast to sop up the broth of bouillabaisse.

FOR THE CHICKEN-BROTH MAYO (MAKES ABOUT 2 CUPS)

1 tablespoon olive oil

3 garlic cloves, chopped

2 whole scallions, chopped

1 jalapeño chile, stemmed and chopped

Coarse kosher salt

1 cup chicken broth

2 tablespoons sherry vinegar

1 large egg

1 large egg yolk

2 teaspoons Dijon mustard

1 teaspoon Sriracha

1¼ cups grapeseed oil

Juice of 1 lime

Freshly ground black pepper

FOR THE CHOWDER

2 tablespoons grapeseed oil

2 carrots, chopped

2 onions, chopped

2 jalapeño chiles, stemmed, seeded, and minced

1 (2-inch) piece ginger, peeled and minced

1 lemongrass stalk, trimmed, smashed, and minced (see page 28)

3 garlic cloves, minced

2 tablespoons tomato paste

1¼ pounds red-skinned potatoes, peeled and cut into ½-inch cubes

1 cup canned white beans (your choice), rinsed and drained

4 cups clam juice

1 (14.5-ounce) can diced tomatoes

2 tablespoons Worcestershire sauce

1 tablespoon Madras curry powder

2 teaspoons white miso

1 teaspoon freshly ground black pepper

1 bay leaf

2 pounds fish scraps (see headnote)

2 pounds mussels, scrubbed and debearded

1 loaf sourdough bread, sliced and toasted or grilled

FOR THE CHICKEN-BROTH MAYO

1 Heat the olive oil in a small saucepan over medium heat. Add the garlic, scallions, jalapeño, and a pinch of salt and cook until the vegetables are softened, about 4 minutes. Add the broth and vinegar, turn the heat up to medium-high, and bring to a simmer. Simmer until the liquid is reduced to about 2 tablespoons, 12 to 13 minutes. Take the pan off the heat and cool to room temperature.

2 Put the egg, yolk, mustard, and Sriracha in a food processor and whir until completely mixed and smooth. Add the vegetables and liquid from the pan and puree. With the processor running, pour in the grapeseed oil in a slow steady stream to make an emulsified sauce. To finish, add the lime juice and salt and pepper to taste. Scrape the mayo out into a bowl, cover, and refrigerate until you're ready to serve. It will keep for 3 days.

FOR THE CHOWDER

3 Heat the oil in a large pot over medium heat. Add the carrots, onions, jalapeños, ginger, lemongrass, and garlic and cook until the onion is softened, about 8 minutes. Add the tomato paste and cook, stirring constantly, until the tomato paste turns brick red, about 1 minute.

4 Add the potatoes, beans, clam juice, tomatoes, Worcestershire, curry powder, miso, pepper, and bay leaf and stir well. Bring to a simmer, then turn the heat down to medium-low and simmer until the potatoes are very tender and all the flavors have melded, about 1 hour.

Discard the bay leaf. You can make the chowder base several hours or even a day ahead. Leave it covered on the stove for an hour or two, or cover and refrigerate.

5 To finish, bring the chowder base to an active simmer over medium-high heat. Stir in the fish and spread the mussels over the top. Cover and simmer until the fish is cooked and the mussels are all opened, 5 to 7 minutes.

6 Divide the chowder between soup plates and serve with the toast and mayo.

SCRAPPY FISH CHOWDER ROYALE

You can fancy this chowder up big-time.

▶ Bring a pot of salted water to a boil. Add a 1½-pound lobster, cover, and bring the water back to a boil. Boil for 3 minutes, then take the lobster out of the pot and let it cool for a few minutes.

▶ Heat a stove-top grill pan over medium-high heat.

▶ Pull the claws off the lobster and crack them with the back of a chef's knife. Cut the lobster in half lengthwise, spoon out the tomalley, and stir it into the chowder. Grill the lobster body, cut side down, for 3 minutes. Grill the claws for 3 minutes per

side. When the lobster is cool enough to handle, pull all the meat out of the lobster body and claws and chop it.

▶ Toss 8 head-on shrimp with olive oil and season with salt and pepper. Grill the shrimp until cooked through, 2 to 3 minutes per side. While the shrimp are grilling, cut a lemon in half and put it on the grill to char. Squeeze the lemon over the shrimp.

▶ Garnish the chowder with the lobster and shrimp. And don't forget to serve the legs; they're great for chewing on and sucking out the little bits of meat.

BROWN BUTTER BISCUITS

MAKES ABOUT 30 BISCUITS

I think of all those women whose hands were made for biscuits. They don't measure. Some of them don't even mix a batch of dough; they'll mix whatever fat they're using into the flour and pull the dry stuff to the side of the bowl. They pour some buttermilk into the other side of the bowl and make the biscuits one by one, stirring a little wet and a little dry together by feel, then patting it smooth and round. Their biscuits are always perfect.

For those of us who don't have biscuit hands, I'm giving you measurements. And some brown butter to up the ante.

→ **This makes more brown butter than you'll need for the recipe. Save it to fry eggs or to drizzle over steamed asparagus.**

---

12 tablespoons (1½ sticks) cold unsalted butter

2 cups all-purpose flour, plus more for rolling

1 tablespoon baking powder

¼ teaspoon baking soda

1 teaspoon coarse kosher salt

¾ to 1 cup buttermilk

1 Preheat the oven to 375°F.

2 Cut 8 tablespoons (1 stick) of the butter into small pieces and put them in the freezer.

3 Cut up the remaining 4 tablespoons butter and put them in a small skillet (something light colored is better than cast iron here because it will be easier to see when the butter browns) over medium heat. When the butter melts, start swirling it in the pan. The butter will sputter while the water cooks out, and the solids will separate. Keep cooking and swirling until the solids have sunk to the bottom and browned and the butter smells nutty. Keep a constant eye on this so the butter doesn't burn. This will take about 6 minutes. Pour the butter out into a small bowl—and make sure you've got all the browned bits.

4 Whisk the flour, baking powder, baking soda, and salt together in a bowl. Take the butter out of the freezer and work it into the dry ingredients with your fingers until it resembles very coarse oatmeal with some larger bits of butter. Stir 2 teaspoons of the brown butter into ¾ cup of the buttermilk, add it to the dry ingredients, and stir the dough with your hand, kneading it a little. Add more buttermilk if you need it to make a cohesive dough that leaves the bowl clean.

5 Dump the dough onto a floured surface and pat it into an even disk with smooth edges. Roll out to ¼ inch. Cut biscuits with a 2-inch cutter and set them, barely touching, on a rimmed baking sheet. Gather up the scraps, form another even disk, roll out, cut out more biscuits, and add them to the baking sheet.

6 Brush the biscuits with some more of the brown butter and bake until risen and nicely browned on the top and bottom (lift one to check), 20 to 25 minutes.

Waste not. Instead of rolling the scraps together and cutting more biscuits, piece them together to make a cat's head biscuit—so called because it's supposed to be the size of a cat's head. This biscuit should go in the center of the baking sheet, with all the other ones surrounding it.

Family meal at Rooster may be something you grab on the run, or it may be the time when everyone gets together to get the final details about that night's event or to learn about changes in schedules or be reminded about how even though there's a problem with the air conditioning, the customers need to be happy. Everyone listens—maybe with one ear and the other ear for a buddy—and fuels up for the night ahead with something good for the taste buds.

BAKED MANICOTTI

SERVES 8 TO 10

I love the combination of pork and collards, creamy cheeses, and tomatoes in the filling of these pasta tubes. And the cheese sauce takes the baked pasta far beyond what you'd get with a plain white sauce.

When we're sitting around the table after we've eaten, I always think, "We've got to make these more often." Make them for your family.

FOR THE FILLING

½ cup olive oil

1 red onion, chopped

4 garlic cloves, chopped

1 pound collard greens, stemmed and chopped

2 tablespoons balsamic vinegar

2 teaspoons fennel seeds

Coarse kosher salt and freshly ground black pepper

2 teaspoons dried oregano

1 pound ground pork

1 (14.5-ounce) can crushed tomatoes

½ cup ricotta

½ cup mascarpone

FOR THE CHEESE SAUCE

1 tablespoon unsalted butter

1 red onion, sliced thin

1 garlic clove, minced

2 tablespoons all-purpose flour

4 cups (1 quart) heavy cream

1 cup milk

½ cup mascarpone

½ pound cheddar cheese, shredded

⅓ pound (1½ cups) Parmesan cheese, grated

¼ teaspoon freshly grated nutmeg

¼ teaspoon ground cloves

Coarse kosher salt and freshly ground black pepper

TO FINISH

2 (8-ounce) boxes dried manicotti noodles

FOR THE FILLING

1 Heat ¼ cup of the olive oil in a large skillet over medium-high heat. Add the onion, half the garlic, and the collards and cook until the collards start to brown, about 8 minutes. Add the vinegar, fennel seeds, and salt and pepper to taste and cook until fragrant, about 2 minutes. Turn off the heat and stir in the oregano. Scrape into a large bowl.

2 Add the remaining ¼ cup olive oil to the skillet. Add the remaining garlic and the pork, season with salt and pepper, and cook over medium-high heat, stirring constantly to break up the meat. When the meat is in tiny crumbles and no longer pink, you can stop the constant stirring; just give

Make them for your family.

the pork an occasional stir until it's browned, about 10 minutes. Add the tomatoes and bring to a simmer. Turn the heat down to medium-low and simmer until very thick, 8 to 10 minutes. Scrape into the bowl with the collards and cool to room temperature. Stir in the ricotta and mascarpone.

FOR THE CHEESE SAUCE

3 Melt the butter in a large pot over medium-high heat. Add the onion and cook, stirring often, until it's starting to brown, 6 to 7 minutes. Stir in the garlic and cook until fragrant, about 30 seconds. Add the flour and cook, stirring, for 1 minute. Pour in half the cream and cook, stirring, until the sauce thickens and comes to a simmer. Pour in the remaining cream and the milk and cook, stirring, until the sauce boils. Turn

the heat down to low and add the mascarpone and cheeses. Whisk until the cheeses melt and the sauce is smooth. Turn off the heat and whisk in the nutmeg, cloves, and salt and pepper to taste. Keep covered at the back of the stove while you finish the casserole.

TO FINISH

4 Preheat the oven to 350°F. Butter a 9-x-13-inch baking dish—be generous. Set up a large bowl of cold water.

5 Bring a very large pot of water to a boil. Salt the water generously and cook the manicotti until just shy of al dente. Use a spider or slotted spoon to transfer the manicotti to the cold water (the noodles are likely to break if you dump them in a colander). When the noodles are cool, lift them out onto a kitchen towel.

6 Put the filling into a pastry bag (you don't need a tip) or a zip-top bag (cut off a corner) and stuff the pasta with the pork and collard filling. You'll have enough filling for 22 noodles. Layer half the pasta in the baking dish and spoon over half the cheese sauce. Make another layer with the rest of the pasta and spread the remaining cheese sauce over the top.

7 Cover the manicotti with aluminum foil, set the baking dish on a rimmed baking sheet to catch any spills, and bake for 30 minutes. Remove the foil, turn the oven temperature up to 400°F, and bake until browned and bubbling, about 15 minutes. Let it sit for at least 15 minutes before serving.

UNCLE T'S MEAT- BALLS

SERVES 4

The staff first tasted these meatballs when we started to develop the recipe for Streetbird, my second Harlem restaurant, and they were a favorite right out of the gate. They're tender, with an extra-crisp exterior, and served on a rich, thick ragu with a spoonful of ricotta and a shower of lemon zest.

Toasted sourdough bread means everyone can be a member of the clean-plate club.

Of course, I think of my Uncle T, who took me fishing when I was young. But the Uncle T here is universal, a tribute to every Italian-American uncle.

FOR THE MEAT SAUCE

⅓ cup chopped onion

¼ cup chopped carrot

¼ cup chopped celery

2 teaspoons olive oil

½ pound ground beef

½ pound ground pork

½ teaspoon hot red pepper flakes

2 tablespoons tomato paste

¾ cup chicken broth

¼ cup dry white wine

1 (14.5-ounce) can crushed tomatoes

½ teaspoon sugar

1 teaspoon grated lemon zest

1 teaspoon chopped fresh oregano

Coarse kosher salt

FOR THE MEATBALLS

1 pound boneless, skinless chicken thighs, cut into chunks

¼ pound chicken livers

½ cup dry bread crumbs

½ cup heavy cream

1 large egg

2 teaspoons fresh lemon juice

½ teaspoon chopped fresh oregano

½ teaspoon chopped fresh thyme leaves

½ teaspoon ancho chile powder

Coarse kosher salt

FOR SERVING

Peanut oil for frying

Ricotta cheese

Grated Parmesan cheese

Grated lemon zest

Freshly ground black pepper

Toasted country or sourdough bread

FOR THE MEAT SAUCE

1 Put the onion, carrot, and celery into a food processor and process until very finely minced.

2 Heat the oil in a saucepan over medium-high heat. Add the beef and pork and cook until browned, about 8 minutes. Stir constantly at the beginning. Once the meat is in small crumbles and is no longer pink, you can stir occasionally.

3 Add the minced vegetables, the red pepper flakes, and tomato paste and cook, stirring, for 1 minute. Add the broth and wine and cook, stirring and scraping to deglaze the pan, for 2 minutes. Add the tomatoes and sugar and bring to a simmer. Turn the heat down to low and simmer until very thick, 50 minutes to 1 hour.

continued on page 320 →

4 Stir in the lemon zest and oregano and taste for salt. You can make this a day ahead. Add the zest and salt after you reheat the sauce.

FOR THE MEATBALLS

5 Put the chicken thighs and livers through a meat grinder (start with the thighs) or grind them in batches in a food processor.

6 Mix the bread crumbs, cream, and egg together in a large bowl. Let sit for a few minutes so the bread crumbs can soften.

7 Add the ground chicken and livers, the lemon juice, oregano, thyme, ancho chile powder, and a big pinch of salt. Mix well. Cover and refrigerate for 30 minutes.

8 Preheat the oven to 350°F. Line a rimmed baking sheet with parchment.

9 Roll out 16 golf ball–sized meatballs. Put them on the baking sheet and bake until cooked through, 30 minutes.

TO SERVE

10 Heat ⅓ inch of peanut oil in a cast-iron skillet over medium-high heat. Add the meatballs and fry until browned and crisp all over, about 3 minutes total.

11 Spoon a generous amount of the sauce into the bottom of four shallow bowls. Top each with 4 meatballs, a spoonful of ricotta, and some grated Parmesan. Finish with a sprinkling of lemon zest and a grind or two of pepper. The toast is for wiping up the sauce.

CHICKEN-SKIN POP

This is a great snack for family and friends.

▶ Bring a saucepan of water to a boil. Add the skin from 6 chicken thighs, bring back to a boil, and blanch for 1 minute. Drain and dry the skin on paper towels.

▶ Fill a saucepan one-third full with peanut oil. Set the pan over medium-high heat and heat the oil to 360°F. Dust the skins with a teaspoon of Chicken Shake (page 84) and dredge lightly in flour. Fry the skin until brown and crisp, 3 to 4 minutes. Drain on paper towels and season immediately with salt. The skins will continue to crisp as they cool.

▶ Pop ½ cup popcorn in 3 tablespoons peanut oil in a large heavy pot over medium heat. Dump the popcorn into a big bowl, drizzle in a little melted butter, and add a teaspoon of Chicken Shake. Toss. Crumble in the chicken skins and toss again.

Pop!

CHINA-TOWN CHICKEN

SERVES 4

This is our take on classic Chinese-American takeout—crisp bits of fried chicken thighs in a sweet and spicy sauce. It's easy to do at home. And it's good!

→ **There's some heat here, but you have cooling green beans as an antidote.**

→ **The classic Chinese technique of marinating the chicken, then giving it a quick deep-fry before stir-frying is called** *velveting*. **It makes the meat tender and silky.**

FOR THE MARINATED CHICKEN

2 large egg whites

1 tablespoon soy sauce

1 tablespoon Shaoxing wine or dry sherry

1 tablespoon vodka

1 tablespoon baking soda

1 pound boneless, skinless chicken thighs, cut into 1-inch pieces

FOR THE SAUCE

½ cup freshly squeezed orange juice

½ cup chicken broth

2½ tablespoons rice vinegar

1 tablespoon soy sauce

2 teaspoons tomato paste

½ teaspoon sesame oil

4 garlic cloves, minced

1 (3-inch) piece ginger, peeled and minced

1 tablespoon brown sugar

1 teaspoon hot red pepper flakes

FOR THE COATING

½ cup cornstarch

½ cup all-purpose flour

2 teaspoons baking powder

2 teaspoons coarse kosher salt

TO FINISH

Peanut oil for frying

2 tablespoons grapeseed oil

1 small garlic clove, sliced

4 dried red chiles

2 teaspoons sesame seeds

1 cup chopped (½-inch) green beans, blanched for 3 minutes

1 mango, peeled and cut into 1-inch cubes; or 1 (8-ounce) can pineapple chunks, drained

2 whole scallions, chopped

½ cup chopped peanuts

1 teaspoon cornstarch dissolved in 2 teaspoons water

FOR THE MARINATED CHICKEN

1 Whisk the egg whites, soy sauce, wine, vodka, and baking soda together in a bowl until frothy. Add the chicken and stir to make sure it is all coated. Cover and refrigerate for 2 hours.

FOR THE SAUCE

2 Combine all the ingredients in a saucepan. Bring to a simmer over medium-high heat. Turn the heat down to low and simmer for 20 minutes.

FOR THE COATING

3 Whisk all the ingredients together in a shallow bowl.

TO FINISH

4 Fill a large saucepan one-third full with peanut oil. Set over medium-high heat and heat the oil to 360°F.

Who put ham hocks and greens on a pizza?

5 Working in batches, lift the chicken out of the marinade, letting any excess drip off. Dredge in the coating, shaking off excess. Fry until golden brown, about 3 minutes. Keep an eye on the heat and adjust it to keep the oil between 350° and 375°F. Drain the chicken on a rack set over a rimmed baking sheet.

6 Heat the grapeseed oil in a large skillet over high heat. Add the garlic, chiles, sesame seeds, green beans, and mango and stir-fry until the green beans start to color, about 3 minutes. Add the chicken, scallions, and peanuts and stir-fry for 2 minutes.

7 Pour in the sauce and bring to a boil, stirring. Add the cornstarch slurry and continue to cook until the sauce thickens and coats everything evenly, about 30 seconds.

8 Divide among four plates and serve hot.

COLD PIZZA

If we're real busy, we'll order in—there's great pizza to be had in Harlem. Other times, the pies will be a group effort. Our pastry chef, Charlene Johnson, will tell sous chef Tristen Epps that she's making pizza dough, and Tristen will check on what's left over and turn it over to a couple of line cooks for them to make magic. Or if we have interns working in the kitchen, Tristen may tell them to make some dough and show their stuff.

Whether it's bought or however it's made, the pizza will be out for everyone by 3:45. It will be a while before the dance begins. The wait staff will be busy wiping the glassware; when they can take a break they'll grab a slice. Cooks have dinner prep to deal with, so they'll dash in and out of the kitchen, catching a bite on the sly. Hostesses are always busy, whether or not we have a customer in the house. Snatches of conversations fly across the room. Shout-outs for the folks who made the pizza that day. Interns beam. Someone talks about how he makes pizza dough, and someone else will smack him down 'cause hers is better. *Who* put ham hocks and greens on a pizza? If the pizza's delivered, talk turns to the best slice in New York. The best pie in Los Angeles. Or Raleigh. Or Kingston.

These are the times when I just like to sit back and watch this crazy group of people who make the Red Rooster enjoy themselves. I know that by the time they got to eat it, the pizza was cold. It always is.

We all need comfort, and that's what these sweet potatoes are. They've got their natural sweetness and the sweetness of honey. But then there's a little bite from the garlic and chile powder. What's great is that you can make them ahead and just leave them out while you're doing something else. Serve them warm. Serve them at room temperature.

GARLIC 'N' HONEY ROASTED SWEETS

SERVES 4 TO 6

1 Preheat the oven to 400°F. Line a rimmed baking sheet with parchment.

2 Toss the sweet potatoes with the olive oil, salt, chipotle chile powder, cumin, thyme, and garlic.

3 Spread the sweet potatoes out in a single layer on the baking sheet. Roast for 20 minutes. Stir, dot with the butter, and drizzle on the honey. Roast until the sweets are caramelized and tender, another 20 minutes.

4 Lift up the parchment and slide the sweets into a serving dish. Serve warm.

2 pounds sweet potatoes, peeled and cut into ½-inch half moons

¼ cup olive oil

1 teaspoon coarse kosher salt

1 teaspoon chipotle chile powder

1 teaspoon ground cumin

2 sprigs thyme

4 garlic cloves, smashed

2 tablespoons unsalted butter, cut into pieces

2 tablespoons honey

We have about 155 staff members at Rooster. Then there are the musicians, the amazing handymen, the talented florists, the accountants—who are not dull. We are a tribe of 200 people who make other people come together.

FAMILY VALUES

If Kingsley does it, it's curry and West Indian dishes; if Cyed does it, it's Asian.

Most restaurants have a family meal before the shift begins. It's a time when you learn about the daily specials—and sometimes even taste them. You catch up with other employees and the chef offers a home-style meal. There's a pre-shift meeting after the family meal when our managers—Reggie and Angela—talk about what's going on in the neighborhood. Sometimes we have a theme for the week, we talk about a review and tips on service. Here at the Rooster, we have two family meals a day: one at ten-thirty in the morning for the lunch shift; the other at three-thirty before the dinner hour. The sous chef decides the family meal. If Kingsley does it, it's curry and West Indian dishes; if Cyed does it, it's Asian. More often than not, musicians come and eat with us. Wynton Marsalis is setting up and grabs a chicken wing. Sometimes, a neighbor down on their luck or just curious stops in and eats a bowl of curry.

"Girl! Come check this." Charlene, Jamie, and Zee are huddled around a poster. It's a picture of Cornelius Locke with his gloves up.

He's a great person—very humble, very sweet, and a boxer. Tenth in the world, fourth in the country, I've been told. He's also a runner at the Rooster. But the ladies don't seem overly concerned about that.

"So you know he's thinks he's all that, now." They nod in unison, but that conversation quickly changes into one about whose kid is going to what school. Did your kid get into that charter? Are we going to set up a play date? Idle gossip that flares to a point every now and again circles around to who may be sleeping with who, and if that's true what does it mean. I try not to listen.

Lissette, our bartender, comes downstairs with two drinks on a tray. "I've done it! Everybody come have a little sip," she says. A crowd forms around the small table where Liz had set the drinks down. It's a spicy drink. Coconut milk and a whiff of cardamom. A plump poached shrimp floats in the martini glass. Charlene reaches the glass first. After a sip or two, she smacks her lips.

"This is not a cocktail. This is soup that'll get you drunk."

"Okay, everybody. Alright. Everybody here? Let's get started." We talk about what happened the night before. This is the time when the front of the house and the back of the house get to meet and everybody congregates. The porters, the chefs, the busboys, the runners, the servers, the bartenders. There's a discussion about the high-profile people who have let us know they are coming and how we will accommodate them. Once Marisa, one of our servers, told me that she felt like working for Rooster is learning a culture. It's a bit of a dance as to how we juggle the celebrities, the businessmen, the tourists, the neighbors.

I've got my mind on all of that. I do. But I can't help noticing who's not here. Jimmy's late and I'm pretty sure this is his twentieth time being late, and I'm positive Rooster has a three-times-late-and-you're-out rule, because I'm the one who created it. Every time I look away, the family gives me this look, this—*Man, do I remember the talking-to Marcus gave me when I was late the second time. Mmm.*

The thing is, I like Jimmy. And I'm not alone. Everybody likes Jimmy. He's a cool neighborhood cat who was in and out of jobs before. He's got this beautiful daughter, four years old. I think he's learning a purpose, he's learning how not to be ashamed of finding a passion.

Just as we are about to break, he walks in. "Sorry, Chef."

"You're late." I say it loud enough that everyone on the dinner shift can hear. "Yeah. I got stopped. Sorry, Chef."

"What happened?"

"Nothing," and he shrugs. "I just got stopped on the way here." I look at him. He's got his chef's pants and chef jacket on, and he wears them with style. To me, he looks like a man on his way to work. I'm not sure how the police saw anything else. This kind of thing has happened so often, that while we don't break into tears, we still, almost as one, surround him. Reggie reaches him first.

"Don't hang your head. We're here."

It's a bit of a dance as to how we juggle the celebrities, the businessmen, the tourists, the neighbors.

GIVING THANKS IN HARLEM

ON A CRISP FALL DAY, I'm sitting with Dapper Dan on his stoop. If someone would have told him that Mike Tyson having a fight with another heavyweight fighter, at four-thirty in the morning in front of his boutique would bring the media and subsequently the law—in the form of now Supreme Court Justice Sonia Sotomayor—into his life and shut down his business, and at the end of the day he would be grateful for it, he would have laughed. Hard. To prove it, he throws his head back and does so. "I would have said, 'grateful?' You have got to be kidding me. But you know? I am thankful. Thankful it happened. Thankful to Harlem." I nod.

Back then, you could stroll a side street and walk by America: Mississippi, Louisiana, Arkansas, Virginia.

If you live in Harlem long enough, you realize sometimes you have to push back in order to push through. If you're Dapper Dan, who was born and raised in Harlem, who opened his boutique on 125th between Madison and Fifth and outfitted hustlers, gangsters, and hip-hop's elite, you appreciate how struggle forces you to walk a different grid. Given the right circumstances, it can transform you into a fashion icon. Dap lounges on his stoop, but he's dressed like his name. His tailored three-piece navy-blue suit fits like a better skin. I swear to God, he's wearing spats, and his yellow socks match his tie, which mirrors the handkerchief that pokes out of his jacket pocket like sunshine. Dap stands up, straightening his flawless suit, then he turns around and looks back at his front door. His son is inside, calling his cadre of private clients, setting up interviews, scheduling a calendar full of red-carpet events and television appearances. Dap's smile is private. Pleased. "Let's walk."

We get three doors away when Dap starts juggling two conversations—one with me, the other with the never-ending stream of people who want to stop him to say hello, to catch up on neighborhood gossip, to invite him to this and that event. "Dap!"

"Dap, how's it hanging, Man?"

If you live in Harlem long enough, you realize sometimes you have to push back in order to push through.

"Dapper, Dapper." When he's not being stopped by our neighbors, he bends at the waist and whispers to me the story of how his parents came to Harlem. His mother was from North Carolina, and his father, in 1910 at age twelve, traveled up north, alone, from Virginia. Back then you could do that, he tells me. Back then, Harlem was a maternal neighborhood. He points to the buildings across the street. Mothers hung out of the windows, watching the kids, "I see you, watch out, Little Man, I see you."

"Couldn't get away with nothing." Something on my face must look dubious, because Dap cracks a smile. "I got away with a little bit." I look around and imagine the Harlem of Dap's childhood. A first-generation child fearless enough to swim in the Harlem River. There was no pier; Harlem used to be a place where you could walk to the shore. Dap's family didn't go to church often, but it didn't matter, since there was gospel on every corner. Whole families grew up in one room; an apartment could house three generations.

Buildings were populated by a Southern town or a state. Back then, you could stroll a side street and walk by America: Mississippi, Louisiana, Arkansas, Virginia.

"Harlem, U.S.A."

"Black Mecca." Dap slips his elegant hands in his pants pockets. "Back then, when you struggled, you threw a party to fix it." Like most families in his apartment building, his mother threw rent parties to help cover the rent. Every Sunday evening, one family in the building would put together a meal that put Thanksgiving to shame. Red rice, potato salad, hoppin' John. In Harlem, even the bars got in the act. They called them bar circles. Groups of friends showed up with platters full of bites of this and that, and in return they were offered two free drinks, which made that third drink they paid for taste so good.

"You know my mother went to the Rooster. The one on 138th."

"Really?"

"Oh, yeah." Dap's mother would take all her extra money and dress up and then walk. And walk. They lived in East Harlem, but in her opinion, the party was happening on Seventh Avenue. She would walk across the park and when she was three blocks away from the Rooster, she'd hail a cab. The original Rooster was that kind of place. You had to arrive in style. Dap whispers that story to me, but the loud laugh that punctuates its end startles. "Everything in Harlem is about style. Everybody wanted it. Especially when you couldn't afford it."

"Everything in Harlem is about style. Everybody wanted it. Especially when you couldn't afford it."

Dap's boutique catered to that desire. Open twenty-four hours a day, Dapper Dan's Boutique's clientele included major drug dealers and kingpins, like Alpo, and hip-hop titans of the day: LL Cool J, Eric B & Rakim, Big Daddy Kane. Everybody wanted to wear fox and leather jackets with the Louis Vuitton logo emblazoned on the back. "Most folks couldn't afford me. But a good salesman knows you got to give people something to aspire to." And when we walk the streets together, I can see that aspiration on display. Two brothers are on the corner conducting business, their hands are quick and confident; their jeans are pressed. An African woman walks arm in arm with her companion, balancing a bag full of shoes on her head. In her ears, on her arms, gold jewelry sparkles. Her head turns, as she watches Dap and me pass her by. She smiles, and I notice her gold tooth matches her earrings.

"A good salesman knows you got to give people something to aspire to."

Hustle combines with beauty, with creativity, with skill. Dap remembers a childhood where his father juggled three jobs to make ends meet, and his mother woke him on Sundays and fed him biscuits and sardines. He convinced barbershop owners to give him their free tickets to the neighborhood ballroom dances. Then he scalped the tickets and with the proceeds bought a new suit and slipped into the Renaissance Ballroom or Connie's Inn. The more he talks to me about Harlem—how the nineteen-sixties and seventies came and so did the riots, how putting up the projects broke up our hood—the more I realize I'm being shown how to strut down the special grid that is particular to Harlem.

All of it—walking with Dap, looking at the old cats who step to him to say hello, the young brothers who look up from the trouble they're up to and say hello, the young woman in heels and three kids in tow—makes me want to say thank you. Life in Harlem is a scramble, but it's also jazz and Symphony Sid. It's Frankie Lymon and Leslie Martin and the Schoolboys. It's Black Mecca and making it. It's Harlem, U.S.A. And it's knowing you can find home even if you weren't born in this country.

Strolling down the street with Dapper Dan, I feel like I lucked into Gordon Parks's images, into Dap's mystique. Every day in the sixty blocks of Harlem is an education. So I'm thankful. Thankful for Crab Man Mike, who still hawks his seafood; thankful for the memories of Pan Pan and M&G. I'm thankful for the ladies who make the tamales in East Harlem, for the Africans who make ginger shaved ice on hot summer days and travel all over our neighborhood to sell them. I'm thankful for the small bars that dot Harlem and give me inspiration, and for the soup kitchens whose presence and generosity remind me to always do more. I'm thankful for Dap's story—it's a tale riddled with fight and grit and style. Mike Tyson fought Mitch "Blood" Green at four-thirty in the morning right on the sidewalk outside the boutique, and that brought media and attention, which in turn brought a fashion industry's scrutiny to a shop in Harlem, and a federal inquiry that brought in Sonia Sotomayor, who led a raid on the shop. Everyone who was there agreed Dap was a gentleman. As if he could be anything less. It was nothing like the things that go down on Canal Street. Every fashion company whose logo he used sued him, and he fought. Close-eyed and swinging, he fought and lost. In 1992 his closed boutique felt like the end of the world but truly was just the beginning. Dap tells us (and yes, I'm listening) that to live in Harlem, it's best not to land on bitter. Land on delicious.

GIVING THANKS PLAYLIST

"ANNIE LEIBOVITZ"   Timbuktu

"VALENTINE LOVE"   Norman Connors featuring
Michael Henderson and Jean Carn

"CHRISTMAS NIGHT IN HARLEM"   Louis Armstrong

"JOYS AND SOLOS"   Fred Ho

HERB-ROASTED TURKEY *with* CRANBERRY GRAVY

SERVES 8, WITH LEFTOVERS

Thanksgiving is the start of the holiday season in Harlem, and 125th Street lights up. Since it's a community day, we partner with our neighbors, the NBA Players Association, to give away roasted turkeys. The first year we did this, our sous chef Michael Garrett stayed up all night, making sure the turkeys would be ready.

We come up with a new recipe each year, and this is a particular favorite. I love the perfume from the lavender and rosemary. The port, red wine, and prune juice that baste the bird give it a mahogany skin, and when you cook cranberries in the pan juices, you've got a killer gravy.

→ Start brining the turkey the day before.

→ Put the neck out on the platter when you serve the turkey—you know someone's going to want it. And save the liver for banh mi (see page 338).

---

8 quarts water

2½ cups fresh orange juice

1 cup coarse kosher salt

¼ cup sugar

1 (12-pound) turkey

½ pound plus 4 tablespoons (2½ sticks) unsalted butter, softened

1 tablespoon fresh rosemary needles, chopped

1½ teaspoons culinary lavender, crumbled, or 1 tablespoon lavender flowers, chopped

1½ teaspoons freshly ground black pepper

1 tablespoon garam masala

4 garlic cloves, peeled and crushed

2 bay leaves

1 (2-inch) piece ginger, peeled, sliced, and smashed

½ cup prune juice

½ cup ruby port

½ cup dry red wine

1½ pounds sweet potatoes, peeled and cut into ½-inch dice

12 pitted prunes, halved

1 cup cranberries

1 Put 2 quarts of the water, 2 cups of the orange juice, the salt, and sugar into a very large pot over high heat and, stirring, bring to a simmer. Add the remaining 6 quarts water and cool to room temperature. Submerge the turkey and refrigerate for 18 hours.

2 Mix 2 sticks of the butter with the rosemary and lavender. Cover with plastic wrap and refrigerate overnight. Take the herb butter and the remaining ½ stick out of the refrigerator 1 hour before you plan on using them.

3 Preheat the oven to 350°F.

4 Pat the turkey dry. Slide your hands under the skin, loosening it from the breast and thighs. Rub the breast and thighs, under the skin,

with the herb butter. Rub the turkey all over with the remaining ½ stick butter. Mix the pepper and garam masala and sprinkle all over the bird. Put the garlic, bay leaves, and ginger into the cavity and tie the legs together.

5 Set the turkey on a rack in a roasting pan and add the neck to the pan. Roast for 2 hours.

6 Stir the remaining ½ cup orange juice, the prune juice, port, and red wine together in a measuring cup. Pour over the turkey. Scatter the sweet potatoes and prunes around the turkey. Slide the pan back into the oven and continue to roast, basting the turkey and stirring the sweet potatoes every 20 minutes, until the thickest part of the thigh registers 165°F on an instant-read thermometer, about 1 more hour.

7 Set the turkey on a carving board and let it rest for 30 minutes before carving. Use a slotted spoon to transfer the sweet potatoes and prunes to a serving bowl.

8 Pour the pan juices into a fat separator. Let sit until separated, then pour the juices into a small saucepan, leaving the fat behind. Bring the defatted pan juices to a boil over medium-high heat. Add the cranberries and boil until the cranberries pop. Taste for pepper (you won't need salt).

9 Put the cranberry gravy into a gravy boat and serve with the turkey, sweet potatoes, and prunes.

It was only after I moved to the U.S. that I began thinking about how powerful and exciting it was that there was a day when everyone was eating the same dish. For me, Thanksgiving points to our spiritual compass.

DAY-AFTER-THANKSGIVING BANH MI

Leftover turkey sandwiches can be a lot more interesting than the usual ones with Swiss cheese and lettuce.

▶ Start by mixing 2 tablespoons cornstarch with ½ teaspoon Aleppo pepper (see page 27) and some salt. Use it to dust the turkey liver and 2 chicken livers (or 6 chicken livers). Heat a slick of grapeseed oil in a small skillet over medium-high heat and sauté the livers until browned and cooked through but still a bit pink inside, about 3 minutes per side. Deglaze the skillet with 1 tablespoon soy sauce, cooking until the skillet is just about dry. Transfer the livers to a cutting board and return the skillet to the heat. Cut an apple into thin slices and sear them for 1 minute per side. Add them to the cutting board.

▶ Cut a crisp baguette lengthwise in half. Cut the livers into pieces, arrange them over the bottom half, and smash them with a fork. Layer on the apples. Shred ½ pound leftover roast turkey and pile it on the sandwich. Top with about ¼ cup each grated carrot and pickled cabbage (I use the Picklz on page 244). Stir 1 teaspoon Sriracha into 2 tablespoons mayo and slather it onto the other half of the baguette. Put the top on, press, and cut in half. It's a great lunch for two.

PAN-ROASTED SWEET POTATOES *with* DRIED CHERRIES *and* WALNUTS

SERVES 4

You gotta have sweet potatoes on a holiday table. With the dried cherries and walnuts, this has the feel of a traditional dish, but you know I had to kick things up with some bacon for lushness and Aleppo pepper for a little bite.

1 tablespoon olive oil

2 tablespoons unsalted butter

2 slices bacon, chopped

1½ pounds sweet potatoes, peeled and cut into ½-inch dice

½ teaspoon Aleppo pepper (see page 27)

½ teaspoon ground turmeric

2 teaspoons honey

1 teaspoon soy sauce

1½ tablespoons dried sour cherries

1½ tablespoons coarsely chopped walnuts

Coarse kosher salt and freshly ground black pepper

1 Put the olive oil, butter, and bacon in a large skillet over medium-high heat. When the butter has melted and the bacon is sizzling, add the sweet potatoes and cook, stirring often, until the potatoes are well browned and just tender, 12 to 14 minutes. Turn off the heat.

2 Stir the Aleppo pepper, turmeric, honey, and soy sauce together in a small bowl, then stir into the sweet potatoes. Add the dried cherries and walnuts and season with salt and pepper. Serve hot or at room temperature.

Smoked hams are ready to eat; you just need to heat them up. I simmer mine in broth, which adds flavor and ensures that the ham won't get dry (which can happen if you just heat it in the oven). Then I stick in some cloves, pack on a mustardy crust, decorate with pineapple, and bake.

Put this ham on a holiday table, and your heart will swell with pride.

→ **Strain the ham broth and freeze it. You can use it later when you're cooking beans or greens.**

THE BIG BAKED HAM

SERVES 8, WITH LEFTOVERS

1 Put the ham in a big stockpot with the onion, garlic, mustard seeds, and broth. Add enough water to cover the ham and bring to a simmer over medium-high heat. Turn the heat down to low and simmer gently—just the occasional bubble—for 2 hours.

2 Preheat the oven to 375°F. Line a rimmed baking sheet with parchment.

3 Cut off the skin if your ham came with it. Score the fat in a diamond pattern; just cut through the fat, not the flesh. Stick the ham with the cloves and put it on the baking sheet. If you're using a half ham, prop it up with crumbled aluminum foil.

4 Whisk the mustard, yolk, honey, maple syrup, ginger, and cinnamon together with 2 tablespoons of the ham broth until smooth. Stir in the bread crumbs. Pack this crust over the top of the ham. Use toothpicks to skewer the pineapple on the ham.

5 Bake the ham for 45 minutes. Let it rest for 30 minutes before carving.

1 (7- to 8-pound) smoked bone-in half ham or smoked picnic ham

1 onion, chopped

2 garlic cloves, peeled

2 teaspoons mustard seeds

2 cups chicken broth

8 whole cloves

½ cup Dijon mustard

1 large egg yolk

2 tablespoons honey

1 tablespoon maple syrup

1 teaspoon powdered ginger

½ teaspoon ground cinnamon

6 tablespoons bread crumbs

1 (8-ounce) can pineapple slices, drained

Much of the staff at Red Rooster comes from the Caribbean, and the passion they have for the food they grew up with has a huge influence on our menu. The coriander, cumin, cinnamon, and curry in this soup is straight from the islands. Jamaican Roti (page 239) is the perfect thing for cleaning your bowl.

LENTIL SOUP
with HAM

SERVES 6

1 Put the shallot, ginger, garlic, jalapeño, and ¼ cup of the water into a blender. Puree to make a smooth paste.

2 Melt the butter in a stockpot over medium-low heat. Add the paste and cook, stirring often, until the water has cooked off and the butter starts to separate from the paste, about 5 minutes.

3 Meanwhile, put the coriander, cumin, cinnamon, and curry powder into a small skillet over medium heat and toast until fragrant, about 1 minute. Add the spices to the pot and cook for 5 minutes, so they can bloom.

4 Add the remaining 9 cups water, the lentils, curry leaves, and thyme and bring to a boil over medium-high heat. Turn the heat down to medium-low and simmer until the lentils are tender, 25 to 30 minutes. Turn off the heat and season with the vinegar and salt to taste.

5 Discard the curry leaves and thyme and ladle out about half the soup. Puree the remaining soup with an immersion blender. Return the rest of the soup to the pot and stir.

6 Put ½ cup chopped ham into each soup bowl, ladle in the soup, and serve.

¼ cup chopped shallot

1 tablespoon chopped ginger

1 tablespoon chopped garlic

1½ teaspoons chopped seeded jalapeño chile

9¼ cups water

4 tablespoons (½ stick) unsalted butter

2 teaspoons ground coriander

2 teaspoons ground cumin

2 teaspoons ground cinnamon

¾ teaspoon Madras curry powder

1 pound black beluga lentils

2 fresh curry leaves (see page 27) or 1 bay leaf

2 sprigs thyme

3 tablespoons apple cider vinegar

Coarse kosher salt

3 cups chopped (½-inch) leftover baked ham (page 172 or 341)

Every restaurant kitchen I've ever known has had an engine, someone who seems to be everywhere doing everything, no matter what his "job" is. Kingsley John is ours. Part chef, part handyman, with a Jamaican patois that's strong and fast ("Mon, whyyoucallsomebody? I fix dot"), he's the heart and soul of the Rooster kitchen.

SQUASH SALAD *with* CRUNCHY QUINOA *and* PUMPKIN SEED VINAIGRETTE

SERVES 4 TO 6

I discovered pumpkin seed vinaigrette when I worked in Austria. I'm using it here in a holiday winter salad of butternut squash, Asian pears, endive, and feta.

FOR THE CRUNCHY QUINOA

1 cup slivered almonds

2 tablespoons quinoa

1 teaspoon sugar

1 teaspoon Aleppo pepper (see page 27)

1 teaspoon coarse kosher salt

FOR THE PUMPKIN SEED VINAIGRETTE

2 tablespoons hulled green pumpkin seeds

1 large egg yolk

3 tablespoons heavy cream

1 garlic clove, chopped

½ cup olive oil

Juice of 1 lime

2 teaspoons pumpkin seed oil; or more olive oil

Coarse kosher salt and freshly ground black pepper

FOR THE SALAD

¼ cup olive oil

1 red onion, sliced thin

2 cups diced (¼-inch) butternut squash

Coarse kosher salt and freshly ground black pepper

⅓ cup water

2 Asian pears, cored and sliced thin

2 Belgian endive, sliced thin

2 tablespoons sherry vinegar

1 cup cubed (½-inch) feta

FOR THE CRUNCHY QUINOA

1 Toast the almonds and quinoa in a skillet over low heat until deep golden, about 15 minutes. Pour into a bowl, toss in the sugar, Aleppo pepper, and salt and cool.

FOR THE PUMPKIN SEED VINAIGRETTE

2 Toast the pumpkin seeds in a small skillet over low heat until golden and fragrant, about 3 minutes. Pour onto a plate.

3 Put the egg yolk, cream, and garlic into a blender and puree until frothy. With the blender running, pour in the oil in a slow, thin stream until emulsified. Add the lime juice and pumpkin seed oil and puree until combined.

4 Pour the vinaigrette into a bowl, season with salt and pepper to taste, and stir in the pumpkin seeds.

FOR THE SALAD

5 Heat the olive oil in a large skillet over medium heat. Add the onion and squash, season with salt and pepper, and cook until the squash is lightly browned, about 10 minutes. Pour in the water and cook until the squash is tender and the water has cooked off, about 15 minutes. Transfer to a salad bowl and cool slightly.

6 Add the pears, endive, and vinegar and toss.

7 Top the salad with the crunchy quinoa and feta. Serve with the vinaigrette on the side.

STEAMED BASS, FIERY NOODLES, LONG BEANS

SERVES 4

This dish was born a few years ago, when Chinese New Year fell during Black History Month. We got to serve it to Fred Ho, the jazz baritone saxophonist who was playing at Ginny's with his band. Noodles and long beans are tossed with mala, a lip-tingling spicy Sichuan sauce, and topped with a piece of soothing steamed fish.

→ **Get long beans at a Chinese market, or substitute green beans.**

---

2 whole (1 pound each) striped bass, cleaned, rinsed, and patted dry

Coarse kosher salt

2 scallions, quartered

2 teaspoons sesame oil

1 pound long beans (see headnote), trimmed and cut into 3-inch pieces

1 pound fresh Chinese noodles

1 cup mala sauce (see page 29) or Chinese chili oil

1 Set a rack in a roasting pan. Pour in 1 inch of water and bring to a boil over high heat.

2 Season the fish inside and out with salt. Stuff the cavities with the scallions, and rub the fish with sesame oil. Set each fish in a shallow bowl.

3 When the water's boiling, set the bowls on the rack and seal the roasting pan tightly with foil. Steam the fish for 8 minutes. Turn off the heat and let sit for 10 minutes. The fish should be barely opaque in the center (make a cut into the fish to check). If the fish isn't done to your liking, steam it for another minute or two.

4 While the fish is steaming, bring a large pot of salted water to a boil. Add the long beans, bring back to a boil, and cook for 30 seconds. Transfer to a bowl with a spider or slotted spoon. Add the noodles to the boiling water, bring back to a boil, and cook for 1 minute. Reserve 1 cup of the cooking water. Drain the noodles and add to the beans. Add the mala and toss, adding some of the cooking water if you need to loosen things up.

5 Scrape the skin off one fish with a spoon. Slide the top fillet onto a cutting board. Grab the tail and lift the bones off. Flip the bottom fillet onto the board and remove the skin. Repeat with the other fish.

6 Divide the fiery noodles and beans between four shallow bowls. Top each with a piece of fish and serve. The fish heads can be the cook's treat, or you can put them out and share.

THE BAMBOO INN

Harlem's Chinese influence began in the nineteen-twenties, but the more recent migration has created an uptown Chinatown in East Harlem today. It may come as a surprise, but there are more Chinese restaurants in Harlem than there are soul food places. When times were bad, Chinese restaurants were here. Good times, and they're still here.

In *Negro Life in New York's Harlem*, Wallace Thurman describes one Chinese restaurant from the Jazz Age. It's the Bamboo Inn, owned by a man called Lee Shu.

> *The other extreme of amusement places in Harlem is exemplified by the Bamboo Inn, a Chinese-American restaurant that features Oriental cuisine, a jazz band and dancing. It is the place for select Negro Harlem's night life, the place where debutantes have their coming out parties, where college lads take their co-eds and society sweethearts and where dignified matrons entertain. It is a beautifully decorated establishment, glorified by a balcony with booths, and a large gyroflector, suspending from the center of the ceiling, on which colored spotlights play, flecking the room with triangular bits of vari-colored light. The Bamboo Inn is the place to see "high Harlem."*

STEWED OXTAILS

SERVES 6

Arthur Golden, father of the Studio Museum's Thelma Golden, was born in Harlem in 1922 and knew the original Rooster. He was part of a generation of hard-working people who left a legacy here, and I hope to honor it. When Thelma called to make arrangements for her dad's eighty-fifth birthday, she said he had one request. Oxtails.

→ Like any stew, this will be even better if you make it the day before you serve it. You'll have lots of sauce, so plan on serving it with grits or mashed potatoes to sop it up. And save leftovers for pasta.

---

4 tablespoons grapeseed oil

6 (4-inch) pieces oxtail (4 to 4½ pounds)

Coarse kosher salt

2 onions, chopped

2 poblano chiles, chopped

1 cup sliced (¼-inch) carrots

3 garlic cloves, chopped

1 (1-inch) piece ginger, peeled and minced

1 bay leaf

½ teaspoon ground cumin

½ teaspoon ground coriander

1½ teaspoons adobo sauce (from a can of chipotles in adobo)

2 cups dry red wine

1 (28-ounce) can crushed tomatoes

2 cups chicken broth

½ cup brewed coffee

1 tablespoon Worcestershire sauce

1 teaspoon fish sauce

1 tablespoon honey

1 tablespoon soy sauce

1 Heat 2 tablespoons of the grapeseed oil in a Dutch oven over medium-high heat. Working in batches, pat the oxtails dry with paper towels, salt them, and brown them well in the oil, 6 to 7 minutes per batch.

2 Pour out the fat in the pan. Add the remaining 2 tablespoons oil, turn the heat down to medium, and add the onions and a big pinch of salt. Cook, stirring occasionally, until the onions are beginning to brown, about 8 minutes. Add the poblanos, carrots, garlic, ginger, bay leaf, cumin, and coriander and cook, stirring once or twice, until very fragrant, about 2 minutes. Add the adobo sauce and wine and bring to a boil. Stir in the tomatoes, chicken broth, coffee, Worcestershire, and fish sauce. Bury the oxtails in the sauce and bring to a simmer. Cover the pot, turn the heat down to low, and simmer, stirring once in a while, until the meat is just tender, about 1½ hours.

3 Uncover the pot, stir in the honey and soy sauce, and simmer until the sauce is silken and the meat is fork tender, about 1 hour. Taste for salt. Discard the bay leaf.

4 Serve in soup plates.

RE-CREATING A NEW TRADITION

My dearest friend, Thelma Golden, is the director and chief curator of the Studio Museum in Harlem. Her passion is finding emerging artists and forging new paths. Here's her story of creating a new family tradition.

When the Rooster opened, it was the first holiday since my mother had passed away. Toward the end of her life, I had tried to replicate the holidays through the dishes she made—even things that I do not eat, like turnips. (For my mother at Thanksgiving, you had to have turnips, so I would make turnips.) My own way to process those last years of her life, her illness, and ultimately my grief was to replicate completely. If I could do my job as a good daughter, if I could make the food, set the table, use her serving pieces, I could re-create it. Then she could see continuity. Even in those years when her appetite was minimal— the act of it for me was important. I didn't have the sense that I had the skill to produce this. I just did it.

him. This was all happening in my head on December 23—poor planning.

In mid-November, I heard Rooster was going to be open Christmas day and some other chefs were invited up. The restaurant wouldn't open officially, but it was going to be a special meal. That was my father's first Rooster experience. That day, not only were they working through the first Rooster menu (which I can remember like the back of my hand), but they also made a few other dishes. And one of them was oxtails.

Oxtails were a food of my childhood. They were something that my grandmother Anna made, here in Harlem. My father described his childhood oxtails as this wonderful meal in a pot, there for a whole day—that's how

---

Oxtails were a food of my childhood. They were something that my grandmother Anna made, here in Harlem.

On the first Christmas after she passed, though, I was torn: I felt that I should try to continue our traditions, but I also felt as if I couldn't do that. I didn't have the physical sense of how I was going to make it happen. But I didn't want to disappoint my father, because I felt that now I needed to do it for

he remembers it. You could leave the pot and come back, and it would still be cooking. And it was something that Anna and my great-grandmother Mimi made and enjoyed as their food. This was the food of Jamaica. This was also the food that they would buy in Harlem. For my father, that was a deeply resonant childhood memory. So that day, when my father ate oxtails, was for me a whole other level of understanding of my own history. It happened in that space, in that early moment. And it will stand for me as an amazing *my* Rooster memory. But also stand in a way that showed me how that menu was looking to touch those different ways and understandings.

I remember that some of the city's most fantastic chefs were in the next booth. And for my father, it couldn't have been a better meal or a better Christmas. It also changed our holiday traditions. Most of our holidays are now spent at the Rooster.

My mother was one of those people who didn't understand people who went to restaurants on holidays. This could have been a moment of a little judgment—"What are you going to a restaurant for?" But, in a way, we're not going to a restaurant. I know that she would understand that—we're going to the Rooster. My father, brother, and I—this is our new family holiday tradition.

IT'S ALWAYS SWEET IN HARLEM

My friend Lana Turner is a reader, writer, sometime poet, thinker, and researcher, with a keen interest in the elements of art and style in black culture and why this meditation matters. A Harlem native, she thinks of herself as a "memory woman"— remembering, remarking, cataloguing, and savoring the past as guideposts for the present, a legacy to pass on to others. Here, the sometime poet ruminates on Harlem's past and present.

Straw–berries
　　Whipped cream
　　　　a hint of sugar
　　　　sprigs of mint
　　　　garnish your visual appeal
　　Small
　　　　cold
　　　　berry-hearts
　　　　sliced
　　I can taste you with a touch.

Within striking distance of the Hudson River, I am on a farm. Upstate. Little wooden basket in tow, my carefully selected berries allow me to revel in the singular pleasure of sitting in the midst of nature's table. I think about my mother whose story would be slightly different. Her memory, fresh with yesterday's pleasures, would set her in a Southern wood, picking wild sweet huckleberries. Under an unapologetic sun, I am content to slowly settle in among the rows. She is in a sylvan wood, making her way through spectral shafts of light with both purpose and pleasure in each step.

We are counterpoints to the other.

And then we are not.

My mother is a collage of things about the kitchen. If she were a weaver, her tapestry would blend an ambrosia of spices and herbs into a cornucopia of banquets. In an undulation of thanksgiving, she summons God in homage as her thread of thanks to bounties past, present, and those yet to come. Refulgent as she hums in search of a song, she gathers ingredients to accent and mold each day.

We are different kitchen women, my mother and I. She is the daily energy of a Christmas dinner—smoked turkey, honeyed hams, roast goose, macaroni and cheese, fried okra, Southern flake biscuits. I am the movement of a buffet at a summer luncheon—cantaloupe soup, salmon mousse, capellini in pesto, melon balls in mint.

My mother is a collage of things about the kitchen.

We are the same as we pick ripe tomatoes, harvest sweet corn, pluck new lemons, and gather summer berries from our traceless gardens. Come spend your life at our tables. There is always more. Laughter and stories are served throughout dessert.

The color of golden honey and caramel cream, she awakens in the misty haze before dawn to paddle her stocky frame to the kitchen. It is her place—by choice. When I was young, I'd awaken early and listen to the sounds of my mother—the opening and closing of cabinet doors that held dishes in an array of patterns worn and chipped, the creaking oven door signaling a check for the goldenness of corn bread, the rattling of a special pot extracted from a precarious nest. It would be a short time from the sounds to the aromas wafting in steady waves throughout the house. There'd be hickory smoked bacon, pan-fried fish, hominy grits, and "juicy eggs" with toast stacked high against a backdrop of guava preserve.

Some of those early mornings held sweet treats. The sound of the electric mixer was the signal. I could hear her beating and mixing, alternately whipping, and knew it had to be the batter for a cake. I was never disappointed. The sound of the wooden spoon against the metal mixing bowl would send me flying.

"I want the bowl!" I'd announce.

"And I want the beaters," my sister would say, finishing second in the race to the kitchen. Running my fingers around the bowl for the thin rims of leftover batter was sweet heaven.

"Wait 'til the cake is ready," Mommy would say.

Once, she decided to try an improvisation of lemon, mint, and ginger ale in her basic pound cake. "It's going to be something," she'd say with the delight of a schoolgirl laden with honors. It always was just as she said—an irresistible delight and, as often, more.

She is the unenforced weight in a tapestry. Tucked within the warp and woof is an obsession of recipes folded and stored within the loom of time. Inside aged hasty creases are scrawls for "spoon bread" and "squash soufflé."

On the discovery of a misplaced grouping, she would say, "I have to put these recipes where I can find them." Her sense of order places this stack topped with directions for the makings of "apple-honey dumplings" into a drawer with lingerie. It is, after all, a drawer she pulls open every day.

Stashed-away recipes in forgotten places are the gifts she gives herself. "Here it is," she can be heard to exclaim, "I've been looking all over for this cranberry-apple soufflé with lemon-nutmeg sauce."

The years of cooking have taught her the secrets of mingling traditions. Now with a little bit of this and a little bit of that she doesn't hesitate to create her own measures—"three pinches past taste," "a broken tablespoon to mix."

The collagist and painter Romare Bearden would often say, "Art goes where there is energy." My mother is an artist. She is the movement floating in swirls of chocolate, the cinnamon of her sweet potato pies, the mango in the spiced chutney. She is the melody of the kitchen.

They found in Harlem a heartbeat that would echo a drumbeat from a time they could not name.

Following the Great Migration's unwritten instructions to head north, my mother and father, Ida Turner and Lee Arthur, landed in 1937's Harlem. The economic meltdown had taken its toll, yet a palpable vibrancy remained. Harlem was alive with its street corner orators, rent parties, and charismatic religious and political leaders vying for attention with ballrooms, nightclubs, speakeasies—with music everywhere. They wasted no time signing up. Donning pinstripe suits, tails, evening gowns, and tiaras, they were members of the likes of the Dukes and Duchesses and the 25 Chauffeurs Club of New York. They romped, stomped, and danced their way over the ballroom floors of the Renaissance (138th Street and Seventh), the Alhambra (126th Street and Seventh), and the Savoy (140th Street and Lenox); claimed a seat in an after-hours club; occasionally dropped by the Red Rooster (138th Street and Seventh); and loved the shows at the Apollo (125th Street between Seventh and Eighth

Avenues). They found in Harlem a heartbeat that would echo a drumbeat from a time they could not name.

My mother found work cooking for Betsey Cushing Roosevelt (President Franklin D. Roosevelt's daughter-in-law). My father butlered for John Hay Whitney (U.S. Ambassador to Great Britain; publisher of the *New York Herald Tribune*; and president of the Museum of Modern Art). Ida was the cook for many other prominent families including that of railroad executive and champion yachtsman Harold S. Vanderbilt, great-grandson of Commodore Cornelius Vanderbilt, and later for actor Burt Reynolds. With Reynolds' family and friends, "Miz Ida" was on a first-name basis while she entertained in Burt's kitchens at *her* table. Meals to warm the heart would often be accompanied by her penchant for making light, fluffy, pretty three-leaf clover-top yeast rolls that would induce Charles Nelson Reilly to propose marriage; encourage Ossie Davis to sing for his supper; and lead Loni Anderson, once married to Reynolds, to love their "girl chats." Ida was always tickled and her presence always in demand. "Miz Ida, are you hiding any more of those yeast rolls?"

Harlem was alive with its street corner orators, rent parties, and charismatic religious and political leaders.

As a young woman in her thirties, Ida landed a coveted wartime job (1944–48) as a team member in the kitchen of the Officers' Club at the United States Naval Air Station, Floyd Bennett Field in Brooklyn. Now a centenarian, she becomes that young Ida again when her eyes light up as she tells about the marinades and gravies she would make from scratch, along with the sheer number of pies and cakes she baked daily. The story always ends with, "You know I have an open invitation to return." Documented in a nineteen-forties photograph, she stands proudly among the culinary staff.

SWEET PLAYLIST

"TELL IT LIKE IT IS"   Aaron Neville

"TEA FOR TWO"   Pink Martini featuring Jimmy Scott

"SISTER SADIE"   Andy Bey & the Bey Sisters

"SUGAH DADDY"   D'Angelo and the Vanguard

"BUMBLEBEE"   Rachel Brown

The more tart the green apple sorbet and the saltier the caramel sauce, the better this dessert will be.

→ **You need a juicer and an ice cream maker for this recipe. And you can pick up citric acid at most health food and vitamin stores.**

THE GREEN VIKING

SERVES 6 TO 8

FOR THE SORBET

1 Core the apples, cut each half into 8 wedges, and toss with the citric acid. Put through a juicer.

2 Measure out 3 cups of the juice and add the sugar, whisking until the sugar is dissolved. Freeze in an ice cream maker according to the manufacturer's instructions.

3 Pack the sorbet into a container, cover, and freeze for at least 2 hours before serving.

FOR THE CARAMEL

4 Put the butter, brown sugar, corn syrup, and condensed milk into a saucepan and bring to a boil over medium heat. Whisk until smooth, then remove from the heat. Whisk in the heavy cream, vanilla, and salt. Cool slightly. You can make the caramel up to 2 weeks in advance. Keep it covered in the refrigerator and reheat before serving.

FOR THE CHEESE WHIP

5 Beat the butter and cream cheese with an electric mixer until smooth. Add the confectioners' sugar and beat until light and fluffy.

TO SERVE

6 Spoon a dollop of the cheese whip onto a dessert plate and cover with cake crumbs. Top with a scoop of the sorbet and a big drizzle of the warm caramel. Serve immediately.

FOR THE SORBET

4 pounds Granny Smith apples

3 tablespoons citric acid

¾ cup granulated sugar

FOR THE CARAMEL

2 sticks (½ pound) unsalted butter, cut in pieces

2 packed cups light brown sugar

1 cup light corn syrup

1 (14-ounce) can sweetened condensed milk

2 tablespoons heavy cream

1 teaspoon vanilla extract

½ teaspoon coarse sea salt

FOR THE CHEESE WHIP

4 tablespoons (½ stick) unsalted butter, softened

2 ounces cream cheese, softened

1 cup confectioners' sugar

FOR SERVING

2 cups pound cake crumbs

SWEET DOG

SERVES 4

When I was growing up in Sweden, we ate a dessert called *semla* on Shrove Tuesday. It was a cardamom sweet roll filled with cooked almonds, and I loved it. Here's my version—a brioche bun filled with almond paste and lots of whipped cream and drizzled with red velvet sauce.

→ **You can buy the buns, so this dessert is quick work. The homemade almond paste won't be as smooth as the stuff from the store, but boy, is it good.**

FOR THE ALMOND PASTE

1½ cups blanched sliced almonds

1½ cups confectioners' sugar

1 large egg white

1½ teaspoons almond extract

½ teaspoon powdered ginger

¼ teaspoon ground cardamom

¼ teaspoon fine sea salt

FOR THE RED VELVET SAUCE

2 tablespoons buttermilk

½ cup white chocolate chips

1½ teaspoons cocoa powder

1 tablespoon liquid red food coloring

FOR THE WHIPPED CREAM

1 cup heavy cream

2 teaspoons granulated sugar

FOR SERVING

4 brioche buns

Confectioners' sugar for dusting

FOR THE ALMOND PASTE

1 Put the almonds and confectioners' sugar in a food processor and process until chopped very fine. Add the egg white, extract, ginger, cardamom, and salt and process until smooth. Scrape into a bowl, cover with plastic wrap, and refrigerate for up to 1 week.

FOR THE RED VELVET SAUCE

2 Warm the buttermilk in a small saucepan over low heat. Add half the chocolate chips and stir until melted. Add the remaining chips and stir until melted. Turn off the heat, add the cocoa powder and food coloring, and whisk until smooth. Serve warm.

FOR THE WHIPPED CREAM

3 Beat the cream and sugar with an electric mixer until stiff. Transfer to a pastry bag fitted with a star tip if you have one.

TO SERVE

4 Slice off the top third of each brioche bun and pull out the center of the bottom. Fill each bun with ¼ cup of the almond paste. Pipe or spoon on a generous mound of whipped cream, covering the almond paste. Put the lids back on, drizzle with the red velvet sauce, and dust with confectioners' sugar.

Forget about chocolate. Our whoopie pies are pistachio cakes filled with fluffy cream cheese frosting perfumed with rosewater. We sell them in our takeaway corner, the Nook, so you can pick them up as a little treat.

WHOOPIE PIES

MAKES 6

FOR THE CAKES

1 Preheat the oven to 350°F. Line two rimmed baking sheets with parchment.

2 Pulse the cardamom and pistachios in a food processor until chopped fine.

3 Whisk the flour and baking soda together. Stir the vinegar, vanilla, and food coloring into the buttermilk in another bowl.

4 Beat the butter and sugar in a large bowl with an electric mixer on medium speed until light and fluffy. Add the egg and beat for 30 seconds. Scrape down the sides of the bowl. Turn the speed down to low and mix in the dry ingredients until just combined. Add the wet ingredients, mix until well combined, and scrape down the sides of the bowl. Mix in the ground pistachios.

5 Use a small (2-tablespoon capacity) ice cream scoop to drop 12 mounds of the batter onto the baking sheets, leaving 2 inches between each. Bake until the cakes have risen and just begun to brown around the edges, 8 to 12 minutes. Cool for 10 minutes, then transfer the cakes to wire racks to cool completely.

FOR THE FROSTING

6 Beat the butter and cream cheese in a large bowl with an electric mixer on medium speed until light and fluffy. Turn the speed down to low and gradually beat in the confectioners' sugar. Add the rosewater, zest, and salt and beat on high speed for 30 seconds.

7 Turn half of the cakes bottom side up and spoon about 3 tablespoons of the filling onto the center of each. Top with the remaining cakes, top side up, pressing down gently to distribute the filling evenly to the edges.

8 Store leftovers in an airtight container for up to 3 days.

FOR THE CAKES

2 cardamom pods

½ cup pistachios

2 cups all-purpose flour

½ teaspoon baking soda

1½ teaspoons distilled white vinegar

½ teaspoon vanilla extract

2 or 3 drops green food coloring

½ cup buttermilk

8 tablespoons (1 stick) unsalted butter, softened

1 cup granulated sugar

1 large egg

FOR THE FROSTING

2 sticks (½ pound) unsalted butter, softened

4 ounces cream cheese, softened

2½ cups confectioners' sugar

1½ teaspoons rosewater

¼ teaspoon grated orange zest

½ teaspoon fine sea salt

BEVY COOKIES

MAKES 12 COOKIES

Television personality and hostess (her Dinners with Bevy have become famous) Bevy Smith is a lifestyle all by herself. She's funny and she's delicious; she's of the world, and she's of Harlem. And she's sweet—just like this cookie packed with chocolate chips and peanuts and topped with melted marshmallows.

2½ cups all-purpose flour

½ teaspoon baking soda

½ teaspoon fine sea salt

2 sticks (½ pound) unsalted butter, softened

1 packed cup light brown sugar

½ cup granulated sugar

2 large eggs

2 teaspoons vanilla extract

1 cup semisweet chocolate chips

1 cup dry-roasted peanuts

2 cups mini marshmallows

Confectioners' sugar

1 Preheat the oven to 350°F. Line two rimmed baking sheets with parchment.

2 Whisk the flour, baking soda, and salt together.

3 Beat the butter and the sugars in a large bowl with an electric mixer on medium speed until light and fluffy. Turn the speed down to low and mix in the eggs and vanilla. Scrape down the bowl. Add the dry ingredients and mix on low until just combined. Stir in the chocolate chips and peanuts with a wooden spoon.

4 Use an ice cream scoop (3-tablespoon capacity) to drop mounds of the dough on the baking sheets, leaving 3 inches between each. Bake until the edges are golden brown, 8 to 10 minutes. Cool on the baking sheets on racks. The cookies will keep in an airtight container for up to 1 week.

5 When you're ready to serve the cookies, arrange them on a baking sheet and pile 10 to 12 mini marshmallows in the center of each cookie. Brown the marshmallows with a kitchen torch or under the broiler. (Watch carefully if you're using the broiler; you don't want to burn the marshmallows.)

6 Dust the cookies liberally with confectioners' sugar and serve.

FRI DJ STORMIN NORMAN
SAT GINNYS LIVE MUSIC
SUN GOSPEL BRUNCH
MS BONCELLA LEWIS
EVENINGS
NATE LUCAS
RECOLLECTION 35
MAKE IT MESSY 16.99
AMBESSA TEA GIFTSET 36
AMBESSA TEAS 9
RED ROOSTER IS PROUD TO OFFER A COMPLIMENTARY GIFT WITH
EVERY PURCHASE MADE WITH MASTERCARD
ASK YOUR SERVER OF R DETALS
Food!
red rooster
AMBESSA

RUM CAKE

MAKES 1 (9-X-13-INCH) CAKE

Rum, rum, and more rum. The boozier you make this cake, the better it is!

→ **Serve with the leftover pastry cream or the best vanilla ice cream. And some berries, if you'd like.**

FOR THE PASTRY CREAM

¼ cup heavy cream

2 large egg yolks

2 tablespoons cornstarch

⅓ cup granulated sugar

1 cup milk

½ vanilla bean, split, seeds scraped

FOR THE CAKE

2 cups all-purpose flour

2 teaspoons baking powder

1 teaspoon salt

½ cup milk

½ cup Myers's dark rum

2 teaspoons vanilla extract

8 tablespoons (1 stick) unsalted butter, softened

1½ cups granulated sugar

½ cup vegetable oil

4 large eggs, at room temperature

FOR THE SOAKING SYRUP

8 tablespoons (1 stick) unsalted butter

½ cup Myers's dark rum

¼ cup water

1 cup granulated sugar

½ teaspoon ground cardamom

½ teaspoon ground cinnamon

½ teaspoon powdered ginger

½ teaspoon vanilla extract

FOR THE BRÛLÉE

¾ cup turbinado sugar or Sugar in the Raw

FOR THE PASTRY CREAM

1 Whisk the heavy cream, yolks, cornstarch, and 1 tablespoon of the sugar in a large bowl until smooth.

2 Put the remaining sugar, the milk, and the vanilla seeds and pod in a saucepan and bring to a simmer over medium heat. While whisking, drizzle half of the hot milk into the beaten yolks. Return the tempered yolks to the pan and cook,

stirring, until the pastry cream thickens. Remove the vanilla pod.

3 Scrape the pastry cream into a bowl. Place a piece of plastic wrap directly on the surface of the cream so a skin doesn't form, and refrigerate for at least 1 hour (or up to 5 days).

FOR THE CAKE

4 Preheat the oven to 350°F. Line a 9-x-13-inch baking dish with parchment.

5 Whisk the flour, baking powder, and salt together. Mix the milk, rum, and vanilla together in a measuring cup.

6 Beat the butter in a large bowl with an electric mixer on medium speed until light. While beating, add the sugar gradually and beat until light and fluffy. Beat in ½ cup of the pastry cream, then beat in the vegetable oil. Beat in the eggs one at a time, scraping down the bowl after each addition. Turn the mixer

speed down to low and mix in half the dry ingredients. Mix in the wet ingredients, then the remaining dry ingredients.

7 Scrape the batter into the pan, even it out, and give the pan a rap on the counter to release any air bubbles. Bake until a skewer comes out clean, 20 to 25 minutes. Cool on a rack for 10 minutes.

FOR THE SOAKING SYRUP

8 Put all the ingredients *except* the vanilla into a saucepan and bring to a simmer over medium heat. Turn the heat down to low and simmer for 5 minutes. Remove from the heat and stir in the vanilla.

9 Turn the cake out onto a rack, peel off the parchment, and flip it right side up onto a rimmed baking sheet. If the cake has domed, use a long serrated knife to even the top. Poke the cake all over with a fork and brush one third of the syrup over the top. Invert the cake onto a second baking sheet and brush with another third of the syrup. Let the cake sit for 10 minutes. Flip the cake back onto the first baking sheet and brush on the remaining syrup.

FOR THE BRÛLÉE

10 Sprinkle the turbinado sugar evenly over the top of the cake. Use a kitchen torch to melt and brown the sugar. You can also brown the sugar under a broiler; just keep an eye on it and move the baking sheet around so the sugar browns evenly.

RED VELVET CAKE

MAKES 1 (10-INCH) LAYER CAKE

It's likely that this Southern classic started out in New York—at the Waldorf Astoria. The Adams Extract Company of Austin, Texas, printed up a recipe to promote sales of red food coloring.

You'll find red velvet cakes all over Harlem, but we're real proud of our version. With its beautiful color and rich cream cheese frosting, it's an ideal party cake. Indeed, it's become a centerpiece dessert for Juneteenth celebrations.

FOR THE CAKE

4 cups cake flour

6 tablespoons Dutch-processed cocoa powder

2 teaspoons baking soda

2 teaspoons fine sea salt

2 sticks (½ pound) unsalted butter, softened

4 cups granulated sugar

4 large eggs, at room temperature

2 cups buttermilk

1 tablespoon distilled white vinegar

¼ cup liquid red food coloring

1 teaspoon vanilla extract

FOR THE FROSTING

2 sticks (½ pound) unsalted butter, softened

8 ounces cream cheese, softened

4 cups confectioners' sugar

2 teaspoons vanilla extract

¼ teaspoon grated lemon zest

½ teaspoon fine sea salt

FOR THE CAKE

1 Preheat the oven to 350°F. Spray two 10-inch round cake pans with pan spray.

2 Whisk the flour, cocoa, baking soda, and salt together.

3 Beat the butter and sugar in a large bowl with an electric mixer until very light and fluffy. Beat in the eggs one at a time, scraping down the bowl after each addition.

4 Add half the dry ingredients and mix on low speed until combined. Add the buttermilk, vinegar, food coloring, and vanilla and mix. Add the remaining dry ingredients and mix until the batter is smooth.

5 Divide the batter between the baking pans and give each pan a couple of raps on the counter to release any air bubbles. Bake until a cake tester comes out clean, 25 to 30 minutes. Cool in the pans on racks for 10 minutes. Then turn out the cakes and cool on racks completely.

FOR THE FROSTING

6 Beat the butter and cream cheese in a large bowl with an electric mixer on medium-high speed until light and fluffy. Turn the speed down to low and beat in the confectioners' sugar, 1 cup at a time. Add the vanilla, zest, and salt and beat on medium-high until fluffy.

TO ASSEMBLE

7 Use a long serrated knife to slice the dome off the top of each cake, making the cake layers even. If you like, crumble the scraps onto a rimmed baking sheet and reserve.

8 Set one layer on a cake plate and frost the top. Set the second layer on the first and frost the sides and then the top of the cake. Press the crumbs into the sides of the cake, if desired.

PICKLED PEACH *and* PLUM COBBLER *with* WARM VANILLA SAUCE

MAKES 1 (9-X-13-INCH) COBBLER

We've gone old-school here, with a batter that rises up between the fruit as it bakes. But while the technique may be old fashioned, the flavors are anything but. Tangy pickled peaches and bright fresh plums are softened by the sweetness of the warm vanilla sauce.

FOR THE PICKLED PEACHES

5 peaches, halved and pitted

2 cups sherry vinegar

2 cups water

3 cups sugar

½ teaspoon mustard seeds

½ teaspoon ground turmeric

½ teaspoon powdered ginger

1 star anise

FOR THE BATTER

8 tablespoons (1 stick) unsalted butter

1 cup all-purpose flour

1 cup sugar

2 teaspoons baking powder

¼ teaspoon fine sea salt

⅔ cup milk, at room temperature

1 large egg, at room temperature

FOR THE FRUIT

½ pound plums, cut into wedges

½ cup sugar

FOR THE WARM VANILLA SAUCE

4 large egg yolks

½ cup sugar

Fine sea salt

1 cup heavy cream

1 vanilla bean, split lengthwise and seeds scraped

FOR THE PICKLED PEACHES

1 Put the peaches cut side down in a casserole dish.

2 Bring the vinegar, water, sugar, mustard seeds, turmeric, ginger, and star anise to a boil in a saucepan over medium-high heat. Stir to dissolve the sugar. Pour the brine over the peaches and cool. Cover and refrigerate for at least 6 hours. You can make this a day ahead.

FOR THE BATTER

3 Preheat the oven to 375°F.

4 Cut the butter into pieces and drop into a 9-x-13-inch casserole. Slide it into the oven to melt the butter.

5 Whisk the flour, sugar, baking powder, and salt together in a bowl. Whisk the milk and egg together in another bowl. Pour the wet ingredients into the dry and whisk until the batter is smooth. Pour evenly over the melted butter. *Do not stir.*

FOR THE FRUIT

6 Drain the pickled peaches and cut them into wedges. Toss the peaches, plums, and sugar together. Scatter the

fruit evenly over the batter. *Again, do not stir.*

7 Bake until the cobbler is golden brown and a skewer comes out clean, 20 to 30 minutes. Cool on a rack.

FOR THE WARM VANILLA SAUCE

8 When you're ready to serve the cobbler, whisk the yolks, sugar, and a good pinch of salt until light.

9 Bring the cream and vanilla seeds to a simmer in a saucepan over medium heat.

10 While whisking, pour about half of the cream into the yolks. Turn the heat down to medium-low. Return the tempered yolks to the saucepan and cook, whisking constantly, until the sauce thickens, 3 to 5 minutes. Do not let the sauce boil.

11 Spoon a puddle of sauce onto a dessert plate and top with a serving of cobbler.

BANANA PECAN PIE

MAKES 1 (10-INCH) DEEP DISH PIE

Banana cream pie and pecan pie are both Southern classics. Combine them and add a layer of chocolate and you have a dessert that will remind you of the kind of childhood you wish you had.

FOR THE CRUST

8 tablespoons (1 stick) unsalted butter

1 (11-ounce) box vanilla wafer cookies (Nilla wafers)

1 vanilla bean, split lengthwise

FOR THE GANACHE

4 ounces bittersweet (64 percent cacao) chocolate, chopped fine

½ cup heavy cream

FOR THE FILLING

½ cup granulated sugar

½ packed cup light brown sugar

6 tablespoons (¾ stick) unsalted butter, softened

3 large eggs, at room temperature

¼ cup light corn syrup

2 tablespoons maple syrup

2 cups pecan halves, toasted and coarsely chopped

½ teaspoon ground cinnamon

¼ teaspoon freshly grated nutmeg

¼ teaspoon ground cloves

½ teaspoon fine sea salt

1½ bananas

Warm Vanilla Sauce (page 370)

FOR THE CRUST

1 Preheat the oven to 325°F.

2 Cut the butter in pieces and melt in a small saucepan over low heat. Cook, stirring occasionally, until the milk solids brown and the clarified butter darkens some, about 10 minutes. Don't let it burn. Scrape out into a bowl, making sure you get all the browned bits.

3 Crumble the wafers into a food processor and pulse to make coarse crumbs. Scrape the seeds out of the vanilla bean and add to the processor (save the pod for another use) along with the butter. Pulse until all the crumbs are moistened. Scrape out into a 10-inch deep-dish pie plate and press evenly across the bottom and up the sides.

4 Bake the crust until lightly browned, about 5 minutes. Cool on a rack.

5 Turn the oven temperature up to 350°F.

FOR THE GANACHE

6 Put the chocolate into a medium heatproof bowl.

7 Bring the cream to a simmer in a small saucepan over medium heat. Pour the cream over the chocolate and let it sit for 1 minute. Whisk gently, starting from the center and working out, until the chocolate is melted and the ganache is smooth.

8 Pour the ganache into the crust and brush it evenly across the bottom and up the sides. Let it set while you make the filling.

FOR THE FILLING

9 Beat the sugars and butter in a large bowl with an electric mixer until fluffy. Beat in the eggs, one by one, scraping the bowl after each addition. Add the corn syrup and maple syrup and beat until smooth. Stir in the pecans, cinnamon, nutmeg, cloves, and salt.

10 Slice the bananas thin and layer them evenly over the ganache. Pour in the filling and shake the pie to even it out.

11 Bake for 5 minutes. Turn the oven temperature down to 325°F and bake until the filling is set, 35 to 40 minutes. Cool on a rack for at least 1 hour before slicing.

12 Serve slices on puddles of the warm vanilla sauce.

BLONDE *and* DARK MUD *with* BOURBON RASPBERRIES

MAKES 1 (10-INCH) PIE

Southern housewives seemed to have started making mud pies—dark as the banks of the Mississippi River—in the nineteen-seventies. It wasn't long before their popularity spread, creating variation upon variation. When we opened, Jimmy Lappalainen convinced me that we had to have our own mud to play with. So here it is: dark ganache topped with mocha mud made blonde with cream cheese and mascarpone in a cookie and pretzel crust.

It's a party!

→ **The pie needs to set overnight, so start the day before you plan on serving.**

FOR THE CRUST

3 ounces (1 cup crushed) pretzels

9 ounces (½ cup crushed) Bevy Cookies (without the marshmallows; page 364) or chocolate chip cookies

½ packed cup light brown sugar

2 tablespoons unsalted butter, melted

FOR THE GANACHE

4 ounces bittersweet (64 percent cacao) chocolate, chopped fine

¾ cup heavy cream

FOR THE FILLING

2 cups milk chocolate chips

2½ cups heavy cream

½ cup milk

¼ cup brewed espresso or strong coffee

2 cardamom pods

2 whole cloves

2 vanilla beans, split lengthwise and seeds scraped

½ teaspoon powdered ginger

½ teaspoon fine sea salt

4½ teaspoons powdered gelatin

½ pound cream cheese, softened

½ pound mascarpone cheese, softened

FOR THE BOURBON RASPBERRIES

½ packed cup light brown sugar

Grated zest and juice of 1 orange

2 cups raspberries

3 tablespoons bourbon

FOR THE CRUST

1 Preheat the oven to 325°F.

2 Crumble the pretzels and cookies into a food processor and pulse to make coarse crumbs. Add the brown sugar and butter and pulse until all the crumbs are moistened. Dump the crumbs into a 10-inch deep-dish pie plate and press evenly across the bottom and up the sides.

3 Bake until the crust is lightly browned, 8 to 10 minutes. Cool completely on a rack.

FOR THE GANACHE

4 Put the chocolate into a medium heatproof bowl.

5 Bring the cream to a simmer in a small saucepan

over medium heat. Pour the cream over the chocolate and let it sit for 1 minute. Whisk gently, starting from the center and working out, until the chocolate is melted and the ganache is smooth.

6 Pour the ganache into the crust and brush it evenly across the bottom and up the sides. Let it set while you make the filling.

FOR THE FILLING

7 Put the chocolate chips into a heatproof bowl.

8 Bring 2 cups of the cream, the milk, espresso, cardamom, cloves, vanilla seeds and pods, ginger, and salt to a boil in a saucepan over medium heat.

9 Strain the cream over the chocolate chips. Let it sit for 1 minute, then whisk until smooth.

10 Sprinkle the gelatin over the remaining 1/4 cup heavy cream. Let it soften for 10 minutes. Add the gelatin to the chocolate cream and whisk until completely combined.

11 Beat the cream cheese and mascarpone in a large bowl with an electric mixer on low speed until smooth, 2 to 4 minutes. Turn the speed up to medium-low, add the chocolate cream, and beat until perfectly combined, with no streaks of white. Scrape the bowl as necessary.

12 Pour the filling into the crust, cover with plastic wrap, and refrigerate overnight.

FOR THE BOURBON RASPBERRIES

13 Put the brown sugar and orange juice into a skillet over medium heat and cook, stirring, until the sugar dissolves. Add the raspberries and turn the heat up to high. Add the bourbon and tilt the skillet to ignite it. Let it flame to cook off the alcohol. Turn off the heat, stir in the orange zest, and leave it to rest for 20 minutes before serving.

14 Spoon the raspberries over slices of the pie.

Jimmy Lappalainen was a chef on our opening team. The Lapp in his name points to Jimmy's heritage; he traces his family to the Sami people—Laplanders—who live in northern Finland, Sweden, and Norway. I chuckle when I remember him talking me into making mud. Jimmy's back in Sweden now with his Puerto Rican wife and their kids—who are all fluent in English, Spanish, Swedish, and Finnish. Seems to me he's made his own beautiful mud.

"MONEY DOESN'T BUY IT"

Quiet as it's kept, Kim Hastreiter is so much more than Paper *magazine's iconic co-founder, editor, and publisher. She's a connector, introducing designer Vivienne Westwood and artist Keith Haring, museum curator Thelma Golden and Nigerian designer Duro Olowu. And she's also a bloodhound when it comes to scoping out talent. It feels right to put her conversation alongside the desserts. Kim has always been the cherry on top.*

I was involved with the hip-hop movement very early on. Afrika Bambaataa used to write a column for us. So, I was super into hip-hop. We were the first to cover it in the early days.

People don't know this, but Bambaataa was the start of hip-hop. And he used to have these parties in the late seventies in the South Bronx where he took over these garages. He was a DJ but also an MC. That's how rap began—they used to talk over the DJ. And then of course the fashion came out around the late seventies: On the trains you'd see these outrageous fashions. I'd see these kids from 125th Street, the South Bronx, with these glasses—preppy, like Cazals, but not even Cazals—a Harvard sweatshirt with a giant Mercedes-Benz

these kids were making a political statement. They were wearing icons of white society or logos of white society and they were turning them upside down and saying, "I might not be able to buy a Gucci but I can wear a GG this big or have it printed all over my sweatshirt." It was so genius.

I would write about the fashion, politically, because I thought it was such a political statement. They were saying, "I'm as good as you are—better, because I'm doing this with no money." I never had money either. It's not about money. Money doesn't buy it. I was super excited. . . . I used to love that kind of subversion, coming from people's brains—it's art.

They were saying, "I'm as good as you are—better, because I'm doing this with no money."

---

medallion necklace, gold teeth with a diamond in it, wearing the big fat Adidas with the big fat laces. Or a whole outfit with fake Louis Vuitton velvet from Dapper Dan's. Or a Gucci logo with a Chanel logo. I used to think, *Oh my god, these people are saying the biggest fuck you to Gucci.* In those days Gucci was for old white ladies. It wasn't hip; but it was really expensive. So

There were all these artists around, like Lady Pink. She's still around. She was the one female graffiti artist. There was only one, and she was the one. There was Johnny Ahearn, this amazing artist who used to body-cast people in Harlem. He would make these sculptures of people and put them up on the sides of buildings. His twin brother, Charlie, made the movie *Wild Style*. They were all really involved in the community in Harlem.

When Gucci and Louis Vuitton were taken over in their next iterations by Marc Jacobs and Tom Ford, the first thing the kids did was knock off that and pay homage by creating sweatsuits with double Gs all over them and raincoats with LVs. They were inspired by hip-hop. And then the Koreans started knocking off that. And then it went back on the street. And the big hip-hop stars were buying the real stuff. It's so circular.

There used to be an amazing guy named Mr. Picasso. He would paint all the gates on 125th street, when they were down. If it was a hair salon, he would paint a lady with an amazing hairdo; if it was a drugstore, he would paint something to do with the drugstore; if it was a record store, he would paint a big boombox on it. He was an artist—he was called the Picasso of Harlem. He also did paintings. If you died, you could give him your ashes, and he would mix it into the paint and do a portrait of you for your family. He was a Harlem character.

On Sunday, we used to go up to Harlem when everyone was in church. And you could see all the paintings because the gates were down. That was the day to see the art.

INDEX

Note: Page references in *italics* indicate photographs.

A

Adorno, Raul, 133, 138
aji amarillo paste, 29
ajwain, 27
aleppo pepper, 27
almonds
  squash salad with crunchy
    quinoa and pumpkin seed
    vinaigrette, 344–45
  sweet dog, 362
ancho chile powder, 27
Apollo Theater, 274–75
appetizers
  beef kitfo with awase, *60,* 61
  cauliflower frites with green
    mayonnaise, 56–57
  coconut fluke ceviche, 146
  corn bread, 63, *65*
  crab in a lettuce cup, 176
  deviled eggs with chicken-skin
    mayo, 200, *201*
  fish croquettes, 58, *59*
  fried green tomatoes with
    buttermilk dressing, 217
  pig ears with hot mustard, 54, *55*
apples, in the green viking, 361
arepas, charred char, 156–57
avocados
  charred char arepas, 156–57
  coconut fluke ceviche, 146
  róbalo a la parrilla (grilled sea
    bass) with jicama slaw, 147
awase, *60,* 61

B

bacon
  the breakfast, 266–68, *267*
  dip, Brussels sprouts with, 295
  double-dragon rice with grilled
    shrimp, 116–18, *117*
  freezing, 113
  jerk, and baked beans, 112–13
  La Marqueta pork tack tack,
    158–59
  mace gravy, 88
  -peanut pork chops, 214, *215*
Bamboo Inn, 349
banana leaves, 30
banana pecan pie, 372–73
Barrow, Ben, 71
beans
  baked, and jerk bacon, 112–13
  the breakfast, 266–68, *267*
  charred summer succotash with
    cooling yogurt, 218–19
  cheese broth, 120
  fava, prepping, 219
  green, and spicy sweets, 170
  long, steamed bass, fiery noodles,
    346, *347*
  roti, 239
  spring pea pasta, 294
beef
  Aunt Grete's, 175
  kitfo with awase, *60,* 61
  marrow dumplings with
    charred broccolini and chiles,
    126–28, *127*
  neck, braised, 171

Obama's short ribs, 168, *169*
  stewed oxtails, 350, *351*
  Uncle T's meatballs, 318–20, *319*
beets, blackening rub, and peanuts
  too, catfish with, 206–8, *207*
berbere, 27
biscuits, brown butter, 314–15
bloody mix, 53
bourbon
  brown-stoner, 47
  fig and pear, 47
  negroni, 51
  nutmeg, 47
  raspberries, blonde and dark
    mud with, 374–75
bread pudding, andouille, 260, *261*
bread(s)
  Aunt Maybel's ham buns with
    chocolate gravy, 270–71, *272*
  brown butter biscuits, 314–15
  chicken-fat challah with
    cracklings and onion,
    97–98, *99*
  corn, 63, *65*
  corn, crumb vinaigrette, 64
  favorite Sunday toast, 269
  roti, 239
brioche buns
  buying, 30–31
  in sweet dog, 362
broccolini, charred, and chiles,
  marrow dumplings with,
  126–28, *127*
broth, bird, 78
Brussels sprouts with bacon
  dip, 295

burrata, about, 30
butter, spiced, 62
Butts, Calvin, 106

C

cabbage
  spicy Haitian (picklz), 244
  see also sauerkraut
cakes
  red velvet, 368, *369*
  rum, 366–67
catfish
  with blackening rub, beets, and
    peanuts too, 206–8, *207*
  and pecans, 114, *114*
cauliflower
  frites with green mayonnaise,
    56–57
  house pickles, 244
  mac and greens, 119–20, *121*
ceviche
  coconut fluke, 146
  shrimp, sour tomato soup with,
    143–44, *145*
Chapman, Andrew, 192, 220–21
char, charred, arepas, 156–57
Chase, Leah, 74
cheese
  baked manicotti, 316–17
  blonde and dark mud with
    bourbon raspberries, 374–75
  broth, 120
  burrata, about, 30
  creamy grits, 180
  La Marqueta pork tack tack,
    158–59
  mac and greens, 119–20, *121*
  mascarpone, about, 30
  migas, 309
  queso fresco, about, 30
  tomato-watermelon salad with
    burrata and tomato seed
    vinaigrette, 242
Cherry Heering, in brown-
    stoner, 47
chestnuts, canned, 31
chicharrón, 32
chicken
  bb roo, sandwich on a potato roll,
    90–91, *92*

bird broth, 78
bird funk and chicken liver
    butter, 82–84, *83*
  -broth mayo, 310–11
  Chinatown, 322–23
  -fat challah with cracklings and
    onion, 97–98, *99*
  fried yardbird, 85
  hot gumbo with tripe and rice,
    290–91, *292*
  just fry the damn bird!, 87, *89*
  lemon, with green harissa
    and roast eggplant puree,
    94–96, *95*
  ramen, 79
  shake, 84
  shrimp, bird, and grits, 204–5
  -skin mayo, 200, *201*
  -skin pop, 320
  Uncle T's meatballs, 318–20, *319*
  and waffles, yep, 210–12, *211*
  wild wild wings, 80–81
  see also liver(s)
chile(s)
  and charred broccolini, marrow
    dumplings with, 126–28, *127*
  double-dragon rice with grilled
    shrimp, 116–18, *117*
  Fresno, pickled, 244
  green harissa, 94–96, *95*
  grilled, vinaigrette, 150–51
  jerk bacon and baked beans,
    112–13
  killer collards, 123
  pescado wrapped in banana
    leaves with green sauce, 148
  Red Rooster hot sauce, 243
  spiced maple syrup, 212
  spicy sweets and green beans,
    170
chipotle chile powder, 27
chipotles in adobo, 29
chocolate
  banana pecan pie, 372–73
  Bevy cookies, 364
  blonde and dark mud with
    bourbon raspberries, 374–75
  gravy, Aunt Maybel's ham buns
    with, 270–71, *272*
coconut
  fluke ceviche, 146

milk, buying, 31
  whipped cream, preparing, 31
collards
  andouille bread pudding,
    260, *261*
  baked manicotti, 316–17
  killer, 123
  mac and greens, 119–20, *121*
cookies, Bevy, 364
corn
  bread, 63, *65*
  bread crumb vinaigrette, 64
  charred summer succotash with
    cooling yogurt, 218–19
  -oyster soup, 202
corn flour, 26
cornmeal
  buying, 26
  charred char arepas, 156–57
  corn bread, 63, *65*
cornstarch, 26
crab
  fish croquettes, 58, *59*
  in a lettuce cup, 176
  spring pea pasta, 294
Crab Man Mike, 177
cranberry gravy, herb-roasted
    turkey with, 336–38, *337, 339*
croquettes, fish, 58, *59*
cucumber(s)
  crab in a lettuce cup, 176
  green papaya salad, 118
  and radishes, pickled, 245
curry leaves, 27
curry paste, Indian, 29

D

Dapper Don, 329–33
desserts
  banana pecan pie, 372–73
  Bevy cookies, 364
  blonde and dark mud with
    bourbon raspberries, 374–75
  the green viking, 361
  pickled peach and plum cobbler
    with warm vanilla sauce,
    370–71
  red velvet cake, 368, *369*
  Rooster donuts with sweet
    potato cream, 186–87

rum cake, 366–67
sweet dog, 362
whoopie pies, 363
dips and spreads
awase, *60*, 61
bird funk and chicken liver
butter, 82–84, *83*
for chicken wings, 81
see also mayonnaise
donuts, Rooster, with sweet potato
cream, 186–87
drinks
bloody rooster, 53
bourbon negroni, 51
brown-stoner, 47
dark and stormier, 48
rum rum punch, 51
the Savoy, 50
yes, chef, 46
dumplings, marrow, with
charred broccolini and chiles,
126–28, *127*

E

eggplant
charred, and spinach, lacquered
halibut with, 183–85, *184*
roast, puree and green harissa,
lemon chicken with, 94–96, *95*
egg(s)
the breakfast, 266–68, *267*
deviled, with chicken-skin mayo,
200, *201*
on egg, 263
favorite Sunday toast, 269
migas, 309
pickled, 245
ramen, 79
shrimp, bird, and grits, 204–5
tomato, Sunday, 264, *265*
Eliot, Marjorie, 298–99

F

fig and pear bourbon, 47
filé powder, 29
fish
canned sardines, about, 32
catfish and pecans, 114, *114*

catfish with blackening rub,
beets, and peanuts too,
206–8, *207*
charred char arepas, 156–57
chowder, scrappy, 310–11
chowder, scrappy, royale, 311
coconut fluke ceviche, 146
croquettes, 58, *59*
lacquered halibut with
charred eggplant and spinach,
183–85, *184*
pescado wrapped in banana
leaves with green sauce, 148
róbalo a la parrilla (grilled sea
bass) with jicama slaw, 147
steamed bass, fiery noodles, long
beans, 346, *347*
trout with ginger and citrus,
178–79
whole fried, with grits,
180–82, *181*
fish roe spread, 32
fish sauce, 29
Flack, Roberta, 195–97
Fleming, Derek, 105
flours, 26
fluke ceviche, coconut, 146
fritters, day-after, 151
fruit. *See specific fruits*

G

Gabriel, Charles, 100–101
garam masala, 28
Garrett, Michael, 75
ginger
beer, homemade, 46
dark and stormier, 48
fresh, working with, 28
pickled, 31
yes, chef, 46
"Ginny's," 194–97
goat
favorite Sunday toast, 269
stew, curried, 236, *237*
grains, 26
see also cornmeal; grits;
quinoa; rice
Golden, Thelma, 352–53
grapes, in the Savoy, 50

green beans and spicy sweets, 170
green papaya salad, 118
greens
crab in a lettuce cup, 176
mustard, and kraut, ham hocks
with, 124, *125*
ramen, 79
see also collards; spinach
grits
the breakfast, 266–68, *267*
buying, 26
cordero (lamb) and, with grilled
chile vinaigrette, 150–51
creamy, 180
day-after fritters, 151
pimiento gritty cakes, 205
shrimp, bird, and, 204–5
gumbo, hot, with tripe and rice,
290–91, *292*

H

halibut, lacquered, with
charred eggplant and spinach,
183–85, *184*
ham
the big baked, 341
buns, Aunt Maybel's, with
chocolate gravy, 270–71, *272*
hocks with mustard greens and
kraut, 124, *125*
leftover, ideas for, 174
lentil soup with, *342*, 343
shoebox, 172–74, *175*
harissa, green, 94–96, *95*
Hastreiter, Kim, 376–77
herbs
drying, 27
pescado wrapped in banana
leaves with green sauce, 148
for recipes, 27–29
horseradish, 28
awase, *60*, 61
bloody mix, 53
hot sauce, Red Rooster, 243

I

Indian curry paste, 29

J

jicama slaw, róbalo a la parrilla
(grilled sea bass) with, 147

K

kelp, dried, 30
ketjap manis, 29
kimchi, buying, 31
kitfo, beef, with awase, *60*, 61
Korean hot pepper paste
(gochujang), 29
Korean rice cakes
about, 31
roasted turnips *dduk*, 296, *297*

L

lamb
(cordero) and grits with grilled
chile vinaigrette, 150–51
day-after fritters, 151
rack of, b-crusted, 216
lavender, culinary, 28
Legend, John, 73
lemon
chicken with green harissa
and roast eggplant puree,
94–96, *95*
pickle, 32
lemongrass, 28
lentil(s)
black beluga, about, 30
ham hocks with mustard greens
and kraut, 124, *125*
soup with ham, *342, 343*
lettuce cup, crab in a, 176
liver(s)
chicken, butter, and bird funk,
82–84, *83*
day-after-Thanksgiving banh
mi, 338
fried, and onions with mustard–
pickled melon for Maya
Angelou, 238
Uncle T's meatballs, 318–20, *319*
lobster, in scrappy fish chowder
royale, 311
Lucas, Nate, 160–61, 277, 280–84

M

mace gravy, 88
Mala sauce, 29
maple syrup
grades of, 31
spiced, 212
marrow dumplings with
charred broccolini and chiles,
126–28, *127*
mascarpone, about, 30
mayonnaise
chicken-broth, 310–11
chicken-skin, 200, *201*
green, 57
Maysles, Albert, 240
Maysles, Rebekah, 246
meat. *See* beef; goat; lamb; pork
meatballs, Uncle T's, 318–20, *319*
melon
mustard-pickled, 245
tomato-watermelon salad with
burrata and tomato seed
vinaigrette, 242
migas, 309
mirin, 26
miso, 29
Mitchell, Billy, 274–75
Moses, Robert, 136
mussels, in scrappy fish chowder,
310–11
mustard
hot, pig ears with, 54, *55*
-pickled melon, 245
types of, 26
mustard greens and kraut, ham
hocks with, 124, *125*
mustard oil, 30

N

noodles
fiery, steamed bass, long beans,
346, *347*
ramen, 79
nori and dried kelp, 30
nutmeg bourbon, 47

O

Obama, Barack, 163–65
oils, specialty, 30
okra
house pickles, 244
pickled, 32
onion(s)
and cracklings, chicken-fat
challah with, 97–98, *99*
and liver, fried, with mustard–
pickled melon for Maya
Angelou, 238
oxtails, stewed, 350, *351*
oyster(s)
coconut fluke ceviche, 146
-corn soup, 202

P

pantry ingredients, 25–32
papaya, green, salad, 118
pasta
baked manicotti, 316–17
cheese broth, 120
mac and greens, 119–20, *121*
spring pea, 294
pastes, stocking pantry with,
29–30
peach, pickled, and plum cobbler
with warm vanilla sauce,
370–71
peanut(s)
-bacon pork chops, 214, *215*
Bevy cookies, 364
blackening rub, and beets too,
catfish with, 206–8, *207*
chile-lime, 176
pear and fig bourbon, 47
pea(s)
pasta, spring, 294
and rice, good for a crowd, 241
pecan(s)
banana pie, 372–73
catfish and, 114, *114*
peppers
charred summer succotash with
cooling yogurt, 218–19
green mayonnaise, 57
Red Rooster hot sauce, 243
see also chile(s)

pickled ginger, 31
pickled okra, 32
pickles at the Rooster, 244–45
pickling spice, 28
pies
  banana pecan, 372–73
  blonde and dark mud with
    bourbon raspberries, 374–75
pig ears with hot mustard, 54, *55*
pineapple
  the big baked ham, 341
  jerk bacon and baked beans,
    112–13
  rum rum punch, 51
  yes, chef, 46
pink curing salt, 28–29
pistachios, in whoopie pies, 363
plantains on the side, puerco en
    cerveza (pork in beer) with,
    154–55
plum and pickled peach cobbler
    with warm vanilla sauce,
    370–71
plum sauce, 29
popcorn, chicken-skin, 320
pork
  baked manicotti, 316–17
  in beer (puerco en cerveza),
    plantains on the side, 154–55
  block-party ribs with sweet q
    sauce, 234–35
  chops, peanut-bacon, 214, *215*
  marrow dumplings with
    charred broccolini and chiles,
    126–28, *127*
  pig ears with hot mustard, 54, *55*
  tack tack, La Marqueta, 158–59
  Uncle T's meatballs, 318–20, *319*
  see also bacon; ham; sausages
potato(es)
  Aunt Grete's beef, 175
  charred char arepas, 156–57
  fish croquettes, 58, *59*
  marrow dumplings with
    charred broccolini and chiles,
    126–28, *127*
  scrappy fish chowder, 310–11
  see also sweet potato(es)
potato flour, 26

poultry. *See* chicken; turkey
pumpkin seed
  oil, 30
  vinaigrette, 344–45

Q

queso fresco, about, 30
quinoa, crunchy, and pumpkin
    seed vinaigrette, squash salad
    with, 344–45

R

radishes and cucumbers,
    pickled, 245
Rakiem Walker Project,
    108–10, 130
ramen, 79
ras el hanout, 28
raspberries, bourbon, blonde and
    dark mud with, 374–75
Red Rooster
  black art at, 104–5
  cocktails served at, 41–43
  Downstairs at the Rooster,
    192–97
  El Barrio night, 133–41
  family meals at, 301–7, 326–27
  fried chicken served at, 70–75
  Latin Night, 140–41
  Obama fund-raising dinner at,
    163–65
  original restaurant, 36–39
  planning phase, 39–41, 220–21
rice
  double-dragon, with grilled
    shrimp, 116–18, *117*
  jasmine, for recipes, 26
  and peas, good for a crowd, 241
  and tripe, hot gumbo with,
    290–91, *292*
rice flour, 26
rice powder, 27
roti, 239
rum
  cake, 366–67
  dark and stormier, 48
  rum punch, 51

S

salads
  crab in a lettuce cup, 176
  green papaya, 118
  squash, with crunchy quinoa
    and pumpkin seed vinaigrette,
    344–45
  tomato-watermelon, with
    burrata and tomato seed
    vinaigrette, 242
sambal oelek, 29
sandwiches
  bb roo chicken, on a potato roll,
    90–91, *92*
  day-after-Thanksgiving banh
    mi, 338
sardines, canned, 32
sauces
  awase, *60,* 61
  green harissa, 94–96, *95*
  hot, Red Rooster, 243
  salsa roja, 309
  stocking pantry with, 29–30
  wing, 80
  see also mayonnaise
sauerkraut
  buying, 155
  ham hocks with mustard greens
    and kraut, 124, *125*
  puerco en cerveza (pork in beer),
    plantains on the side, 154–55
sausages
  andouille bread pudding,
    260, *261*
  fish croquettes, 58, *59*
  hot gumbo with tripe and rice,
    290–91, *292*
  Sunday tomato eggs, 264, *265*
sea bass
  grilled (róbalo a la parrilla) with
    jicama slaw, 147
  pescado wrapped in banana
    leaves with green sauce, 148
Shaoxing wine, 26
shellfish
  fish croquettes, 58, *59*
  scrappy fish chowder, 310–11
  scrappy fish chowder royale, 311
  see also crab; oyster(s); shrimp
shichimi togarashi, 28

shrimp
  bird, and grits, 204–5
  ceviche, sour tomato soup with,
    143–44, *145*
  dried, about, 30
  grilled, double-dragon rice with,
    116–18, *117*
  hot gumbo with tripe and rice,
    290–91, *292*
  marrow dumplings with
    charred broccolini and chiles,
    126–28, *127*
  powder, about, 30
  scrappy fish chowder royale, 311
soups
  corn-oyster, 202
  lentil, with ham, *342, 343*
  ramen, 79
  scrappy fish chowder, 310–11
  scrappy fish chowder royale, 311
  sour tomato, with shrimp
    ceviche, 143–44, *145*
spices and spice mixes, 27–29
spinach
  and charred eggplant, lacquered
    halibut with, 183–85, *184*
  green mayonnaise, 57
squash salad with crunchy quinoa
    and pumpkin seed vinaigrette,
    344–45
Sriracha, 29
stew, curried goat, 236, *237*
stewed oxtails, 350, *351*
St-Germain liqueur, in brown-
    stoner, 47
Streater, Ginny, 221

sweet potato(es)
  cream, Rooster donuts with,
    186–87
  garlic 'n' honey roasted
    sweets, 325
  herb-roasted turkey with
    cranberry gravy, 336–38,
    337, 339
  pan-roasted, with dried cherries
    and walnuts, 340
  spicy sweets and green
    beans, 170

T

tomato(es)
  cherry, pickled, 244
  eggs, Sunday, 264, *265*
  fried green, with buttermilk
    dressing, 217
  salsa roja, 309
  soup, sour, with shrimp ceviche,
    143–44, *145*
  -watermelon salad with
    burrata and tomato seed
    vinaigrette, 242
tomato juice
  bloody mix, 53
  bloody rooster, 53
tomato paste, 29
tomato powder, 29
tripe and rice, hot gumbo with,
    290–91, *292*
trout with ginger and citrus,
    178–79

turkey
  day-after-Thanksgiving banh
    mi, 338
  herb-roasted, with cranberry
    gravy, 336–38, *337, 339*
Turner, Lana, 355–59
turnips, roasted, *dduk*, 296, *297*

V

vinaigrette, corn bread crumb, 64
vinegars, for recipes, 25
vodka
  bloody rooster, 53
  the Savoy, 50
  yes, chef, 46

W

waffles, chicken and, yep,
    210–12, *211*
Walker, Rakiem, 106–10
wasabi powder, 28
watermelon-tomato salad with
    burrata and tomato seed
    vinaigrette, 242
whoopie pies, 363
Wilson, Melba, 188–89
wines, for cooking, 25–26

X

XO sauce, 30

Y

yuzu kosho, 30